Contemporary Australian cinema

MANCHESTER
UNIVERSITY PRESS

For Sarah, Jake and Sam

Contemporary Australian cinema

An introduction

JONATHAN RAYNER

distributed exclusively in the USA by St. Martin's Press

MANCHESTER UNIVERSITY PRESS   Manchester and New York

Published by Manchester University Press
Oxford Road, Manchester M13 9NR, UK
and Room 400, 175 Fifth Avenue, New York, NY 10010, USA
http://www.manchesteruniversitypress.co.uk

Distributed exclusively in the USA
by St. Martin's Press, Inc., 175 Fifth Avenue, New York,
NY 10010, USA

Distributed exclusively in Canada by
UBC Press, University of British Columbia, 2029 West Mall,
Vancouver, BC, Canada V6T 1Z2

British Library Cataloguing-in-Publication Data
A catalogue record is available from the British Library

Library of Congress Cataloging-in-Publication Data applied for

ISBN 0 7190 5326 9 *hardback*
    0 7190 5327 7 *paperback*

First published 2000

07 06 05 04 03 02 01 00   10 9 8 7 6 5 4 3 2 1

Typeset in Photina with Frutiger
by Northern Phototypesetting Co Ltd, Bolton

Printed in Great Britain
by Biddles Ltd, Guildford and King's Lynn

Contents

4 The male ensemble film

5 New glamour, new Gothic: Australian films in the 1990s

Conclusion

Illustrations

All illustrations courtesy of The Ronald Grant Archive

Preface

This book is intended to offer introductory readings of some of the well-known and less well-known feature productions coming out of Australia since the revival in the national film industry at the end of the 1960s. The interpretations of the texts and the careers of their makers are considered in relation to the emergence of an indigenous film culture and the construction of national identity. The majority of the films examined in this book have had theatrical or video releases in the UK, and many have also been screened on the terrestrial television channels. Therefore, the films chosen for analysis represent a range of productions of acknowledged critical and aesthetic standing. Lesser or more recent features sharing or developing the generic features of earlier famous and successful films are included for practical, critical comparison. Australian films enjoy considerable popularity with British and European audiences, and as well as suggesting texts suitable for study within academic courses, an aim of this book is the encouragement and consolidation of interest in a distinctive, enjoyable English-language cinema, whose products are readily accessible to devotees and students alike.

Acknowledgements

I would like to thank the following people for their assistance and support during the development and completion of this book: Dr Graeme Harper for his invaluable advice on the drafts; Dr Andrew Hassam for some additional materials; Professor Steve Neale for faith in Mr Fourteen Hours; Dr Bryan Burns for his friendship; and my colleagues and students at Wrexham and Sheffield.

Abbreviations

AFC   Australian Film Commission
AFDC Australian Film Development Corporation
AFFC Australian Film Finance Corporation
AFI   Australian Film Institute
AFTRS Australian Film, Television and Radio School
BEF   British Empire Films (distribution arm of the Greater Union
       Organisation theatre chain)
CFU   Commonwealth Film Unit (later Film Australia)

Introduction

The nationalities of cinema

The acceleration of abstraction, while it is certainly the main factor evident in the historical development of the arts during the twentieth century, is not the only one. The force that counters this estheticism[sic] is our continuing sense of the political dimension of the arts: that is, their direct connection to the community, and their power to explain the structure of society to us.[1]

The analysis and discussion of a national cinema represents the

1   *The Man from Snowy River*

pursuit of three more or less elusive entities: a national identity, a filmic culture and a commercial, industrial context. Even this identification of subject areas must undergo a further multiplication. Many national sub-groups may define alternative identities, and trace their overt or covert expression through the medium of film. Film style or content in narrative and non-narrative modes are usually defined in relation to accepted, international techniques of visual communication. In practice, the standard to which all other national forms of film expression are compared is that of Hollywood, and the American film industry casts an equally long shadow in economic terms.

The examination of the progression of a national film industry's development, through analysis of the individual products punctuating the process, always represents a formidable and multi-faceted task. The debate must strike a balance between acknowledging the variation and reining in the generalisation, yet the broad strokes of a critical appreciation are attractive, because of the unifying interpretation they can offer. Despite the fragmentation of nationality and society, this interpretative effort reunites the national representation and the represented community, a wider film culture and individual film artistry. A reading of examples of cultural continuity and artistic evolution which find cinematic expression provides the map on which landmark films, of national, societal and individual significance, can be located. A recognition of the range of cinematic products and styles emanating from a particular country will always be related to (and limited by) consideration of the circumscribed cultural and commercial bases which give rise to them. Nonetheless, linkages have been and continue to be sought between a country, its citizens and society, and filmic reflections and representations of them. In a socio-historical sense, films represent simply another series of cultural texts in which the influences of movements and events can be traced. In a socio-economic sense, the same films represent evidence of commercial trends and consumerist tastes. In a formalist analysis, adherence to or divergence from structures of narrative, conventions of genre or signatures of authorship (the evidence of the medium's 'abstraction', compared to its cultural relevance or political bias) can be studied within these delineated texts. Films of any era or nationality can be as fertile, since they refer, inevitably, to other films, eras and nationalities. Film's circumstances of communal production, its mixed art/industry status, and its reflexive and polyphonous form, precipitate or demand an individual, ungeneralised and interdisciplinary reading. The counter-currents identified by Monaco, as the poles of pure artistic development and cultural critical debate, largely define the oppositions discernible in the analysis of the significance of national cinema movements. Reconciling filmmakers and genres, film texts and eras, conventional forms of representation and (post)modernist revision, and national stereotypes and notional identities forwarded for myriad political or cultural reasons should take account of, rather than attempt to dispel, their attendant tensions:

The shared, collective identity which is implied always masks a whole range of internal differences and potential and actual antagonisms. The concept of national cinema is equally fluid, equally subject to ceaseless negotiations: while the discourses of film culture seek to hold it in place, it is abundantly clear that the concept is mobilised in different ways, by different commentators, for different reasons.[2]

Keeping pace with the medium's abstraction, and plotting the intersections of political, cultural and societal influences upon it, permit an effective criticism of national cinematic development. Aesthetic compositions on the individual scale, national constructions with political motivations, and cultural representations ranging from the simple and exclusive to the complex and diverse, coexist and await criticism within a national cinema's 'explanation of the structure of society'. With this kind of approach, the critical exercise might resemble a catalogue of the national cinema's diverse flora and fauna, and not a partial, generalised and symbolic 'map' of the territory which has spawned them.

The prehistory of Australian cinema

The ideal of a national cinema, and the critical methods mobilised in its appreciation, are used to categorise the proliferating film industries which distinguish themselves culturally, verbally or formally from Hollywood, the American multi-national cinema. Nations with emergent film cultures, those with long-standing and successful film industries, and those with histories of fitful production and uncertain direction in filmmaking, all share problematic relationships with the dominant American film culture of production and consumption. The history of filmmaking in Australia, through several cycles of expansion and contraction, epitomises the difficult relationships smaller film industries enjoy with Hollywood, which inspires and competes with them, providing a norm from which they can differentiate themselves or which they can (usually unsuccessfully) seek to emulate. A mature acknowledgement of these pervasive conditions lay behind the calls in the 1970s for a revival of indigenous film-making in Australia:

All other domestic film industries stand, in relation to the American industry, in the same relationship as the Aboriginals to the main-stream of Australian culture: they have been disinherited, and need massive injections of support and a special program of re-education if they are to preserve the remnants of their history and identity. Like the Swedish, German, Canadian and British film industries, the Australian film industry is underdeveloped – an oppressed minority group.[3]

As in the case of the major European film industries, Australia's history of filmmaking represented a source of nostalgia, pride and regret for those who sought the rebirth of the national cinema during the 1970s.

The record of Australian filmmaking achievements from the beginnings of cinema at the end of the nineteenth century to the end of the silent period includes claims for some notable 'firsts'. *The Story of the Kelly Gang* (Charles Tait, 1906) is forwarded as the original feature-length film narrative, pre-dating competitors in America and Europe:

Billed as 'The Sensation of the Year – the greatest, most thrilling, and sensational moving picture ever taken', it was to justify its claim at the box office and in motion picture history. It took six months to make – and was 'upwards of three quarters of a mile long'.[4]

The Salvation Army's production *Soldiers of the Cross* (Joseph Perry/Herbert Booth, 1900) enjoys a similar status. Although not a feature as such, it represented an inventive and compelling combination of filmed reconstructions of Biblical stories, scored music and slide presentations to accompany edifying lectures, with the entire programme lasting two and a half hours.[5] Irre-spective of the validity of the claims for these spectacles and the accuracy of information relating to them, they can be taken as representative of a vital and innovative film industry, well attuned to its local audience. However, as with many European film cultures competing with the burgeoning American industrial edifice, the years immediately before and after the First World War were a watershed for indigenous production. As standard-ised, quantity production became institutionalised in America, so small-scale, independent producers and cottage industries else-where found themselves outclassed and overrun by the ubiqui-tous Hollywood product. However, audience preference for imported films was only one factor among several which initiated the decline:

The years before the First World War were the most productive for Australian cinema, with a quantitative peak in 1911 that has not been equalled since. But by 1913 production had declined, and it did not recover until the heavy input of government finance in the 1970s. The cultural imperialism of the U.S.A. and Britain has often been blamed for causing the failure of the feature film industry by acquiring a stranglehold over Australian theatres and denying local film-makers access to the screen ... The collapse in production had nothing to do with audience response; it was a myth spread by the enemies of local production that Australian films were 'below standard' and that Australian audiences did not want to see them. On the contrary, the feature film industry was the victim of a struggle for power within the distribution and exhibition trades.[6]

The downturn in local production was followed and exacerbated by the departure of some Australian actors and technicians for work overseas. With competition between distributors and exhibitors making it difficult for those films that were made to reach an audience, concerns were voiced (as in other countries swamped by the influx of Hollywood films) about the threat of erosion of moral and cultural values. As in the case of the United Kingdom, these anxieties eventually gave rise to government intervention, with the establishment in 1927 of a Royal Commission of Enquiry tasked with examining the film industry's organisation and practices. In another parallel with Britain, a quota system was proposed to buttress production, assisted by taxation and duties imposed on imports. However, factors outside the country as well as the local industry again proved decisive in negating the benefits of such initiatives:

Although its main recommendations came to nothing, the Royal Commission provided a strong indirect incentive to production, and in anticipation of government action, 1928 became the most productive year for Australian feature films in a decade. Production soon ceased, however, because of the technological and financial barriers to sound.[7]

For the next twenty years, Australian film production continued, but at such a low level as to be negligible. Studios after the Hollywood pattern were created at the start of the sound era when, as elsewhere, the economic effects of the Depression led to mergers and centralisation which disfavoured the small producers. Ken G. Hall's studio Cinesound Productions existed on a 'self-supporting basis, with the income from one film providing the finance for the next'.[8] A second attempt at quota legislation stimulated another short-lived boom in the mid-1930s, and preferential treatment of films from within the Empire under the rules of the British Quota Act of 1927 ensured a market to sustain the limited level of production. With the coming of Second World War, production was given over to newsreels, propaganda and government information films, engendering another illusory boom period. However, instead of creating opportunities for Australia's pre-eminent feature directors (Ken G. Hall and Charles Chauvel), the post-war period saw Australia and its screens the object of a concerted but not unanticipated invasion:

Most of the important feature films in the twenty years after the war were made by British and American companies. For the Americans, Australia was little more than an exotic background for dramas that reflected their own preoccupations and that could mostly have been made in America itself ... Australian feature films virtually disappeared by the end of the 1950s.[9]

The two decades preceding the 1970s revival saw further evidence of cultural imperialism, technological advances and restrictive industrial practices, all of which mitigated against the maintenance, let alone expansion of indigenous production. Paradoxically, the profits from exhibition and the patterns of Australian cinema-going were encouraging, if only for foreign concerns. The duopoly existing in the exhibition sector was dominated by Australian subsidiaries of American companies,[10] which were themselves vertically integrated with US-owned distributors:

In 1965 there were still more than a thousand picture theatres across the nation grossing some $50 million for exhibitors. Of this amount, nearly half was remitted directly overseas through distributors. In 1967, all major film distributors, with one exception (BEF), were wholly-owned from the United States. As Australians, on a per capita basis, were the world's leading cinema-goers, the importance of the local market was obvious.[11]

The irony of Australian enthusiasm for visits to cinema screens bereft of indigenous productions was not lost on the lobbyists, who called for financial commitment from the government to recreate a national cinema. Australian television had also been colonised by British and American products, but Australian-made programmes began to provide positive and popular images of the country and its inhabitants on the one hand, and the impetus for a creditable and controllable national image on the big screen on the other. The production and transmission of Australian images were perceived as vital to counterbalance the 'sociological influence of imported material'[12] and allow the emergence of local creative talent. Perhaps more than a national industry, Australia as an institution required a national identity, consisting of images of itself, emanating from its own culture and reflecting the characteristics of its population. By the end of the 1960s, the momentum of the lobbyists had been matched by a governmental commitment (of funds as well as rhetoric) to the ideal of a new Australian film industry. Financial support in the form of grants would begin to assist in the realisation of feature and experimental films:

In 1972 the Whitlam Labour Government brought to an end 23 years of Liberal, right of centre rule, which had devoted only a small effort to culture and the arts. But a Tariff Board Inquiry set up by John Gorton, the Liberal Prime Minister, made a complete survey of the industry and recommended financial help. Which eventually led to the establishment, in 1970, of the Australian Film Development Corporation, which in four years of bank-like activity co-ordinated the financing for 54 cinema and 42 television film projects.[13]

However, the notion of a national cinema serving a purely nationalistic agenda was countered by the pragmatism of the market place, which Australian viewers themselves did so much to support. Some commentators were in favour of an artistic film industry dedicated to broadcasting authentic images of Australia and Australians. This would be less extreme than the contemporary New German cinema, a defiantly non-commercial national film industry populated by individualistic directors. Their opponents placed commercialism over artistry, and demanded that the new films should be able to turn a profit nationally and internationally. This polarisation between 'film as industry and commerce vs. film as art'[14] has dominated Australian filmmaking since its renaissance, but is illustrative of comparable debates affecting other, similarly beleaguered national film industries. However, irrespective of the particular commercial or artistic emphasis, the emergent Australian New Wave was blessed or cursed with a national mission:

whether the notion of art or industry prevailed at a given moment of pro-industry rhetoric, the underlying notion that film served the identification and refinement of essential Australianness was the confident starting point for everybody.[15]

Inconveniently, the definitive version of Australian-ness was and is obstinately elusive. Without exaggeration, the subsequent period of filmmaking from 1970 until the end of the century can be appraised as a sequential evaluation of possible candidates, and/or a running battle between their sponsors and their critics. If the existence and maintenance of an indigenous film industry in competition with America are not problematic enough, its choices of subject and forms of representation can exacerbate the situation. Conversely, the very diversity which such introspection and self-interrogation reveal can form the basis of genuine, beneficial and progressive national representation:

Australian cinema serves as a vehicle of popular socialisation and as a forum for telling uncomfortable truths about its society. Australian films and film institutions negotiate cleavages of ethnicity, gender, race, class and nation. It is an *object of knowledge* which narratively and discursively connects Australia, society, the cinema, genre and various cultural differences.[16]

Representing the nation

Theoretical interest in the cinema has recently tended to focus on notions such as 'distanciation', 'anti-illusionism', 'audience-participation'. The feeling is that the cinema ought to raise the consciousness of the spectator, demystify and instruct him about (political) reality and the ideological function of the cinema itself ... this is a discussion about the cinema as an institution within a certain society. But it is also ... about how art, and in particular, the cinema relates to society and individual consciousness via the aesthetic processes themselves.[17]

The ideological purpose behind the dominant representations and images of nationhood produced by the Australian cinema is linked indelibly to enduring colonial, cultural associations. The stereotypes of Australian-ness which emerged in early, successful or favoured cinematic representations have entered the consciousness of local and foreign audiences. Consequently they form as benchmark from which subsequent images can diverge or derive power from contrast or comparison. Even under circumstances of indigenous production, the framework of cinema often remains a First World institution, from which emanate coercive or reductive identifications which reaffirm the colony's inferior situation.

Cinematic representations of a nation too often begin (and end) with images of the prevailing, consensual social structure, reinforcing existing power bases associated with gender and ethnicity. In the case of Australia, the definition of the nation and its distinctiveness have been prejudiced from their inception by the country's colonial origins. The pre-eminent British influence, within the primarily European origination of the population until the 1970s, was stamped upon the images of the colonisers themselves and has had inevitable repercussions in relation to the representation of everything and everyone else:

The images by which Australia is instantly recognized in the world at

Contemporary Australian cinema

large are of men, of *white* men, and the establishment and promotion of these images has had certain corollaries, both in cultural products and in the life of the country. Among these corollaries have been the suppression of the role of women, relegated to the sidelines in most recent Australian films, neglect -in fact and fiction – of the country's Aboriginal population and its history, and a playing up of the Australian male's engagement with a demanding natural environment.[18]

This utilitarian stereotype of the national identity and set text for the national cinema presupposes the de-selection of feminine and Aboriginal characteristics, and the preference for certain environments, activities and relationships (between the men and the land, between male 'mates' and rivals, between men and males of other nationalities, and perhaps lastly between men and women). Its pervasiveness across eras and genres of the Australian cinema (comedies like *They're A Weird Mob* (Michael Powell, 1966) and *Crocodile Dundee* (Peter Faiman, 1986), pseudo-Westerns such as *The Overlanders* (Harry Watt, 1946) and *The Man from Snowy River* (George Miller, 1982), and period films like *Breaker Morant* (Bruce Beresford, 1979)), testifies to its durability as a successful and sanctioned character type. However, the American slant of Miller's and Faiman's films (conceived along commercial, Hollywood-inspired lines) and the British emphasis in Powell's and Watt's underline the extent to which this identity is imposed from without as much as asserted from within. The stereotype and its attendant subject matters of rural life, endurance and inseparable nationality and masculinity have persisted as popular and viable features of Australian cinema. Yet the greater national and international popularity of representations conceived in opposition to this orthodoxy (qualifications or contradictions of nationality, ethnic origin, environment and masculinity seen in *Death in Brunswick* (John Ruane, 1990), *Strictly Ballroom* (Baz Luhrmann, 1992), and *The Adventures of Priscilla, Queen of the Desert* (Stephan Elliott, 1994)) suggests the inadequacy and instability of this institutionalised national character. Australian cinema's conceptions of national identity can be arranged chronologically, generically and textually in relation to the original white, masculine representation, and its development can be charted through the proposal of varied alternatives. The initial limitation in the portrayal of the exploits and experience of the rural white male has given way to a no less commercial, no less contrived but considerably more variegated depiction. As such, the recent past and immediate future of Australian filmic representation constitutes an illustrated enquiry into the propriety and pertinence of differing screened nationalities:

the Australian cinema since the 1970s has resolutely set about problematizing its national identity, taking on, or perhaps 'trying on' successive identities, holding together apparently incompatible national cultural and political objectives and using the nation as a means of questioning and interrogating its very national possibility and merit as such.[19]

In order to comprehend this evolutionary process, a return to antecedent representations is necessary, along with an interpretation and appreciation of their currency and contemporaneity.

The valuable territory

Examining the rural white male stereotype in its landmark representations establishes the basis (by deference or default) of subsequent images of identity. The Anglo-American influence is significant in the shaping and perception of this version of Australian-ness, both inside and outside the country itself. *The Overlanders* (Harry Watt, 1946) stands out as a progenitor of the male Australian character, seen unabashedly from the Mother Country. The film's titles trumpet it as 'Ealing Studios' First Australian Production ... Filmed in Australia with the full co-operation of the Commonwealth Government and the Federal and State Governments'.

The objectification of the country and the categorisation of its inhabitants are inseparable from the perspective and timing of the film's narrative. It records the epic cattle drives across the northern half of the Australian continent during the Second World War, made necessary by the fear of a Japanese invasion in 1942. In addition to the military commitment of men from the colony, the country is a vital agricultural resource for the entire British Empire. The 'bullocks' it rears are 'more important than bullets' in the context of total war, yet the men who tend and drive them incarnate the same characteristics of endurance, reticence and individuality inculcated by ANZAC propaganda. Fighting and driving are equally valid 'war jobs' within the sphere of colonial service and obeisance. Either as an asset or an instrument in the conflict, the landscape and its resources embody unity and sacrifice in Imperial service: 'Space, scorched earth and space was Australia's final weapon.' Rather than destroy the cattle prior to invasion, Dan (played by Chips Rafferty) decides to attempt a 1,500 mile cattle drive across three states. Whereas poster images warning of the threat have stated that 'Safety demands Obedience', Dan's laconic *dis*obedience actually serves the greater good and reaffirms the national stereotype simultaneously.

Despite the concentration of emblematic Australian characteristics in the figure of Dan, the film's portrayal of the necessary, united and democratic action entails the recruitment of the non-white, the non-male and the non-Australian to the cause. The two-year trek is undertaken without question by Jacky, an Aborigine who defers to Dan as 'Boss'. Similarly the accompanying farmer's daughter Mary Parsons is granted 'a man's wage' for doing a male drover's work. The inexperienced British sailor nick-named 'Sinbad' is also allowed to join the company, once Dan has dispelled his delusions about Outback life: 'Nothing romantic about us, y'know. We don't carry guns or shoot up rustlers. We're just plain cattlemen – hard yakka and hard tucker.'

This statement of difference from American cowboys is significant, because of the film's comparability with the Classical Western in terms of landscape and activity. The diffidence of Dan's demeanour and his pragmatism drain the trek of one type of (melo)drama in order to instil it with an alternative, nationally determined heroism. In this respect Watt's film contrasts with *The Sundowners* (Fred Zinnemann, 1960), an Anglo-American co-production which transplants the Western's motifs to Australia wholeheartedly and uncritically.

If Dan's reserve is as stereotypically British as it is Australian, then it is fully attuned to the film's documentary aesthetic and its retrospective propagandist tone. The circumscription of national identity occurs elsewhere, as in the males' unexpected deference to matriarchal authority (the farmer's wife Mrs Parsons breaks up fights between the drovers and reprimands their drunkenness as a dereliction of duty). Likewise, the population of the Northern Territory is stated as 'five thousand whites', with the 'black fellas' and particularly the 'wild blacks' dismissed or relegated to part of the fauna. Ironically, the clearest statement of Australian patriotism (aside from unequivocal colonial obedience) is couched in the terms of Western frontiersmanship. Dan responds scathingly to Corky's draft prospectus for the 'Northern Territory Exploitation Company':

'We've exploited our south for a hundred years and torn the heart out of it. The Territory's far too valuable to be messed about by get-rich-quick schemes like yours. I say let's save the north from what we've done to the south ... Leave it to Australians. Ordinary Australians like Bill [Parsons] and his family. It's a national job, Corky, too big for little people like you.'

The preservation of the unsullied landscape as a national resource, entrusted to the likes of the dedicated, hard-working and stoical Parsons family, combines contradictory Western ideals (the desert being made to flower and the wilderness being left unchanged by the encroachment of civilisation). The admiration Dan inspires as a national icon (simultaneously pitting himself against and yet respecting the landscape, using and conquering it for the fulfilment of national pride and colonial duty) seems to suggest that the ambiguous goal of preserving the Territory for true patriots is attainable. The concomitant denial of the Territory's indigenous population, who are not involved in the global conflict but are the likely victims of the region's exploitation, is not explored. Treatment of the natural landscape throughout the Australian cinema reflects this ambiguity. The natural settings of bush, desert and mountain are classified and interpreted syntactically. On the one hand the landscape appears as a source of national pride, the origin of difference, the crucible of Australian pioneer character and the catalyst which unifies disparate communal elements. On the other it represents uninhabited void, an antipathetic vacancy symbolising the partiality and ephemerality of European colonial settlement.

Dan's characterisation as the national stereotype is unambiguous: he is taciturn but decisive, skilful but undemonstrative, individualistic but dutiful. This incarnation of admirable qualities summarises the requirements of the nation and reinforces the assumptions of the Empire. The best Australian defies authority to serve the greater good, and uses his innate skills and the resources of the land to define himself and defeat the distant enemy. Just as representation of national character is limited to the masculine icon, so national identity is restricted by the stipulations of Commonwealth membership.

The big country

In the last period of vigorous Australian film production prior to the revival of the 1970s, local filmmakers had concentrated on country's connection to its cultural fountainhead:

Ken Hall and Charles Chauvel's cinema of the 1930s projected Australia's 'British' character. Such an identity 'united' both the English migrant and the (older) Australian, just as it marginalised the minority settler ethnicities ... Generically, textually and content wise the Australian cinema of the 1920s and 1930s was obsessed by its British relation.[20]

Deference to the Northern hemisphere and discussion of the creation of a multicultural Australia emerge twenty years after *The Overlanders* in *They're A Weird Mob* (Michael Powell, 1966). The conservatism of inherent Britishness has been absorbed into an establishment structure distrustful of foreign immigrants, while the stereotype of the ordinary male Australian is urbanised, ironised and exaggerated. The country and people are seen from the outside, from the perspectives of the newly-arrived immigrant and the British filmmaker, and this approach mimics the reactions of Sydney residents to the 'New Australians', based on prejudices and reinforced by first impressions.

The film opens with the positioning of subject and object. Images of schoolchildren studying a model globe, which turns to reveal the Australian continent at the bottom of the world, are accompanied by a authoritative voice-over: 'Australians live down under. Like flies on the ceiling they never fall off.' A child tilts her head to look at the underside of the globe, and pictures of Sydney streets are duly inserted, upside down. When the narrator points out, 'Of course, they see themselves like *this*', the image rotates and rights itself, but the patronising tone of the mock-documentary is maintained through a series of illustrative vignettes which attempt to decipher particularities of custom and idiom. These exemplify the Australian male's innate sexism and predilections for drinking, gambling and hunting which the film proper explores in detail. However, the catalogue of 'weirdness' functions rather as a reminder of truisms, and an acknowledgement of certainties in the definition of both Britishness and Australian-ness. These are strengthened by the comedic national anthems by Reen Devereaux which accompany the opening and closing credits:

In this man's country a man doesn't dream in the sun,
There's many manly things that must be done.
A man's gotta prove he's a man and he can
In this land that is shiny and new,
So shorten your shorts, bare your chest, get a tan,
Catch a fish, paint a boat, build a barbecue,
A king-size barbecue, that takes a big, big steak,
The Antipodean man must eat,
Under king-size skies and the king-size flies
While the missus shrivels up in the heat.

After the orientation provided by this combination of travelogue and parody, the film follows the experiences of 'Nino Culotta', a New Australian from Italy. From his arrival Nino is met with a mixture of impatience (in the attitudes of immigration officials, police, taxi drivers and hotel staff), and forbearance (tolerance from the ordinary Australian males that he works with on a building site). Nino is forced to accept manual labour because the Italian-Australian magazine he is supposed to work for has gone bankrupt while he is in transit. As such, the building work he takes on becomes symbolic on numerous levels. Initially it is simply a source of income to support himself and repay the debts incurred by his relations at the magazine. However, this is also indicative of a perceived as well as actual debt that the migrants owe to their new home country. The Australian labourers welcome Nino, providing the chance for him to prove himself in an unaccustomed job and offering him hospitality in their homes. His willingness to join the group (in working and drinking) quickly makes him an honorary Australian male. The building of new homes (next to the property of a Chinese immigrant) to which he contributes also symbolises the creation of the New Australia. At the comic level, he constructs furniture for himself in his temporary lodgings from the piles of unsold magazines. The ultimate expression of symbolic construction is Nino's planning and building of his own house (with the help of his new mates) on his own piece of land.

The group Nino joins (comprising Joe the foreman and his men Dennis and Jimmy) incarnates the stereotype outlined by the film's opening songs and images. Like Dan they are in awe of the authority wielded by their wives, but the emblematic skills and self-reliance of the bushman are undermined by their return from a rainy hunting trip with only one dead rabbit between them. This trophy is thrown onto a silver tea tray Joe's wife has brought out for entertaining Nino, whose European refinement is highlighted elsewhere by the use of a fork to eat cake. In this group, the modesty and laconic demeanour of Dan gives way to a lackadaisical attitude, where work is endured rather than enjoyed and enthusiasm is reserved for the national recreations identified at the opening. At the site Jimmy opines that Nino will 'conk out by lunchtime' if he carries on working with such unseemly eagerness, but he later dismisses Joe's idea of replacing him and the other 'moody bastards' with a mechanical digger: 'Cost you more than us mate, and it won't go and have a beer with you.'

Nino's assimilation is signalled by Dennis' defence of him in the face of another contractor's prejudice, but he remains distinct from the other males in his attitudes to courtship. The marriages of Joe and the others are seen as a continuum of drudgery, with freedom and enjoyment only achievable through duplicity or drunkenness. These relationships appear to have neither a passionate beginning nor a rancorous end, simply a perpetual dreariness and resignation on the part of both partners. Nino's romantic pursuit of Kay Kelly, the daughter of a building magnate (played by Chips Rafferty) provokes scorn from some quarters ('they're all alike in the dark'), but his fervour succeeds in eroding her reserve. Initially her prejudice against him parallels that of other establishment figures, but under his influence she changes her wardrobe and her hair style, adopting European fashions and losing her (British) restraint. Kay's father is won over too, when he recognises in Nino an 'Australian' candour, self-assurance and commitment to self-improvement in the new land comparable to his own. Under these circumstances the formality of their meeting evaporates, and the men remove jackets and ties in order to drink. By comparison, Kay's meeting with Nino's adoptive family (Jimmy, Dennis, Joe and his wife) is stilted and farcical, until Nino shouts for beer in place of the tea and meringues which have failed to impart any sophistication. Nino's assimilation as a true Australian male, Mr Kelly's recognition of this and Kay's acceptance of it, are crowned with the unification of the classes, cultures and sexes in a final drunken party. The conceptualisation of Australian-ness propounded at the opening is therefore ratified at its conclusion. Australia is a country with 'room for everyone' only inasmuch as cultural, sexual and class difference can be submerged in the stereotype, adopted by men, endured by women, and broadcast and recognised overseas, as the final (inverted) image of the Sydney Harbour Bridge suggests. The lack of discrimination in relation to the film's representation can be gauged from its massive box-office success in Australia and New Zealand, in comparison with its failure in Italy and Great Britain.[21]

The Australian abroad

By the mid-1960s and 1970s, the very idea of Australia as British had definitively – if unevenly – changed ... Some famous revival films of the 1970s and early 1980s embody these dedominionising strategies. In *The Adventures of Barry McKenzie*, *Gallipoli*, *Breaker Morant* an Australian identity and culture was defined against the British. In *Barry McKenzie* the British/Australian relationship had become banal – a point of differentiation represented by competing stereotypes. The very idea of Australia as British – and England as home – is set up as a conceit to reveal its sheer implausibility and as a lame plot excuse to put the fantastic and grotesque Barry McKenzie abroad as the half-wit 'Aussie innocent'.[22]

The perceptions of Australians and Australian-ness at home and abroad have undergone inevitable change, and also enjoyed unanticipated reinforcement, in the years since Powell's film. The earliest commercial films of the revival, the 'Ocker' comedies, thrived on the further exaggeration of the vulgar, brash and uncultured version of masculinity at the heart of *They're A Weird*

Mob. As considerable box-office successes, films such as *Stork* (Tim Burstall, 1971) and *The Adventures of Barry McKenzie* (Bruce Beresford, 1972) magnified the art-versus-commerce conflict, since the latter was entirely funded by the newly-formed Australian Film Development Corporation. They also capitalised on the market for sex comedies and built on earlier Australian films centred on the fish-out-of-water character.[23] These X-rated 'adult' comedies perpetuated certain aspects of the national characterisation as defined to date. The predisposition to drink, allied to irrepressible energy, innocence and a specific corporeality, combine in the character of Barry to mobilise the film's scatological humour. The innocence or inexperience of the Australian male was qualified in *Alvin Purple* (Tim Burstall, 1973), by the addition of numerous sexual encounters. The eponymous hero, like the central character of the British comedies *Percy* (Ralph Thomas, 1971) and *Percy's Progress* (Ralph Thomas, 1974) finds himself beset by insatiable females. All of these films rely on the recognition as much as the rewriting of prevalent stereotypes. While local and international success for disadvantaged national cinemas is clearly dependent on the use of such representational shorthand (cf the depiction of the emotionally inarticulate and class-bound British in *Four Weddings and A Funeral* (Mike Newell, 1995)), the perpetuation of such images can dignify rather than ironise their reductiveness:

McKenzie is a camp comedy of a by then outdated Australian masculinity ... In many ways, the film can be regarded as a 'rewriting' of *They're A Weird Mob* (Powell, 1966). It encourages not so much 'identification' with its Australianness, but a suspending of illusionist belief, thereby producing a fantasy of the 'hyper-Australian' intersecting with an equally 'hyper-Britishness'.[24]

While undoubtedly there was and is a 'happy mutuality'[25] between British and Australian representations of Australianness (and Britishness) underpinning as well as undermining cultural communication and comprehension, *Barry McKenzie* was both old-fashioned in its circumscription of both nationalities, and contemporary in its attitude towards the vestiges of the British heritage. The irony of its humorous treatment, like that of *They're A Weird Mob*, is sometimes lost in the popular recognition and acceptance of its treatment of national stereotypes. Two succeeding films, depicting the solitary Australian either abroad or at home and successful at home and overseas, stressed the contrasting commercial and generic influence of America in Australian cinema in the 1980s.

The Man from Snowy River (George Miller, 1982) touches upon many aspects of national identity and Australian culture encountered in the representations of stereotypical Australian-ness already mentioned. The men of the mountains exhibit skills in horsemanship and frontier resourcefulness to rival those of *The Overlanders* and the heroes of the Hollywood Western. Their life in the mountain environment is seen as demanding and rewarding, and it sets them apart within the country even as the characteristics they embody define the country to outsiders. The narrative basis for the film is the poem by A.B. 'Banjo' Paterson, enshrined on school curricula as an important literary and cultural text. However, these artistic roots belie the film's shrewd commercial crafting, which sets it apart from the near-contemporary literary adaptations and period dramas approved by the Australian Film Commission as fitting expressions of the new film culture. Its American credentials (through the involvement of 20th Century-Fox and the casting of Kirk Douglas), its full espousal of the format and iconography of the Western, and its inception by the creative team of Geoff Burrows and George Miller (with considerable experience in production and direction for Australian commercial television), are indicative of its wholehearted commitment to popular success.[26]

Jim Craig is the titular hero, who works with his father on a unprofitable mountain farm. To raise money they attempt to trap a herd of wild horses ('brumbies') led by a stallion, but accidentally Jim's father is killed and their mare Bess is run off by the stallion. Jim is forced to seek work in the lowlands, to 'earn the right' to return to live in the mountains, and vows to recover Bess and capture the brumbies. The wild horses have been used graphically from the film's title sequence as romantic symbols of the freedom of the mountains and Jim's destiny in mastering them both. Entering the service of an American cattleman named Harrison, Jim gains respect for his skills with horses but is dismissed because of the growing affection between him and Harrison's daughter Jessica. However, when Harrison's prize colt is also lost to the brumby stallion, Jim proves his worth by recovering all the horses singlehandedly, and claims Jessica as his reward. The unflattering conflation of Jessica with the brood mares as the hero's bounty underlines the chauvinistic tone. This is also extended to the valuation of the landscape, which despite putative respect is tamed in the same way as the wild animals and the initially liberated future spouse. Jim is endowed with an heroic and archetypal status by his origins and his skills, which are proved superior to those of every other cattleman including the mythic figure of Clancy. As the most famous stockman of them all, Clancy's costume and characterisation within Miller's film define him as a mid-Atlantic merger of the Australian stereotype and the Marlboro Man. Clancy is played by Jack Thompson, an actor as well known and inseparable from images of Australian masculinity in films of the revival as Chips Rafferty had been to a previous generation. In an echo of Rafferty's character in *The Overlanders*, Clancy is given a speech similar to Dan's defence of the Territory, when he opposes Harrison's plans to exploit the Snowy River country. The argument between the two older men is settled by Jim's interjection, that 'you might sooner hold back the tide than tame the mountain'.

The success of the film is remarkable (or perhaps inevitable) given its predictability in narrative, characterisation, melodramatic manipulation and ideological conservatism:

> In its disjunctions, its cliches bordering on the camp, its hamming-up, its firm situation with the genres of film and television ... it was obviously not a 'well made' film. There is however a sneaking suspicion that its spell, the pleasure that audiences obviously draw from the film, has to do, somehow, with the fact of that poor script, that staginess, those touching animal cliches like a thousand movies before it ... They were appreciating, as Geoff Burrowes, the producer, was quick to point out, the very scenes that critics had lambasted as banal.[27]

O'Regan identifies the aspects of popular culture articulated by the film as shared, and as undeniably Australian as American. The myth of the frontier common to both cultures has been repackaged in a mechanical, formulaic way, to restate and update its unassailable national value:

> *The Man* is not a reassertion of the pioneer legend A.B. Paterson attempted to create. *The Man* is self-consciously a spectacle film with a flagrant disregard of the values and perceptions of the times. Harrison rails against feminism. Jim talks in the language of animal liberation when he breaks in the colt from Old Regret. Clancy admonishes the predatory Harrison in terms that make sense only within an ecological frame of reference ... European settlement is registered, not as a raping of the landscape, but as a fact. Further it is *Australian* and not European. There is no European gentility to be incorporated or overcome in this film. The settlers are not fighting against the bush. They are not maintaining and retaining in a ridiculous fashion their Europeanism in a hostile, alien environment. They are quite simply there and they manifestly belong there.[28]

The film's relatively enthusiastic reception in America can be attributed to its star, its clear generic lineage, its undemanding narrative and the bonus of a quaint exoticism. (Simon Wincer, the executive producer of *The Man from Snowy River*, has been able to repeat its salient features in other commercial Westerns he has directed in subsequent years, such as *Lonesome Dove* (ABC-TV, 1989), *Quigley Down Under* (1990) and *Lightning Jack* (1994).) In Australia, its enormous success represents a conjunction of commercial proficiency, generic acquaintance and popularity, and reductive, positivist nationalism. A similarly cynical combination of textual features and cultural factors underpinned the success of the other Australian hero abroad in the 1980s.

Crocodile Dundee (Peter Faiman, 1986) and its sequel (*Crocodile Dundee II* (John Cornell, 1988)) again foreground the American influence on attempts to commercialise the output of the Australian cinema. The generic basis is again the Western, with the additional narrative element of Paul Hogan's Outback hero being transported to New York, where the fish-out-of-water comedy resembles a sanitised version of *McKenzie* in Manhattan. Hogan's deadpan comedic persona established through television and advertising is tailored to the ironic male characterisation, but his heroism, adaptability and suitability as a romantic hero are all asserted unambiguously by the film's conclusion. Dundee's nickname is derived from an apocryphal story which tempts Sue the American journalist to Australia to meet him. The embellishment of this tale devalues him, but only momentarily. His manifest skills with animals, his knowledge of the land and understanding of Aboriginal culture (through tribal adoption) all confirm him as an embodiment of the Australian male stereotype. This character might be drawn as much as a parody as a paragon of nationality and masculinity, and could be excused as such. However, the presence of Wally (John Meillon), the clearly fake hero aspiring to the same status, serves to revalidate Dundee as the genuine article.

Dundee's adventures at home and in America offer an (albeit milder) repetition of Barry McKenzie's formative encounters. Sexual, racial and cultural differences are seen to crumble before the naivety and ignorance of the old-fashioned 'real man'. His shortcomings in experience and etiquette are compensated by an uncomplicated nature, a broad grin and a big knife. Activity (drinking, chasing, rescuing) is always preferred to contemplation. Sue's eventual selection of Dundee over her effete fiancé is secured by her running after him through the city streets, and violently dispatching muggers along the way. As a further development of this, the sequel simply increases the proportion of stunts and chases and heightens its resemblance to many other undistinguished Hollywood action films. The mixture of morally satisfying violence, semi-mock heroics and romantic narrative that the film incorporates succeed in making the national international, or alternatively encapsulate the questionable national stereotype in thrall to Hollywood centrism. The archetypal Australian-ness of the character is thus both foregrounded and negated simultaneously:

Crocodile Dundee ... wearing a costume that would seem more at home on Harrison Ford in a Steven Spielberg adventure, arrives in New York as a Candide and leaves it as Rocky.[29]

As further evidence of the conservatism behind the stereotype and the film, the treatment of the Aboriginal characters provokes particular criticism. Mick Dundee's appropriation of (and improvement upon) Aboriginal lore and custom is as objection-able as the contemporaneous television series Bush Tucker Man. Mick is portrayed as a 'better' Aborigine than the people them-selves. In the first film, he participates in rituals and moves more silently than the city boy Nev (played by David Gulpilil). Aboriginal spirituality is also ridiculed when Sue asks to take a photograph of Nev. In the sequel Mick capitalises on the loyalty of tribal people (led by Ernie Dingo) who refuse to track him on behalf of the villains. When the tables are turned the villains are terrified by threats that the Aborigines might eat them. O'Regan compares Hogan's character with that of Chips Rafferty in The Phantom Stockman:

Aboriginality – its skills and bush lore – is lent to the white leads, enabling them to be 'super' men, at one with the landscape ... This cannibalisation of Aboriginal knowledge systematically disadvant-ages the indigenous black, who is stripped of any superior under-standing of and competence in the natural environment.[30]

Ironically, the international success of the Crocodile Dundee films, particularly in America, represented the attainment of a coveted level of proficiency in commercial, narrative filmmaking which notable figures in Australian film criticism had long desired. The apparent incapability of revival films to fulfil the requirements of classical Hollywood narrative form (and thus achieve the con-comitant box office returns) was a source of frustration, even though divergence from such norms was inevitable in the estab-lishment of a definitive Australian subject and the search for a particular national filmic idiom in which to express it. In com-paring the inconclusive narrative and ambiguous allusion of the Australian film Picnic at Hanging Rock (Peter Weir, 1975) with the clarity, linearity and unequivocal closure of the American film Witness (Peter Weir, 1985), McFarlane and Mayer conclude that the pretension towards art cinema in the former has been replaced by maturer storytelling techniques in the latter.[31] While such an evaluation of *Witness* is questionable in itself, the fact remains that the formal and commercial effectiveness of *Crocodile Dundee* is reliant on the simplification, obfuscation or denigration of important cultural specificities. The cost of creating national film texts and a representative film culture, whether through aesthetic or commercial pursuits, is never purely financial.

Reading the national cinema

The pervasiveness of foreign cultural influences (British and American) is discernible in the history and pre-history of the Australian revival. The particular impact of Hollywood models, American commercial goals and popular filmic genres is most evident in films incorporating the emblematic white Australian male stereotype. While the Hollywood Western is a clear inspiration in many cases, the utilisation and revision of other Hollywood genres is a major trend within the Australian revival. Additionally, the independent development of several indigenous film genres has been an important feature of recent production, and has helped to punctuate and bracket the streams of feature production that have evolved since 1970. These Australian genres have been identified and evaluated (the Australian Gothic, the period film, the male ensemble film[32]) and are worthy of consideration both in their own right and in their intersection with other conventionalised forms (science fiction, fantasy and horror in comparison with the Gothic, the heritage film and literary adaptation in connection with the period film, and the war film and rite of passage in relation to the male ensemble). More recently, an aesthetic and thematic trend (rather than a genre proper) has emerged in the examples of *Strictly Ballroom*, *The Adventures of Priscilla, Queen of the Desert* and *Muriel's Wedding* (P.J. Hogan, 1994), which foregrounds elements of the camp, the kitsch and the retrospective idolisation of 1970s Glamour. Such chronological, stylistic and thematic groupings are important in the interpretation of national filmmaking, not simply as consistencies which underpin generalisations but as continuities in communication between the subject(s) and object(s) of cultural representation:

the concern is with what the films are about. Do they share a common style or world view? Do they share common themes, motifs or preoccupations? How do they project the national character? How do they dramatise the fantasies of national identity? Are they concerned with questions of nationhood? What role do they play in constructing the sense or the image of a nation? One of the most productive ways of exploring national cinema from this perspective is in terms of genre analysis, for the processes of repetition and reiteration which constitute a genre can be highly productive in sustaining a cultural identity.[33]

By extrapolating from the persistent (though not original or primary) forms of national representation, and the correspondences of indigenous and imported generic output, this study seeks to interpret the contemporary Australian cinema. This entails the reading of individual films within the context of identifiable, evolving indigenous and transmuted imported genres, and tracing the promotion and propagation of disparate national images. In adopting the generic categories suggested by Australian commentators, this interpretation of the new Australian cinema concentrates on the pervasive problematisation of national identity apparent within contemporary production. Some films defy straightforward generic classification, and in some cases this difficulty prompts a re-examination of both individual texts and broader categories. Just as the physical landscape is regionalised, urbanised and politicised, and the human landscape is demarcated along lines of gender, race and ethnicity, so the film industry and its products are both divided and yet made to cohere along generic, auteurist and ideological lines.

Notes

1 James Monaco, *How to Read a Film* (revised edn) (Oxford, Oxford University Press, 1981), p. 6.

2 Andrew Higson, *Waving the Flag: Constructing a National Cinema in Britain* (Oxford, Clarendon, 1995), p. 5.

3 Jan Dawson, Australian Film Culture, *Cinema Papers* no. 12 (1977), pp. 307, 373 (p. 373).

4 Eric Reade, Australian Silent Film 1904–1907: The Features Begin, in John L. Fell (ed.), *Film Before Griffith* (London, University of California Press, 1983), p. 88.

5 Andrew Pike and Ross Cooper, *Australian Film 1900–1977: A Guide to Feature Film Production* (Melbourne, Oxford University Press, 1980), pp. 5–6.

6 Ibid., p. 4.

7 Ibid., p. 116.

8 Ibid., pp. 199–200.

9 Ibid., p. 263.

10 Liz Jacka, The Film Industry in Australia: Trends in the Eighties, *Media Information Australia* no. 42 (1986), pp. 17–21 (p. 17).

11 Graham Shirley and Brian Adams, *Australian Cinema: The First Eighty Years* (revised edn) (Sydney, Currency Press, 1989), p. 221.

12 Interim Report of the Film Committee, Australian Council for the

Arts (1969), in Albert Moran and Tom O'Regan (eds), *An Australian Film Reader* (Sydney, Currency Press, 1985), p. 171.

13 Gideon Bachmann, Films in Australia, *Sight and Sound* vol. 46 no. 1 (1976–7), pp. 32–6 (p. 33).

14 Susan Dermody and Elizabeth Jacka, *The Screening of Australia Vol. I: The Anatomy of a Film Industry* (Sydney, Currency Press, 1987), p. 35.

15 Ibid., p. 27.

16 Tom O'Regan, *Australian National Cinema* (London, Routledge, 1996), p. 10.

17 Thomas Elsaesser, Narrative Cinema and Audience-Oriented Aesthetics, in Tony Bennett, Susan Boyd-Bowman, Colin Mercer, Janet Woollacott (eds), *Popular Film and Television: A Reader* (London, BFI, 1981), p. 270.

18 Brian McFarlane, *Australian Cinema 1970–1985* (London, Secker & Warburg, 1987), p. 48.

19 O'Regan (1996), p. 69.

20 Ibid., p. 312.

21 Ken Hall, Strategies for An Industry – Television and Co-production, in Moran and O'Regan, p. 160.

22 O'Regan (1996), p. 313.

23 Shirley and Adams (1989), p. 242.

24 O'Regan (1996), pp. 51–2.

25 Ibid., p. 56.

26 Pike and Cooper (1980, pp. 134–5) note the commercial crafting and American influence of an earlier version *The Man from Snowy River* (Beaumont Smith/John K. Wells, 1920).

27 Tom O'Regan, *The Man From Snowy River* and Australian Popular Culture, in Moran and O'Regan (eds) (1985), p. 244.

28 Ibid., pp. 245, 247.

29 Philip Adams, A Cultural Revolution, in Scott Murray (ed.), *Australian Cinema* (St Leonards, Australia, Allen & Unwin, 1994), p. 68.

30 Tom O'Regan, Fair Dinkum Fillums: The *Crocodile Dundee* Phenomenon, in Susan Dermody and Elizabeth Jacka (eds), *The Imaginary Industry: Australian Film in the Late '80s* (North Ryde, AFTRS Publications, 1988b), p. 171.

31 Brian McFarlane and Geoff Mayer, *New Australian Cinema: Sources and Parallels in American and British Film* (Cambridge, Cambridge University Press, 1992), pp. 54–60.

32 See Susan Dermody and Elizabeth Jacka, *The Screening of Australia Vol. II: Anatomy of a National Cinema* (Sydney, Currency Press, 1988a), pp. 29–74.

33 Higson (1995), p. 6.

2

Australian Gothic

Origins

The category of Australian Gothic covers a broad range of film texts, with the first representatives appearing in the early 1970s at the same time as the 'Ocker' comedies. The films given this label share a variety of common characteristics, but the best known examples (*The Last Wave* (Peter Weir, 1977), the *Mad Max* trilogy (Dr George Miller, 1979/1981/1985), *Shame* (Steve Jodrell, 1987)) illustrate the variations in setting, characterisation

Georgia

and mode that the films essay. The environments chosen for drama cover the contemporary cityscape in *The Last Wave*, the isolated rural community in *Shame*, and the deserts of the post-apocalyptic future in *Mad Max*. The narratives borrow freely from recognisable popular genres (science fiction in Miller's films, the Western in Jodrell's, the horror film in Weir's), and transplant their protagonists to create unease and alienation (a middle-class lawyer encounters Sydney's Aboriginal underclass in *The Last Wave*, a female barrister from the city meets local corruption and injustice in *Shame*, and Max the young cop becomes divorced from society and family in the vain battle against encroaching anarchy). The enumeration of such differences can be extended even further, when one takes into account the debt to Hitchcock (in *The Plumber* (Peter Weir, 1978)) and to the political/investigative thriller (*Heatwave* (Phillip Noyce, 1981), *Deadly* (Esben Storm, 1990)). Instead of a genre, Australian Gothic represents a mode, a stance and an atmosphere, after the fashion of American Film Noir, with the appellation suggesting the inclusion of horrific and fantastic materials comparable to those of Gothic literature. These characteristics are shared by films which are otherwise derived from disparate sources (arguably a willingness to revise and parody the conventions of one or more established genres is another key Gothic feature). However, three thematic concerns which permeate all the films related to the Gothic sensibility provide links across the distinctions of era, environment and character. They are: a questioning of established authority; a disillusionment with the social reality that that authority maintains; and the protagonist's search for a valid and tenable identity once the true nature of the human environment has been revealed. These themes are themselves interlinked, and reflect a doubt or dubiety in the assertions of national character and confidence in national institutions which characterised earlier examples of Australian film.

Two films which are credited with marking the re-emergence of Australian filmmaking and inspiring further production are *Walkabout* (Nicolas Roeg, 1970) and *Wake in Fright* (Ted Kotcheff, 1971). Although neither were directed by Australians, their specific settings and casts helped to re-establish the technical support for the Australian industry, and coincidentally their narratives and *mise-en-scène* laid the foundations for the appearance of Australian Gothic in the remainder of the 1970s. Roeg's film charts the odyssey of two schoolchildren across the vastness of the Outback. The teenage sister (Jenny Agutter) and her younger brother are marooned far from civilisation following their father's suicide, after he has failed in his attempt to kill them. They are befriended by an Aboriginal boy (David Gulpilil), who saves them from thirst and starvation and leads them back towards white habitation. However, the girl misinterprets the Aborigine's dance of courtship as a prelude to rape, and her rejection prompts him to hang himself. In the film's epilogue, years after their safe return to the city the girl (now married to an affluent husband) recalls as in a dream the Edenic freedom of the interlude away from civilisation. The impact of the film derives from its allegorical potential, not simply to discuss the loss and exploitation of natural innocence in the Australian landscape, but to allude to the spiritual bankruptcy of Western civilisation in all its manifestations. At one level the Australian landscape appears as the ultimate blank slate, unmarked by (non-Aboriginal) culture and antithetical to human encroachment. By re-entering the pre-lapsarian landscape, the children return to a guiltless and uncomplicated life. However, the flora and fauna are seen to be alien and threatening (the blank immensity of the desert is populated by monstrous lizards and insects, features pools which appear and disappear without warning, and is traversed by an alien human whose language, customs and intentions are unknown). If the landscape contains an unfathomable menace (present in nature, projected onto the Aborigine, repressed in the girl), then the city the children have left is portrayed as an abstraction of the same primitive, innate qualities:

Roeg begins his film with an eerie, alienated, anthropological view of civilised man. Over a disjunctive soundtrack (a radio talk on etiquette and snatches from Stockhausen's 'Hymnen' punctuated by an 'unnatural' or at least un-urban silence), commuting businessmen scurry in and out of their glass office blocks, soldiers march on parade, a housewife hacks up offal in her stainless steel kitchen, and rows of schoolgirls chant out their consonants in a breathing class: a series of sounds and images which suggest that modern man has not transcended the rituals of the tribe but merely perverted them.[1]

The imperceptible difference between modern and traditional societies is encapsulated in Roeg's dislocation of music and image throughout the film's exposition. Radio reports and static are overlaid with Aboriginal music and the school elocution lessons, and traffic noise accompanies a view around a brick wall which leads into the heart of the desert. The thousands of years of human development are at once inconsequential, in the endless repetition of communal behaviour and hierarchical structure, and insuperable, as the fatal breakdown of communication between innocence and inhibition attests. At the same time, the character of modern humanity and its advances are portrayed as both vicious (unconscionable killing of wildlife for fun rather than sustenance) and ridiculous (the clear blue swimming pool seen below the girl's adult home is built only yards from the ocean). *Walkabout* manages to balance these anomalies through its portrait of the timeless land, indifferent rather than aggressive towards human incursion. It evokes lyricism and transcendence in place of coherent narrative or commentary, presenting 'familiar antitheses (noble savage and corrupt society, paradise lost and urban hell) ... as images rather than ideas'.[2]

As the other parent of the Gothic, *Wake in Fright* approaches similar principles from an alternative angle. Again the validity and stability of the human environment imposed on the natural is an important issue, but instead of concentrating on emblematic child characters, Kotcheff's film focuses on a typical rural community. The film's relentless gaze centres on the debasement of the population of an isolated town, whose decline into barbarism is viewed (and paralleled) by an outsider. An English teacher leaves his Outback school for the holidays, planning to spend his time and earnings with his girlfriend at the coast. As he waits for a connecting train in the secluded town of Bundunyabba, he becomes embroiled in illegal gambling and loses all his wages. Thereafter, the unremitting hospitality of the locals includes him in their endless drinking and debauchery, culminating in his involvement in a bloodthirsty kangaroo hunt. The young Englishman's inexorable slide from aloof reserve into full participation in the futile, mindless and violent pastimes of 'the yabba' rubbishes distinctions of class, race and education which his incongruous presence in the Outback had previously upheld. His initiation into the all-male group is completed by copying his 'mates' in slitting a kangaroo's throat, and by being given his own gun for future hunts. His final degradation at the nadir of control and consciousness, is his attempted suicide after being sexually assaulted by the town's alcoholic doctor. Significantly, the doctor can be seen as the embodiment of societal collapse, since his decline and assimilation into the town's culture prefigures the teacher's degeneration. However, the teacher survives and recuperates before travelling back to his job a sadder and wiser man.

Wake in Fright foregrounds rural towns and eccentric communities as the breeding grounds of the Gothic. The normal camaraderie of drinking and hunting comes to define characters and fill lives in such isolation. Since civilisation supports survival, the hunt becomes a savage and senseless ritual, arising from disregard of the landscape and inspiring self-loathing. Paradoxically, the civilisation the town represents actually threatens survival in a different way, as the loss of direction and identity the town's way of life engenders leads to a soaring suicide rate. The local policeman turns a blind eye to this, recording the deaths as 'accidental', and similarly overlooks the gambling ring despite its contribution to the town's despair. That this character is played by Chips Rafferty represents one of the film's greatest coups. The stoicism and forthrightness of Dan from *The Overlanders* becomes, in this incarnation, a blank denial of the bleakest truth. The policeman can insist on a minute's silence in the town's pub on Anzac Day, but also refuse to recognise the implications of other national characteristics on the town's imploding population. Taken together, these two films outline many of the narrative devices, much of the iconography and the majority of the themes explored in the true examples of Australian Gothic. *Walkabout* identifies the natural landscape as a source of anxiety and regret, and the modern world as the tainted inheritance of civilisation. At the same time, the land and its ecology are seen as the victims of ravaging tribal instincts debased and exaggerated by the advancement of technology. In *Wake in Fright* the rural existence of the stereotypical Australian male is stripped of mystique and individualism, as the Outback town is portrayed as the repository of warped or degenerate tendencies, dark reflections of accepted characteristics:

Wake in Fright turned a deliberately blind or jaundiced eye towards the beauty of the interior landscape; it was about the impoverished terrain of white, civilised humanity in that overwhelming emptiness. *Walkabout* is its Siamese twin, facing the opposite direction but from the same point. Urban Australia, coastal city and small inland town, is seen as a perverse denial of the essential truth of Australia. In this film, the interior is still brim full of a spiritual infinitude which answers the needs of Eurocentric mankind escaping from a shrinking Europe.[3]

As recent and successful antecedents to indigenous film production, these films are credited with an influence and a pertinence because, not in spite, of their non-Australian directors.[4] They itemise the subject matter of Australian Gothic: the pre-existing landscape, the human social construct, the human authority exerted more or less successfully on both, and the reaction of disempowered individuals to this spectacle.

The Gothic rural community

White country communities ... have come to represent all that is bad in the Australian settler culture and which a metropolitan sensitivity can take its distance from: racism, xenophobia, misogyny, violence, intolerance of difference, homophobia and aggressive masculinism in a film-making stretching from *Wake in Fright* ... to *The Adventures of Priscilla: Queen of the Desert*.[5]

The nature of the rural community's secret depravity alters subtly from film to film, but its otherness is a given. For the unsuspecting outsiders who venture by chance or accident into its confines, the insularity of the backwater town is a cause rather than a symptom of fatal difference. The perversity of rural townships and their residents forms the basis of Gothic texts which in other respects reflect debts to generic entertainment, social polemics, fantasy and allegory.

Peter Weir's first feature production *The Cars That Ate Paris* (1974) portrays the Outback town as the seat of deranged authority. Weir had contributed to the inception of Australian Gothic with his independent short film *Homesdale* (1971), which mixed homage to Hitchcock, Pythonesque humour and expressionistic visual style. Its black comedic narrative concerns the experiences of a group of visitors at the hunting lodge of the title. Homesdale is described variously as a 'hospice' and a 'new experiment in togetherness', and the guests seem to be the patients or victims in a bizarre series of tests and torments devised by the asylum staff. The lodge appears to be built on an isolated island, and can therefore be seen to stand for Australia itself, as a forgotten outpost still ruled by an outdated British establishment. The devious combination of public school discipline, religious exhortation and psychological manipulation that the lodge's manager uses to break and mould the minds of the guests builds into a scathing indictment of cynical establishment control. The manager is a caricature of the conservative establishment figures permeating Australian institutions, and similarly the authority he wields is based on archaic notions of team spirit and corporal punishment. However, the varied backgrounds of the guests and their individual neuroses both undermine his complacent world view and serve his darker purposes, as he and his staff home in remorselessly on the weak and the malleable. The manager's nostalgic recollections of the war years are contrasted with a guest's recent and traumatic experiences of combat. While the Vietnam War is never mentioned by name, the resentment of Australian involvement in an American, rather than British, war overseas is clearly implied. The activities at the lodge (disturbing games, tricks played on the guests and an unnerving treasure hunt) culminate in the persecution and humiliation of one inmate. His treatment drives him insane and he kills another guest, but the film's epilogue reveals that he has subsequently become an attendant at the lodge, assisting in the control and torture of others. Authority, as seen in this short fantasy, derives its power from the manipulation and abuse of weakness. The insane are recruited to secure the objectives of the malevolent establishment. The denunciation of the establishment found in the allegory of *Homesdale* can be seen to recur throughout Weir's career of feature films in Australia and America, but in the short term is developed in the characterisation of patriarchal authority in *The Cars That Ate Paris*.

Arthur Waldo appears to be an unlikely hero when he wakes up in the Paris infirmary following a car accident. His brother has died in the car crash on the outskirts of the town, and the trauma has left Arthur incapable of driving. As a result, he is marooned in Paris, and slowly he comes to understand the horrible truth of the town's subsistence on contrived car crashes. Like eighteenth-century Cornish wreckers, the residents of Paris engineer accidents on the surrounding country roads, and the town's barter economy uses a currency of tyres, oil, petrol and parts. Even the occupants of the wrecked cars are absorbed or recycled. Many injured drivers are kept in the infirmary, reduced to vegetables by their injuries or the unknown experiments of the local doctor, and the family of the sinister Mayor (played by John Meillon) is augmented by second-hand, orphaned children. Although his automotive disability prevents him from leaving, Arthur's discovery of the town's dark economy and the danger of him revealing the facts to the outside world are countered by the Mayor's offer of a permanent home, as his adopted (but silent) son. However, the town's fate is sealed by its love-affair with the car, as its rebellious younger generation build exotic spiked vehicles from the wrecks and terrorise the older inhabitants. A civil war develops between the generations, again provoked by the immoral authority of the establishment, and the town is destroyed. Arthur, regaining his manhood by repeatedly ramming a youth's car and killing its driver under the Mayor's direction, drives off gleefully into the surrounding darkness.

Several complex elements are interwoven in this film. Some conventions of science fiction are in evidence, such as background information on a wider societal and economic turmoil (fuel rationing, violent demonstrations, the collapse of the currency and repressive new laws) relayed through radio reports. These hints in *Cars* anticipate the depiction of the breakdown of law and order found in *Mad Max*. In this context, Paris' solution to rural stagnation evinces a ruthless pragmatism, but on a different level the town's murderous economy equates Western consumerism with cannibalism in a fashion similar to *Weekend* (Jean-Luc Godard, 1967). This is seen most clearly in the film's prologue, a dumb show modelled on cigarette advertising in which a photogenic young couple's car ride in the country ends in a fatal accident. At the same time, the film's black humour coexists with motifs drawn from horror films, and the iconography and characterisation of the Hollywood Western:

Paris ... is an outback Australian community not too distant from those little Western towns accustomed to remedial attention from such as Clint Eastwood. The law of the gun, however, has been replaced by the regime of the road, and the vehicles roaring joyously through the streets are close to severing all links with human control ... so encrusted with chromium jaws and spikes that their drivers are lost to view, they charge across the society that fostered and exploited them until it at last collapses.[6]

Arthur's arrival in the town mimics the intervention of the Western hero, who protects the threatened homestead before riding out into the wilderness. However, his diminutive stature and his emasculation (mocked for his inability to drive like a cowboy, too yellow to draw) undermine this expectation. The genre is parodied further when Arthur is enlisted by the iniquitous authorities. Instead of opposing corruption he colludes with it, and is given the job of traffic warden, tasked with making the town a 'decent place for people to park'. This leads to bathetic confrontations in the main street between Arthur and the youths of Paris, whose costumes imitate those of Spaghetti Western villains. Arthur's unheroic portrayal is completed by his destructive rather than redemptive violence at the film's climax. Far from cleansing and saving the town, he aids in its disintegration, and the final exodus of Paris' inhabitants suggests the spread rather than the containment of anarchy. From these disparate ingredients (the conventions of several popular, imported genres wedded to a specific national setting and a universal social commentary) *Cars* emerges as a landmark text in terms of its definition of the Gothic and contemporary Australian-ness:

While it reverts to the oblique and grotesque in its approach to the question of how to be an Australian film, *Cars* doesn't strain for an answer. It is, of course, commenting on something deeply embedded in the Australian ethos: that we would die without our cars, and to prove the point we daily risk dying in them. The spike-encrusted cars coming out of the darkness to prey on civilisation form the crowning image; but *Cars* produces equally suggestive menace of a quieter kind, like the way the Mayor's car with its long fins slides like a shark among the long grass of an otherwise lyric landscape. It works as a suggestive, dark, comic fantasy, uneven in its success, but rich in some of the perversity it unearths from the underside of the Australian psyche.[7]

Jodrell's *Shame* mobilises a similar range of components, using the rural setting, the Western's structure and the immediacy of social commentary in its portrait of another secluded community fractured by prejudice and secrecy. The title represents a deliberate evocation of the archetypal Hollywood Western *Shane* (George Stevens, 1953), in which the enigmatic titular hero brings justice and peace to the nascent civilisation of the plains. Jodrell's film, like Weir's, opens with images of the harmless provincial town set in innocuous countryside, emphasising the incongruity of the institutionalised evil that their central characters uncover. Asta Cadell arrives in another apparently sleepy town following a motorbike accident. While she waits for the delivery of the parts to effect repairs, she becomes aware that the town's female residents have been subjected to repeated sexual assaults by a group of male youths. Further intimidation and the collusion of the local law officers have silenced the women's protests, and no charges have ever been brought against the perpetrators. Asta is also threatened on several occasions but is able to defend herself both verbally and, in the last resort, physically. When she reveals that she is a barrister, she is able to mobilise the voiceless females and encourage them to testify against their attackers. Initially the accused are released when other men in the town pay their bail. However, a desperate attempt by the youths to silence their accusers ends in the death of one of the victims. This final tragedy nearly overwhelms Asta's spirit, but it ensures that all the gang members will now be brought to justice.

Shame derives its structure and its impact from the conventions of the Classical Western and such updates as *Bad Day at Black Rock* (John Sturges, 1954). Its adaptation of the Western model, in which the hero's intervention reveals and cures the town's guilty secret is more thorough and significant than the superficial alterations to the location, era and sex of the central character might suggest. As an avenger of barbaric social inequality, Asta overturns several stereotypes, proving superior to the males in her handling of the motorbike and her fighting abilities. Her costume of black leathers and white T-shirt links her with the rebellious bikers of *The Wild One* (Laslo Benedek, 1953), but morally she incarnates the urban, educated liberal majority appalled at the realities of rural existence. Her determination to bring justice to the town in the face of lies, corruption and grief has an equally dramatic effect on the portrayal of Outback masculinity, epitomised by the police's refusal to rock the boat and the youths' repudiation of any wrongdoing:

As is appropriate in a movie about the systematic denial of reality, we are never shown a rape on screen ... Far from simply exploiting its initial gimmicky premise ... the film instead homes in on its subject with a quite relentless single-mindedness. 'Mateship' has rarely been accorded a more acid depiction in Australian cinema.[8]

While engaging in its withering examination of violent prejudice allowed to go unchecked in the isolated community, *Shame* also recognises the town's economic circumstances as a contributory factor in the women's oppression. Most if not all of the women work in the factory processing hunted kangaroo meat for pet food. The inclusion of this detail equates the rape of the landscape with the dehumanisation of the women, and stresses the helplessness of the women's plight in a town with only one industry and one pastime.

The pervasiveness of sexual tension, and its provocation of other forms of social conflict in rural communities, are also explored in *The Umbrella Woman* (aka *The Good Wife*) (Ken Cameron, 1986) and *Incident at Raven's Gate* (aka *Encounter at Raven's Gate*) (Rolf de Heer, 1988). Both films address the pressures upon spouses and siblings, and the wilful disregard for sensibility or decorum that isolation encourages and indulges. De Heer's film follows Weir's and Miller's in incorporating elements of science fiction, and is similar to *Razorback* (Russell Mulcahy, 1984) and *Tremors* (Ron Underwood, 1989) in its bleakly humorous narrative of an alien visitation afflicting a remote desert town. However, *Raven's Gate* foregrounds its sexual conflicts (a triangle between Rachel Cleary, her husband Richard and his brother Eddie, and competition for the affection of the local barmaid between Eddie and the district cop) instead of assessing the implications of an alien landing. Sexual tensions distract the residents from the increasingly bizarre occurrences in the area. It seems that unpredictable and violent incidents of human origin outweigh in importance those caused by extra-terrestrials:

Rather than inflicting its teasingly putative alien invasion on an average community likely to react with reasonable unanimity and logic, the script makes the courageous assumption that whatever the identity or purpose of the visitors they would remain firmly peripheral to the everyday concerns and preoccupations of earthly country folk (particularly Australians).[9]

The alien presence perhaps inspires the murderous actions of certain individuals, or rather merely arouses their latent tendencies. What is noticeable is that the film ascribes the worst intentions and actions to the most superficially reputable characters (Richard the wronged husband and Skinner the lovelorn policeman) and punishes them with death. Conversely, their antagonists the recidivist younger brother and adulterous/incestuous wife are vindicated by survival. Higher, external authority as characterised by the secretive Dr Hemmings is gnomic and amoral. His fleeting appearances (to hush up the evidence of alien activity and magically restore the Cleary homestead destroyed by the aliens) highlight the conspiracy theorist's distrust of political authority covering up or colluding with extraterrestrials. However, since the aliens kill Richard and Hemmings returns Eddie and Rachel to the refurbished farm, the contributions of both external forces seem more eccentric and benevolent than malign. This perspective on the profound otherness of everyday activity, and the erratic nature of human judgement and perception, are fully developed in de Heer's Gothic defamiliarisation of contemporary urban existence *Bad Boy Bubby* (1993).

As an example combining generic revision, symbolic setting and characterisation and the disconcerting atmosphere of secrecy and guilt, *Summerfield* (Ken Hannam, 1977) encapsulates all the aspects of the Gothic's rendition of rural existence. Dismissed on its release as an inefficient thriller, *Summerfield* attracted adverse criticism for its failure in terms of narrative technique:

it demonstrates the inability, or unwillingness, of the Australian cinema to build on expectations, and effectively resolve the 'problems' developed in the body of the film ... it was a prime example of an Australian film that promised so much in its initial stages, in generic and narrative terms, and failed so comprehensively to fulfil these expectations.[10]

The commercial failure of films like *Summerfield* (or rather the critics' evaluation of failure to meet a commercial, melodramatic rubric) again centres debate on the form and execution of Australian filmmaking. Endings which are downbeat, inconclusive or which run counter to audience expectation can be construed as evidence of recalcitrance (refusing to follow established patterns) or of innovation (diverging deliberately from a Hollywood hegemony of narrative technique). By default an Australian pattern, approach or genre emerges from the rejection of the anticipated and the commonplace. Such a denial of filmic form and audience effect is particularly prevalent and appropriate in the Gothic category, centred as it is on the juxtaposition of mundanity and horror, the banal and the barbaric.

The film's narrative concerns the efforts of a young, single teacher Simon Robinson to discover the hidden truth about a small rural town and the nearby island estate of Summerfield, owned by the reserved Abbott family. Peter Flynn, Simon's predecessor in the local school has disappeared. He believes that the unmarried Jenny Abbott and her brother David are implicated, since he suspects the missing teacher is the father of Jenny's daughter. His investigation reveals that the teacher's car has been hidden by the local policeman, and the secrecy of the town's inhabitants seems to confirm his suspicions. However, his investigation is both motivated and complicated by his growing attraction to Jenny. Simon's 'responsibility' for discovering the truth is established early in the film and is constantly reiterated: the previous teacher's account at the local garage is handed on to him despite his protestations; he finds Flynn's clothes and personal effects have been left in the room he takes at the local hotel. However, his heroic quest is as frequently tarnished by guilt: he succumbs to the sexual advances of the hotel owner's wife, and he injures Jenny's daughter Sally when he knocks her over in his car. Ironically these misadventures further his investigation and his interest, since he learns the town's gossip about the Abbotts in bed and he gains access to Summerfield island to give Sally lessons at home while she recuperates.

The danger he courts in pursuing the investigation is also stressed: Sally tells him 'You've come the wrong way' when he drives over the bridge to the island on his first day, and repeats these words when he knocks her down; when he finds a hubcap from Flynn's car on a nearby headland, he is nearly cut off by the advancing tide. The relevant clues which hint at the real secret (that Sally is the product of an incestuous relationship between Jenny and David) are also scattered throughout the film. Sally paints the same sea birds that David photographs, and their equal talent is ascribed by Simon himself to 'two streams of influence – partly environmental, partly hereditary'. The local doctor tells Simon of Sally's proneness to an hereditary blood disease, and of Jenny's grief and guilt when this was diagnosed. David, in an echo of Hareton in *Wuthering Heights*, kills a litter of kittens on the island since the 'cats in this place are a pretty poor lot – they're all inbred.' The seclusion of the island estate and the incestuous family inhabiting it can be seen to represent the entire island continent, just as the introspection, idiosyncrasy or iniquity of other Gothic rural communities assume an allegorical representativeness. Simon learns that Summerfield has belonged to the Abbott family since their great-great-grandfather, an English sea captain, colonised the island more than a century ago. The connection with this ancestor extends to the colloquial name for the hereditary disease the family carries ('salt water in the blood'), and the lighthouse on the headland which David says has been watched by five generations of their family. Jenny tells Simon how, as children, she and David used to look out over the sea and wonder if the land they could see was America or Britain: 'but it was always the world; the world beyond our world'. Inside the family home, Jenny shows Simon their 'one concession to the past', a room furnished as a colonial time capsule with wood panelling, oil lamps, paintings and a grandfather clock. When Simon breaks a teacup from their best china service, Jenny turns down his offer to mend it since it would be 'imperfect'. The island itself is not only remote from the town and separated by the water, but also defended by high fences and locked gates on the solitary connecting bridge. The film opens and is punctuated by shots of the isolated island, and its array of warning signs.

Simon's investigation culminates in his discovery of Jenny and David making love. After the failure of his attempt to find and kill Simon, David kills Jenny and Sally and then takes his own life. The secret Simon has been driven or encouraged to reveal is at once irrelevant and destructive, denying the suspicions of the town and the hero (but not those of the alert viewer) and punishing guilty and innocent alike:

> *Summerfield* finally fails to satisfy the expectations of either the art-cinema or the generic cinema ... the investigation in *Summerfield* is stripped completely of any personal or social relevance as the investigation does not lead to the discovery of great evil (as in *Chinatown*), at least within the terms presented within the film, since neither Jenny nor David Abbott is presented as a villain. The audience is left with a sense of despair and pointlessness.[11]

In this view, the disappointment of the romantic, melodramatic and investigative expectations of an audience anticipating a thriller narrative is perceived as palpable, and culpable. Similarly, the aspiration towards enigmatic open-endedness (after *L'Avventura* (Michelangelo Antonioni, 1960) or, more pertinently, *Picnic at Hanging Rock* (Peter Weir, 1975)) is inappropriate or inadequate. However, the ambition of Australian film in the revival, seeking both cultural representation and credibility, enlists generic convention, the subversion of expectation and the assumption of art-cinema devices in the cases of Hannam's and Weir's films. (Incidentally, despite being credited with inspiring the cycle of polite 'period' films, *Picnic* shows as strong an affinity with Australian Gothic as Weir's preceding films). Both *Summerfield* and *Picnic* espouse and then discard investigative narratives in the course of examining aspects of Australian culture or consciousness (such as the colonial inheritance and influence of the landscape) in metaphorical terms. The futility of enquiry (which produces no answer to the mystery in *Picnic*, and the wrong answer in *Summerfield*) is sufficient indication that narrative has been sidelined in favour of allusion, metaphor and symbol. This relegation of the narrative affects the characterisation and activity of the hero. Simon's reasoning is specious, his methods are ineffective and his intrusion into the rural mystery (like that of Arthur Waldo and the teacher of *Wake in Fright*) has catastrophic consequences for himself and others. *Summerfield* signals this by illustrating the hero's visual impairment (his dirtied and opaque windscreen leads to the accident which injures Sally). At the film's end, when Flynn reappears unharmed, the full impact of Simon's blindness to the truth and responsibility for the tragedy is shown by the the blackness which consumes the screen gradually until only his eyes remain. The genres these films emulate and parody work against their generic audiences and heroes, as anticipation of their role to influence narrative events meaningfully and conclude them satisfactorily is undermined repeatedly. In place of narrative closure, alternative pleasures are to be derived: in determining the metaphorical significance, the aesthetic sophistication or the formal innovation of these films. The Gothic hero is predicated as a diminution or parody of the active, controlling generic hero of Westerns, thrillers or horror films, and is therefore also a subversion of the stereotype of capable, confident Australian masculinity. From this perspective, treatment of the hero in the most successful Australian Gothic films, which adhere most closely to popular genres and notions of closure and entertainment, warrants special scrutiny.

The *Mad Max* trilogy

The considerable commercial success of *Mad Max* (1979) and *Mad Max 2* (1981) both at home and abroad is attributable to the strong generic basis for their narratives, characterisation and iconography. Elements of the Western (the lone avenging hero, the beleaguered community, the desert landscape with its outlaws), science fiction (the collapse of civilisation in the first film, the vestiges of post-apocalyptic society in the second and third), the biker movie and the police thriller are incorporated with a dynamic combination of self-consciousness and self-parody. As a youthful amalgam of Harry Callahan and Ethan Edwards, Max's heroic tasks grow in stature and destructiveness as the cycle progresses. He moves from avenging the loss of his own family to saving a nascent new society, and finally safeguards the future by rescuing a colony of marooned children in *Mad Max Beyond Thunderdome* (1985). His likeness to the Western hero goes beyond his role as revenger to encompass his similarity to the outlaws he combats. In *Mad Max* the policemen of the Main Force Patrol inhabit the same blank desert, dress in the same fetishised costumes and employ their vehicles and weapons (and vehicles *as* weapons, in an echo of *Cars*) in the same fashion as their adversaries the nomad bikers. Indeed, such equivalence is as crucial to this film's erosion of moral distinctions as it is to its sources and influences. In *Mad Max 2* the hero's inseparability from the bandits who scour the desert is suggested graphically by their shared black clothing and exotic vehicles. This kinship is restated by Pappagallo, the leader of the 'white tribe', who likens Max and the 'dogs of war' to 'maggots living off the corpse of the old world'. Max's heroic posture and achievement is a point of debate within the texts themselves, from the first film's elevation of him to mythic status. His initial appearance is fragmented and tantalising, intertwining his image with the connotations of his car and costume through close-ups of his hands tending the engine, his impassive expression half-shielded by dark glasses, the dashboard and controls:

the film insists ... that here was a screen presence that could stop a story. Max, once he has duly buttoned up, put on his sunglasses and turned the ignition does indeed the stop the chase, stop that part of the story. But the film had predicted this through its cross-cutting and the deliberately different and slow responses of Max. The film had, by marking absence of action on Max's part, created Max as a figure of powerful action.[12]

The frenetic and vain attempts of his colleagues to stop the Nightrider are succeeded by the robotic and efficient actions of Max. Driving at the Nightrider head on without flinching, Max seems to cause an instantaneous, emasculating breakdown in his foe, who crashes fatally soon afterwards. Only when he dismounts to view the resulting explosion does Max remove his glasses and express any emotion. The negation of emotion and masculinity enmeshed with machinery are foregrounded as themes from the character's first appearance.

In principle, the hero's actions and their justification are linked indelibly with the group or ideal he fights to defend. At a superficial level Max's actions always serve a greater good, but in each film the Gothic sensibility intrudes to deny them their dignity. The Main Force Patrol are seen to be fighting a losing battle against the advancing forces of darkness. The highways they protect (the first seen is named 'Anarchie Road') are exacting an ever-increasing death toll. The validity of their lethal pursuits is doubly undermined. The majority take place far from urban areas, and so are valueless as law enforcement, but when a member of the nomads is brought to trial, the vicissitudes of the legal system and the intimidation of the witnesses mean that he must be released unpunished. Conversely, when the first desperate chase 'heads for population', the danger to bystanders comes as much if not more from the police vehicles as the Nightrider's stolen car. Yet the public that is endangered is also made culpable. Arguing parents let their toddler wander onto the highway into the path of the cars. Rather than defending society, the MFP is engaged in a series of escalating confrontations based on personal feuds. In his speeches their leader Chief MacAffee asserts the need for heroes and 'winners' like Max to bolster their disintegrating society, but these make no impression on his best driver. The concept of society and the notion of heroism are both obsolescent. Rather it is the inducement of driving the last V8 interceptor (the very car stolen and driven to death by the Nightrider) that persuades Max to stay.

The robotic professional of the film's opening becomes the 'burnt out shell of a man' we see at its climax (and at the opening of *Mad Max 2*), and though the two portraits share impassivity and ruthlessness, the events of the first film serve to rationalise this mirror imaging. Its story was one of:

mutilation, disempowerment and re-empowerment. Its maiming was carefully choreographed: a hand missing here, a leg there, a leg in plaster, a body beneath a tent in too appalling a shape to be seen. Thus the film inscribed upon the male bodies an almost hysterical anxiety – a fear of literal and symbolic castration.[13]

O'Regan's analysis accounts for the Nightrider's immediate mental collapse, in which loss of emotional control and loss of life are the direct consequences of a challenge to masculine integrity. Max's weakness, and the target of the nomads' vendetta, is his family, his emotional life. While he works, his wife Jessie and their child Sprog represent a source of strength and a haven for retreat, as their home is remote from both the roads and the towns. Significantly, they are attacked when Max is on an indefinite holiday from the force, when the family has become one with the feeble, vulnerable and guilty society. The death of Sprog and the injuries to Jessie are the final examples in the film's catalogue of physical trauma. Goose's broken leg, Charlie's throat injury, and the burning of Goose in the wrecked truck enact the erosion of anatomical humanity as a parallel to the loss of moral and spiritual humanity. Max's refusal to accept the blackened 'thing' under the tent as Goose illustrates a fear of loss of identity that outstrips a fear of death. However, the loss of his family reduces him, in the words of the hospital staff tending Jessie, to a 'zombie'. In place of a peaceful and contemplative Fordian vigil by the graveside (cf. *She Wore a Yellow Ribbon* (John Ford, 1949)), Max draws infernal power from this burial of humanity (cf. *The Searchers* (John Ford, 1956)). It is immaterial that she is still alive if, in Max's mind, her identity and his emotional link to it are lost. Therefore his revenge and his duty merge. The professional automaton of the beginning and the emotionless killer of the ending are rhymed together, just as the V8 interceptor links him conclusively with the nomads of the first film and the bandit tribes of the second. The vengeance he exacts is divorced from the emotional attachment which inspired it, and the heroism and justification of his subsequent deeds become questionable as a result.

In building on the first film's varied generic sources, *Mad Max 2* adopts the format of the Western wholeheartedly. Police sirens and cavalry bugles intermingle in the choreographed attacks by the Humungus' dog soldiers. Attacks on Western forts and wagon trains are restaged in the Australian desert with cars, bikes and trucks. Max survives in the wilderness with the same skills and instincts as the bandits. Like them he is 'mobile enough to scavenge, brutal enough to pillage'. His black leather uniform has degenerated and become as stylised as the costumes of the 'dogs of war', and his likeness to a machine is heightened by the mechanical joint supporting his injured leg. In the 'blighted' desert, Max will 'learn to live again' through a renewed commitment to heroic service, but his re-humanisation is delayed and problematic.

When he first comes across the white tribe's camp and oil refinery, he observes the attacks led by his nemesis Wez dispassionately. He waits for an opportunity, and rescuing one of Pappagallo's scouts provides it. Max seeks to trade the man's life for gasoline, but he dies before an agreement is reached and the white tribe, equating him with the opposition, chain Max up for safety. When he learns that the tribe are searching for a truck to pull their tank of fuel to the coast, he offers his services, but strictly on a business footing. His delivery of the Mack tractor prompts their gratitude and the assumption that he will drive the tanker in their planned break-out. However, Max insists on departing, remaining convinced he has 'all he needs' in his car. Pappagallo points out it contains everything but 'a future', and this is vindicated by Max's brush with death in attempting to escape the Humungus' blockade.

Max is rescued and returned to the camp by the Gyro Captain. Although he is a comic character (his gangling stance echoed in his spidery, fragile flying machine), he acts as a catalyst at crucial moments in the second and third films to prompt or facilitate Max's heroic actions. Bringing Max back to the white tribe provides him with the chance to drive the tanker that becomes the focus of the climactic running battle, but his motivation for doing so is unstated. The eventual showdown with Wez is a component of the battle, but not the reason for joining it. Rather Max resumes his role of defender of society, and as in the first film it is a society of which he cannot be a part and which has little respect for him. Significantly, the members of the tribe who accompany Max on the decoy tanker are those sharing his skills (the impassive Warrior Woman) and his associations (the group's crippled mechanic). These characters mimic Max's emotional and physical disabilities, and both are killed on the suicide mission which allows the new settlers to escape. The battle takes place on the same straight road through a blank, flat landscape which formed the abiding image of the first film. In recommencing his violent, heroic activity, Max confirms the elevation of his role and status implied in his mythic appellation (which was used as the film's title in America) of 'the Road Warrior'. Again his skills bring victory, and again the adversary is destroyed in a head-on collision. The final revelation (perhaps already known to Max) that the tanker was filled with sand, not petrol, underlines the ambiguity of his heroism. Perhaps he has been abused by the society he saves, or perhaps he acknowledges that this is the only way he could save it. Perhaps he would have acted as he did irrespective of the potential benefits for the settlers and glory for himself, and equally perhaps the settlers have merely availed themselves of such contradictions within him.

If the resumption of Max's heroism is obscure, his re-attainment of humanity is also questionable. His emotional connections remain undeveloped. The series of companions which he endures rather than encourages emphasises his distance from community and civilisation. His cattle dog is succeeded by the Feral Kid who, reaching manhood, leads the new tribe and tells Max's story. The irony of the savage child acting as an unwelcome substitute for

Sprog, sharing the hero's environment and skills but eventually integrating with the society closed to Max, increases the ambiguity of Max's motives for action. In *Mad Max Beyond Thunderdome*, his pet monkey saves his life on two occasions (throwing equipment from his camel-drawn wagon when it is stolen by the Gyro Captain, and bringing him water in his exile in the desert). Intentionally or coincidentally, the Gyro Captain's theft furnishes Max with another setting and opportunity for redemptive heroism, in liberating Barter Town from tyranny. Instead he agrees to take part in a political killing instigated by Aunty Entity. In an unexpected return to the moral ambiguities of policing explored in the first film, the survival of her version of civilisation requires Max to murder. However, Barter Town's existence and the harsh law embodied in Thunderdome represent a reaction against the 'maelstrom of decay' and mushrooming of violence to which Max contributed. His sudden compassion for the child-like Blaster leaves him subject to punishment under the town's law, since he fails to capitalise on the only thing he has to trade – his brutal skills.

His expulsion leads him into another potentially heroic encounter, when a lost colony of children mistake him for the saviour who will lead them back to civilisation. Instead of delivering them, he disillusions them, and only their departure without him stings him into reluctant action. The group's eventual arrival in and escape from Barter Town are chaotic. Max's contribution to the battle around the fleeing locomotive is not distinguished, until their party meets up with the Gyro Captain again. His plane is only able to carry the survivors to safety because of Max's willing sacrifice, again driving head-on into Aunty's pursuers to allow the aircraft to get airborne. Although they fly on to the ruins of Sydney where a new society flourishes, Max's heroic efforts are still undercut, since his intervention has destroyed the community of Barter Town and created another society which he cannot join.

If Max's actions and motives have appeared contradictory in the course of the saga, his heroism has been further undermined by the actions and relationships of those around him. In *Mad Max 2* Wez acts as a parallel as well as an opponent to Max through the equation of their skills and losses. Max's lost family is answered by the death of Wez's partner, with his revenge motive mimicking Max's from the first film. At first the Gyro Captain enters the white tribe's camp with the same selfish motives as Max, and also attempts to leave with a female accomplice. However, his lust for her becomes subsumed in the tribe's cause, prompting his crucial contribution to the final battle which is rewarded with the girl and leadership of the new settlement. In the third film the character has a different name but is played by the same actor, and is accompanied by a child identical to him in mannerisms and dress. Therefore, the Gyro Captain can be seen to acquire the dividends of heroism (in a sexual partner, offspring, and leadership status) which Max abjures or loses. Symbolically, as he flies the children to safety, he assumes the role of the long-awaited pilot-saviour which Max had failed signally to fulfil.

As well as a commercial and critical landmark within Australian cinema as a whole, the *Mad Max* trilogy represents an intriguing and fertile saga concentrating on the ambiguities of heroism in an Australian context. The cars which Dermody and Jacka saw as central to the specific, national horror of *The Cars That Ate Paris* are equally crucial to definitions of character and identity in Miller's films. The cars epitomise power, in escape or in pursuit, to enforce the law or break it. Max's being and role are concretised inside the varied vehicles he acquires, and his greatest battles are wordless performances of skilful, aggressive driving in which the man and the manipulated mechanism become inextricably interwoven. At the same time, the cars become deadly traps (viz. the couple's ordeal in their decorated Chevrolet, Goose caught in his harness, Johnny Boy handcuffed to a smouldering wreck, the self-destruction of the V8). At a symbolic level, Max is trapped in his policing job and revenger's role by the V8 interceptor. Its destruction is a necessary precursor to his redefinition as a hero in driving the tanker as a selfless decoy. Throughout the saga the car, like the hero is deified and travestied, customised and caricatured, elevated and undermined as a generic and national icon. The films, despite their distinction from the contemporaneity and spareness of social commentaries like *Shame*, are the epitome of the Gothic in their generic hybridisation, their parodic and black comedic approach, and their subversion of authority and heroism. The series' development from its low-budget, B-picture origins to its big-budget finale is the final irony, as the subversive and exploitative prototype evolves (as does its star) into mainstream Hollywood product.

The urban Gothic

The imperfections and uncertainties of Gothic heroes in the rural environment are repeated by the reclusive and alienated individuals seen in Gothic films in urban settings. In the cases of *Walkabout* and *Shame*, a significant part of the horror resides in the defamiliarisation of natural and human landscapes away from urbanisation. In urban Gothic films, flawed heroes uncover conspiracies, reveal iniquitous forms of authority and experience disconcerting alterations in their circumstances and perceptions. In discussing Peter Weir's treatment of the Gothic in its rural (*Cars*) and urban (*The Last Wave* (1977)) forms, Brian McFarlane identifies the trauma of dislocation which the central characters undergo: 'the ordinary grasp on life that seems to sustain the protagonists is thrown into psychic and emotional disorder'.[14] Disturbance on the personal, emotional and psychological level is echoed by disruption in society, natural order and the physical world. Perceptions of the inner self and outer reality are mistrusted as the known environment falls victim to the unknown or unacknowledged truth.

Weir's *The Last Wave* (along with his near-contemporary television feature *The Plumber* (1979)) is overtly Gothic in tone, drawing upon sources in the horror genre and apocalyptic science fiction. David Burton, a married middle-class lawyer, undergoes a personal crisis when asked to defend a group of Aborigines charged with murder. He amasses information which suggests that, contrary to popular opinion, Aboriginal people in the city have retained their tribal identity and beliefs. At the same time, Sydney and the surrounding country are suffering freak weather conditions, and Burton is increasingly unnerved by a series of disturbing, prophetic dreams. Eventually he learns that all these streams of activity and consciousness are connected. The worsening storms presage an apocalyptic tidal wave which has been predicted by Aboriginal mythology. David's visions impart a second sight because he is the descendant of a prehistoric South American tribe which travelled to Australia in the distant past. The dreams which offer revelations of the future also force David to recognise buried knowledge of his own past:

Situations and experiences, at first random and unconnected as they are usually taken to be in life, become charged with *pan-determinism*: everything has a specific meaning and occurs in relation to a definite order and purpose. David, in retrieving and deciphering the dreams of his childhood (which include a premonition of his mother's death), learns that he is, and always has been, the medium through which the spirit Mulkurul, speaks.[15]

The film establishes a series of juxtapositions: the civilisation of European settlers versus the culture of indigenous peoples; materiality versus spirituality; the superficiality and inadequacy of modern life versus the profundity and unity of traditional society. However, the apparent distinctions between eras, classes, races and life styles are slowly erased as David's subjective vision supplants objective reality.

David shares his prophetic status and inability to alter the inevitable cataclysm with the central characters of other renditions of twentieth-century angst and depersonalisation, such as *Invasion of the Body Snatchers* (Philip Kaufman, 1978). While the fantasy narrative accounts for the interconnection of inward and outward chaos, the use of David's subjective narration also implies that his perspective is unreliable or even deranged. In toying with the reliability of the narrator's vision and suggesting the vulnerability of civilisation, modernity and sanity simultaneously, *The Last Wave* enlists varied stylistic, aesthetic and generic materials. Foremost in its *mise-en-scène* are the Aboriginal artefacts which are central to the murder enquiry and appear in David's dreams. These are at once culturally specific in Australian terms, but are also seen as culturally exclusive, since they are both indigenous and alien to non-Aboriginal Australians. As occult objects they symbolise a threatening otherness under the connotations of the horror film. However, David's alienation from his own culture and attraction to an alternative community, and the use of altered film speeds, freeze frames, distortions in sound and composition to characterise his destabilised perspective, reflect a thematic and stylistic debt to art cinema. The apocalyptic threat of science fiction films, an unfathomable menace emanating from the natural world (reminiscent of *The Birds* (Alfred Hitchcock, 1963)) and the spiritual vacuity of modern life explored in the art cinema, are distilled in this version of the urban Gothic:

As soon as he accepts his true vocation, David sees the wave and becomes its first victim. The wish such a horror film fulfills [sic] is that of *seeing*, and the world view it confirms is that 'the other side' is real. In other words, David is a surrogate for the audience's desire to have, through watching a horror film, a spiritual vision. The satisfaction of being 'first victim' is that one knows the hidden truth.[16]

David's gradual isolation from his own class and society is paralleled by estrangement from his wife and family. The family home becomes the target for disruptive events. The disturbances caused by David's dreams are followed by the racial and sexual tension arising from him inviting his Aboriginal defendant and his spiritual leader into his house. Marital stresses increase in line with the worsening weather, and at the film's climax the house is rent open by storms and flailing trees. The house becomes an effective symbol for both the protagonist's mind and his social milieu, taxed to breaking point in confronting hidden truths and unacknowledged guilt (the eradication of Aboriginal culture, and the inadequacy of the rationalism and materialism which have displaced religious observance). The definition of Weir's central character as a lawyer,[17] who builds on precedence in creating new and individual interpretations, sets him apart from wider society. The establishment's attempts to explain away the storms (by attributing them to the effects of pollution) parallel the ineffective police investigation, which files murder charges when no cause of death can be found:

Neither the seeming solidity of those city blocks nor the pleasant suburban home of the lawyer in the end offer a substantial bulwark against these unknown forces. And this point, made in the film's *mise-en-scène*, provides a physical analogue for its decent, rationalist hero's growing attraction to, and fear of, the mysterious and the irrational.[18]

David's emergence from narrow-mindedness and fascination with other forms of existence and perception is repeated by the heroes of Weir's other films in Australia (*The Year of Living Dangerously* (1982)) and America (*Witness* (1985), *Fearless* (1994), *The Truman Show* (1998)). In comparison, the narrative of *The Plumber* utilises the conventions of the thriller in portraying a psycho-sexual threat to a lone female protagonist. In an echo of *Cars*, black comedy intrudes in the spectacle of Jill, the reserved female academic besieged in her flat by an uninvited plumber. His menacing presence and the disruption of the middle-class home provoke a similar reappraisal of the divisiveness and repressiveness of modern society and class structures. At one point Jill recalls a confrontation with a Beatu man in New Guinea which mirrors the misunderstanding between the girl and Aboriginal boy in *Walkabout*. Jill's reaction to the quasi-sexual threat represented by the plumber and the Beatu man is violent in one case and vindictive in the other. While remaining faithful to the thriller format, in concluding with the 'victim' triumphant, the form and manner of Jill's revenge exhibits a condemnation of authoritarian ignorance and prejudice:

what in fact emerges is a complex examination of the structure of middle-class liberal defence systems. The examination is, if anything, more effective than the one undertaken in *The Last Wave*, because the disrupting factor is less arcane and more believable.[19]

The indictment of suburban, bourgeois insularity is furthered in *The Night the Prowler* (Jim Sharman, 1978). When an ineffectual prowler breaks into her bedroom, Felicity Bannister takes the opportunity to evade her prescribed social role, reject her

respectable fiancé and confound the expectations of her caricatured parents. Her perceived plainness, subservience and conformity are replaced with a nocturnal mastery of the suburbs. Clad
entirely in black leather, she accumulates a circle of disreputable
friends and vandalises the homes of other middle-class families.
Her rejection of accepted values and behaviour is interpretable as
a reaction against the conservative, British-based Australian
establishment epitomised by her repressed and absent father.

The Last Wave's horror treatment of the forces of nature, and
its depiction of modern peoples estranged from their environment,
can be seen as an exaggeration of aspects of *Walkabout*. These features are sensationalised in *Long Weekend* (Colin Eggleston,
1977), in which marital discord (adultery and abortion) links
with disregard for the natural world and prompts supernatural
revenge. Where *The Last Wave* simply alludes to abuse of the
environment and wildlife, Eggleston's film highlights the shallow,
mindless destruction of human development, and equates it with
the country's colonisation:

> *Long Weekend* has a hard-edged, half-surreal approach. In *Long Week-
> end*, crimes against Nature lead to the torment and death of a holi-
> daying couple at the hands of Nature ... *Long Weekend* accords with
> the self-loathing of liberal Australians for their material and spiritual
> sins against the continent.[20]

In comparison, the resolution of marital discord and the empowerment of the female (distinct from the disempowerment of the
male) disarms and simplifies the Gothic into an unchallenged
thriller formula in *Dead Calm* (Phillip Noyce, 1988).

Horror exists in both supernatural and prosaic forms in the
urban Gothic portrayal of institutionalised immorality and wrongdoing. Two contemporary, commercial productions by Antony I.
Ginnane (*The Survivor* (David Hemmings, 1980) and *Harlequin*
(Simon Wincer, 1980)) use the conventions of horror unimagi-
natively, but share the Gothic concentration on the discovery of
conspiracies and secrets supporting a morally bankrupt authority.
In the former, the mysterious crash of an airliner causes the death
of all the passengers and crew except the pilot, Captain Keller.
Aviation and medical authorities are unable to account for the
accident, Keller's survival or his amnesia, which both impedes the
investigation and implies his guilt. A local medium and one of the
press photographers at the scene are afflicted by the restless spirits of the dead, demanding restitution from those responsible for
the crash. Keller's indomitable will, expressed in the indelible
desire to survive the disaster and determine its cause, eventually

unmasks two secrets: that the plane was brought down by a bomb planted by an accident investigation official anxious to preserve his status, and that Keller, far from surviving the crash, has embodied and focused the victims' hunt for revenge. This has been facilitated by his life beyond the grave, which ends once the culprit is exposed and killed.

In *Harlequin* a corruptible politician's leukaemic son is targeted by Gregory Wolfe, a charismatic faith healer. While Senator Rast's rise is masterminded by shadowy figures responsible for the death of his predecessor Eli Steele, Gregory inveigles himself into the affections of the politician's wife through curing her son. The narrative serves as an updating of the story of the Tsarina and Rasputin, with Gregory as an other-worldly figure capable of magic and metamorphosis. His wife's attraction to Gregory and Rast's own extramarital affair threaten to compromise his forthcoming election, and the senator's backers move to eliminate Gregory even as he attempts to convince Rast of his own expendability in their eyes. Both these productions, though styled as unashamedly commercial in comparison with the art film aspirations of *The Last Wave*, continue the Gothic critique of malign and secretive authority. As a producer Ginnane was committed to the commercial impetus behind the revival, with the result that their casts include Australian, American and British actors and their settings and the nationalities of their protagonists are unspecified. Their contemporary critical dismissal (as 'drearily undistinguished' films resembling 'Italian spin-offs from proven American successes'[21]) belies some poignant commentary, such as the bravura opening sequence of *Harlequin*. Through sustained and rhythmic intercutting, Gregory's magic tricks at a birthday party for Rast's son, Steele's disappearance while swimming and the senator's deft handling of journalists' questions at an airport are interwoven and equated. These events do not take place simultaneously, and the correspondence between physical and verbal dexterity, magical and political sleight of hand which effect varying types of vanishing act, is intimated entirely by the editing.

In *Heatwave* (Phillip Noyce, 1981), the ecological, political and materialist criticism of the Gothic film are combined in an investigative thriller narrative reminiscent of *Summerfield*. As in *The Last Wave*, the specious rationalisation of the establishment is opposed by the unfathomable power of nature, as radio reports describe the unceasing hot weather without being able to account for it. The media comment dispassionately on the escalating conflict between developers and home owners in the centre of Sydney, apparently unable or unwilling to draw moral distinctions between the aims and conduct of the two sides. In another echo of Weir's film, the perspectives of the architect Steve West and activist Kate Dean are occasionally rendered through subjective techniques, such as slow-motion, the distortion or elimination of diegetic sound and the repetition of images.

John Houseman, an expatriate building magnate, seeks to demolish an area of terraced housing to make way for a luxurious apartment building named 'Eden'. Steve's design for the project is elegant and expensive, and cannot proceed until the residents of the terraces agree to sell their homes. Those already vacated have been occupied by squatters opposing the scheme, led by Kate and her associate Mary Ford. Unexpected events and vested interests plague the development, and lead Steve to question his involvement: Mary Ford disappears after investigating Houseman's associates; unions boycott the construction and certain tenants refuse to sell; as costs and controversy spiral out of control, the aesthetic 'balance' of Steve's design is sacrificed to the 'balance' of Houseman's accounts; and then the houses of the most resistant residents are destroyed in an arson attack. Having previously been friends with Mary, Steve begins a hesitant affair with Kate as he swaps sides in the conflict.

Against this background the Eden design, based on the shape of an apple tree, provides a symbolic moral focus. As his vision is cheapened, perverted and finally shelved, Steve gains a dispiriting knowledge of the reality of financial expediency. His eyes are opened to the inextricable links between the media, capitalism and legal authority. A perfunctory search for Mary by the police is followed by the planting of incriminating evidence in Kate's house. The newspaper reporter who encourages Steve's attempts to uncover the conspiracy is himself bought off (or more disturbingly, may have manoeuvred Steve in order to further implicate Kate). In place of the criticism of class structure discernible in *The Plumber*, the characters in *Heatwave* are seen to be disadvantaged by class mobility. Steve's illusory idealism is the last vestige of his lower-class aspiration, realised through education and hard work. Conversely, Kate upper-class liberal sympathies are devoted to lost causes. Significantly, both these characters are also connected with Australian cultural influences emphasised in the film. Steve and his partner Robert attend a speech given by an American financier, who describes the Eden project as a union of 'enlightened sponsorship and design genius' which would 'be erected in the States anyday'. In a similar reference to this suspect imported morality, Steve's divergence from Mary's beliefs is attributed to a change of heart during his studies in America.

During the sweltering Christmas holiday which constitutes the narrative's time span, Kate and other protesters are seen listening to the Queen's speech. The contextual irony of the platitudes contained in the address, championing a *British* 'concern for freedom' and 'equality before an impartial law' is matched with the melancholy disinterest of the listeners. The influences on contemporary Australia appear to combine past irrelevances and present threats, with the society afflicted by misplaced adherence to either new or old colonial agencies. Within the country, the power of unelected, profiteering authority appears unassailable. Even as Houseman is bankrupted, his devious lawyer is shot dead and the true emerging villain Molnar is murdered on the eve of his triumph, the film's progression asserts that another financier will step forward to devalue and exploit the project further. The interaction of financial enterprise, legal controls and media representations will continue undaunted. The film's final dispiriting images reveal Mary Ford's body being uncovered on the building site by the torrential rains which accompany the climactic resolution.

Heatwave uses the weather as a reflection and judgement upon human affairs in the same way as *The Last Wave*, and also shares the latter film's subversion of narrative structure and closure in combining generic and art cinema materials (thriller narrative and political and philosophical issues). Representative characters embody issues rather than propel the narrative. Just as *The Last Wave* recruited allusive materials such as features of Aboriginal mythology as alternatives centres of interest to its horror narrative, so *Heatwave* deviates from its investigation in stressing significant elements of *mise-en-scène*:

[It] is basically not interested in developing causality and motivation through the traditional character-centred approach, but places greater emphasis on factors such as colour and the climate as important determinants of meaning. Whereas the classical system subordinates such impersonal aspects to psychological causality, *Heatwave* subordinates the characters to visual style, to camera movement and to the heatwave, which is used as a metaphor for the business, union, political and personal corruption in the film.[22]

In the cases of *Summerfield*, *The Last Wave* and *Heatwave* failure to adhere to classical narrative forms and objectives has been seen as detrimental to the audience's immersion in and emotional satisfaction with the viewing experience they offer. Such a view discounts the direct, contemporary and national relevance of their amalgamation of genre, art and Gothic film elements.[23] In particular Pulleine notes that Heatwave's 'field of vision is specific and compressed ... and this close focus confers a would-be representa-

Contemporary Australian cinema

tive status on events'.[24] In all three films the discovery of the uncanny or the unknown behind the façade of mundanity is linked to a problematic investigation of personal and national identity. This consistent concern within the Gothic makes the rejection of classical American narrative form increasingly significant.

The desire to establish personal beliefs, origins and identity which is implicit in *Heatwave* and *The Last Wave* becomes of central importance in *Georgia* (Ben Lewin, 1988) and *Ground Zero* (Michael Pattinson, Bruce Myles, 1987). In Lewin's film Nina Bailey, a tax fraud investigator, is prompted to delve into her own past after receiving an anonymous invitation to a retrospective exhibition of photographs. Nina's mother reveals that the photographer Georgia White was her natural mother, and that she and her then-husband Bill Karlin adopted Nina after Georgia's mysterious death by drowning. With her mother's identity confirmed at the exhibition, Nina pursues two other (eventually inseparable) enquiries to establish the identity of her father and the cause of Georgia's death. Responsibility for the birth becomes indivisible from guilt for the death. Techniques of subjective narration are present again in the recreation of events in accordance with the testimony of each witness that Nina interviews. Every character involved or implicated in Georgia's life and death offers a version of events, and each is given equal credence through the form of a flashback reconstruction. No single account or character is given precedence, and therefore Nina's and the viewer's interpretative tasks are equally handicapped. The precise evaluation of images becomes the film's most important theme and activity.

Nina's enquiries are inspired initially by the black and white images of the exhibition. A card inviting her to the retrospective arrives unexpectedly at her new address, and connects with a monochrome image of a woman holding a child planted suspiciously in her flat before she moves in. The images and their story precede her literally and metaphorically. The woman in the picture is obscured behind the child, and it is only her adoptive mother's recognition of the same picture at the gallery which confirms that it shows the infant Nina with her natural mother. During tours of the exhibition and the subsequent testimonies, the circumstances of each picture being taken are re-enacted. In the first reconstruction Georgia's face is again hidden behind her camera, but in later flashbacks Georgia is played by Judy Davis, who also plays Nina. (In some ways, this role reprises Davis' performance as Kate Dean in *Heatwave*, and her questing, independent persona first established by the character of Sybylla in *My Brilliant Career* (Gillian Armstrong, 1979)). The doubling of

Georgia and Nina vindicates Nina's parentage and investigation on one level. The suggestion that Georgia was killed because of her involvement in a police undercover operation is supported and paralleled by the dangers Nina encounters in probing her death. Yet on another level, given that all the subjective flashbacks are equally true (and false), Georgia's resemblance to Nina may appear as no more than the daughter's projection and wish fulfilment.

In her search Nina quizzes her adoptive mother's present partner, who gives her Georgia's camera. This proves to be of great interest to Frank Le Mat, a retired police detective who used Georgia to photograph Karlin in the undercover operation. No charges could be brought in relation to allegations of money laundering, illegal property development and murder, since the examination of Georgia's negatives after her death revealed no firm evidence. In tracking down the elusive Karlin, Nina fails to prove that he is her father or her mother's killer, but plays into the hands of Le Mat, who is still fixated with the memory of Georgia and his incomplete case against Karlin. It is possible that either Karlin, or Le Mat or both could have planted the picture and invitation to the retrospective, and funded the mysterious exhibition itself in order to nurture their personal obsessions (Georgia and Nina, and Nina as a replica of Georgia). In doing so they have also prompted Nina to question and probe her own identity for the first time. However, the validity of information garnered from subjective sources (including photographic images) is open to debate. The value of the images themselves has been seen to be contestable, in the context of the gallery's exhibition of photographs and in Nina's job. Early in the film we see her questioning a businessman to prove that he has given nearly worthless paintings to charitable organisations (themselves owned by his parent company) and claimed huge tax write-offs in compensation. Through the course of her investigation and her evaluation of testimonies and reports of the drowning, Nina comes to view personal and social identity as constructed and possessed by others. Georgia now exists only as a series of subjective recollections, unreliable flashbacks and photos which are open to interpretation. This much is implied by the name of the gallery ('Ephemera') exhibiting Georgia's pictures, suggesting that the photos, the people they contain and the meanings they are given are fleeting and arbitrary. In acknowledging this, understanding her own adoption and accepting the impossibility of finding her real father, Nina begins to assemble her own identity. This cannot be dictated by preference (she remarks to Le Mat that she doesn't 'want a murdered mum'), but can be divorced successfully from the expectations of others (evading her adoptive mother's guilt and Le Mat's delusions). When Nina discovers the missing autopsy report, it confirms that Georgia drowned simply because she was drunk when she went swimming off the pier. Le Mat's refusal to accept the facts has driven him to pursue Nina in place of her mother. When he chases Nina onto the road outside her apartment, he is knocked down and killed. The film ends with Nina unable to answer the questions put to her by a policeman at the scene, while others officers collect indefinite and conflicting witness statements. The truth of factual events is seen finally as elusive, indeterminate and relative.

The relativity of values in the interpretation of historical fact is seen in relation to another search for personal identity in *Ground Zero*. Harvey Denton, a freelance cameraman, is encouraged by an anonymous source to investigate the effects of British atomic tests in the Australian desert. The contemporary and national significance of his enquiry (which accompanies a Royal Commission investigating compensation claims from ex-servicemen and Aborigines) is matched by the personal relevance to Harvey and his family. The body of his father, who was believed to have drowned in an accident after filming the Maralinga tests for the Australian Army, has been found inside an irradiated bomber aircraft buried after a test in 1954. Harvey has been transferring his father's films to video for the rest of his family, but both his own and his sister's homes are raided by the Australian secret service. All the films are seized and submitted as evidence to the Commission. Having reviewed the footage remaining within the Army's archives (one newsreel reports 'Australian servicemen get the best view of all: only one mile from ground zero'), Harvey tracks down Prosper Gaffney, a veteran who accompanied his father during the filming and has lived in the desert ever since. They recover a film entrusted to Gaffney by Harvey's father, but are pursued by British and/or Australian agents and by American soldiers now stationed in the same region. Harvey is convinced that the film will substantiate the allegations made by Army and Aboriginal survivors: that nomadic tribes were exposed to lethal radiations levels during the tests and that their bodies were recovered and hidden in the aftermath. Ironically, the bellicose Australian chairman of the Commission, the caricatured British governmental representative and the head of the Australian intelligence services find themselves in agreement in impounding the film, but it is found to be fogged irretrievably through exposure to fallout. However, on his return home Harvey discovers that his father's last film, sent through the post by his sister and not found by the security services, contains scenes of Aboriginal bodies being examined at a secret Army base.

Ground Zero builds on the example of *Heatwave* in giving a Gothic treatment to documentary drama materials. Factual titles at beginning and end detail the duration, scale and legacy of the tests, and deliberately short-circuit the suspense that its thriller format might otherwise engender. While the ending vindicates both Harvey's and his father's efforts to uncover the truth, the damage on the national and personal scale is irreparable: the tribal lands of Maralinga are contaminated, Harvey's father is dead (probably murdered by the authorities) and Harvey himself will be subject to state surveillance for the rest of his life. Instead of Gothic allegories of malign influence and corrupt authority, *Ground Zero* gives a Gothic treatment to present political realities. The American soldiers in the desert are linked to a news report Harvey watches, in which President Reagan and Prime Minister Hawke are seen renewing the ANZUS defence treaty. Sighting the pursuing soldiers, Prosper remarks: 'Nothing changes, only the accents and the uniforms.' Although set in 1984, the film's relevance to its time of production and the crisis in ANZUS membership (caused by New Zealand's refusal to allow visits by nuclear-armed American warships) is very clear. In the past and the present, Australian governments have colluded in the colonial subordination of their country. Australian servicemen and indigenous peoples alike have suffered as a result, and though different their cultures and laws have strengthened the atmosphere of secrecy (the Official Secrets Act silences service personnel, and cultural taboos prevent Aborigines discussing their dead). Linking the Gothic with polemical documentary, and subverting conventions of narrative and genre in ways different from *Heatwave* or *Summerfield*, *Ground Zero* succeeds in uniting the urban and rural Gothic strands, and in connecting the colonial subjection of Aboriginal and non-Aboriginal Australia. Pattinson's and Myles' film was well received at the Berlin International Film Festival in 1985.

In bridging the rural–urban divide, dramatising a contemporary, documentary issue (Aboriginal deaths in custody) and again reworking aspects of the thriller format, *Deadly* (Esben Storm, 1990) represents an efficient, melodramatic and commercial realisation of the Gothic trend in Australian film. The central character of Tony Bourke, a police detective who is tainted by service in the city and redeemed by probing a rural crime, makes *Deadly* as much Australian Noir as Australian Gothic in its similarity to *On Dangerous Ground* (Nicholas Ray, 1951). Tony is sent from the city to the rural town of Yabbabri to investigate an alleged suicide. While working on the drug squad he has been responsible for the accidental shooting of a female addict during a street chase, and has been demoted to uniformed duties. However, if he can explain away Jimmy Bryant's death in custody to the satisfaction of Police Commissioner Stewart, he will be given his old job back.

In keeping with the Gothic portrayal of insularity and bigotry, the film is unflinching in the characterisation of rural social issues. The self-destructive activities which the local sergeant Mick Thornton ascribes to the Aborigines ('Drinking and fucking's all they think about') are equally represented amongst the white population. Mick's wife Irene points out that the drinking is a 'symptom', not the illness itself. This is encapsulated in a damning, half-comedic sequence in which, in the course of their investigation, Mick and Tony attempt to get as drunk as the blood tests show Jimmy was in order to ascertain if he could really have hanged himself. Any moral superiority the outsider from the city may assume (as in *Shame*) is unattainable, given Tony's guilt over his fatal shooting. In any case, Mick equates junkies and 'boongs' as social irritants which confront the police, but points out affably that at least in his area they kill themselves and 'save you the trouble'.

During his enquiry Tony uncovers personal and national histories associated with the town, which emphasise *Deadly*'s thorough and complex combination of Gothic plots and motifs. Jimmy's death in custody echoes the case of Craig Burns, who died in the same police cells thirteen years previously. Behaviour in the Aboriginal settlement near Yabbabri reflects the endless repetition of drinking, decline and death in conflict with the establishment. Poignantly this is connected to the monument at the town's centre, a statue of 'Major Mitchell' who killed seventeen blacks in a 'dispersal' two generations before, which becomes a focus for Aboriginal protests. The town is built on and defined by prejudice, and acts as a magnet for examples, victims and perpetrators. The unquestioned maintenance of racism is exhibited from Tony's arrival, when the local who drives him to town from the airport swerves to try and knock down an aged Aborigine by the roadside. The deaths of Jimmy and Craig are matched on a different level by the experience of Daphne, who has come to the town to trace her Aboriginal mother. She was forcibly adopted by a white family when her natural mother was deemed unsuitable, was institutionalised and also died prematurely. In an echo of the frequent, suspicious deaths in Bundunyabba, Daphne asks Tony: 'Do you call it suicide or murder, when one is destroyed by the system?'

The town's attempted assimilation of Tony is apparent in Mick's invitation to a kangaroo hunt, after the fashion of *Wake in Fright*. However, Tony continues his investigation and in so doing alienates his fellow officers without gaining the trust of the Aboriginal commuity. His eventual solution of the case reveals the interconnection of all the personal and political strands, with the resolution of the film's narrative enhancing its polemical stance. Mick Thornton is found to have been responsible for Jimmy's death, because of an affair between Jimmy and his wife Irene. The resulting child has been adopted by Irene's sister Siobhan, who is married to an Aborigine, Wally Nobody. Wally and Siobhan are ostracised by both Aboriginal and non-Aboriginal communities. The mixed marriage is condemned from both sides, and their family withholds the physical evidence (Irene's daughter Rose) on which revelation of the town's secret is dependent. As a police tracker, Wally was shunned because of his involvement in the Craig Burns case, earning him the soubriquet 'Nobody'. (In this respect Wally is similar to the character of Ross in *Shame*, who is alone in standing up to the local mob after his wife is attacked). The couple's social non-existence, coupled with their crucial narrative and symbolic significance (as an unpopular but inevitable integration of the factions), illustrates the film's successful negotiation of melodramatic structure and social relevance. The past histories of Craig and Daphne are linked effectively with the present death of Jimmy and the uncertain future of Rose. Likewise, the discovery of one town secret induces the revelation of another. As the then sergeant in Yabbabri, Commissioner Stewart was responsible for Craig Burns' death, which Thornton had helped to cover up at the time. In Yabbabri, the wider prejudices and specific cases are seen to converge over three generations. Tony takes a truth about prejudice back to the city, just as decades earlier Stewart had brought bigotry with him out of the country. The film ends on an affirmation, with a full investigation into Craig Burns' death promised and Tony united with Daphne and Jimmy's brother. However, the tensions it recognises and foregrounds are not entirely dispelled. Its melodramatic characterisation and conclusion emphasise rather than diminish the social issues it has addressed. The materials of the thriller's microcosm are clearly germane to the political and societal macrocosm:

[*Deadly*] played with the liberal social problematisation of structural racism in a country town, as a pretext to fool the audience and retrain them to see the 'real' crime behind the casual statistic: the police officer's crime of passion ... Aboriginal-white relations are redrawn mythically as family matters. They are not 'out there' – but where they belong in the (Australian) famly ... *Deadly*'s take is that the reality of Aboriginal/white sexual relations, elicit desire, love, passion is just as structural to the history of country towns and families as police and rednecks who need race awareness training supplied from the city.[25]

Deadly circumvents criticism of its narrative technique or commercial crafting by consummating its plot threads and the protagonists' representative characteristics in a satisfying and conclusive resolution. However, it also avoids the dangers of simplifying or defusing the social questions it raises. As a Gothic text it incorporates nearly every motif, plot or device found in previous examples: critiques of the urban and rural environments; investigations into parentage and identity; the bankruptcy of establishment structures and authority; the institutionalization of immorality; social ills articulated through conflicts between communities and generations; and the problematisation of heroic intervention.

Conclusion

The criticism of the human environment found in the Gothic encompasses a revised appreciation (and frequent *de*preciation) of the heroic figure who attempts to intervene meaningfully in its re-organisation. Reappraisal of the hero is perhaps the key Gothic characteristic, since it coexists with re-negotiation or abandonment of conventional narrative form. Rejection of classical narrative is linked to a desire to examine the present form and pertinent origins of identity. This can be seen in the examples of *The Last Wave* and *Summerfield*, in which identity is explored metaphorically on personal and national levels. In the case of *Heatwave* the desired distance from American influence explicit in the text parallels the film's implicit distance from classical narrative in its form. The hero is reconsidered throughout the Gothic, with his disempowerment and the inversion or subversion of his actions being significant in relation to the optimism of previous masculine, Australian representations. They are also significant in relation to the American genres and generic heroes that the Gothic revises and undermines. Since it first appeared near the start of the revival and because famous examples are derived from adolescent genres like horror and science fiction, the Gothic may seem to be a limited and exploitative product. However, as a heterogeneous genre or trend, Australian Gothic represents a precocious examination of filmic form and national identity, iconoclastic in its approach to national stereotypes and genre conventions. Its exploration of masculinity, identity, nationality and social reality in fantastic and metaphoric forms is expressed through generic hybridisation and narrative subversion, and represents an individual and innovative response to the revival's problematisation of Australian-ness.

Notes

1 Jan Dawson, *Walkabout*, *Monthly Film Bulletin* vol. 38 no. 455 (1971), pp. 227–8 (p. 227).

2 Ibid., p. 228.

3 Susan Dermody and Elizabeth Jacka, *The Screening of Australia Vol. II: Anatomy of a National Cinema* (Sydney, Currency, 1988a), p. 81.

4 Scott Murray, Australian Cinema in the 1970s and 1980s, in Scott Murray (ed.), *Australian Cinema* (St Leonards, Allen & Unwin, 1994), pp. 72–3.

5 Tom O'Regan, *Australian National Cinema* (London, Routledge, 1996), p. 266.

6 Philip Strick, *The Cars That Ate Paris*, *Monthly Film Bulletin* vol. 42 no. 496 (1975), pp. 101–2 (p. 102).

7 Dermody and Jacka (1988), pp. 95–6.

8 Verina Glaessner, *Shame*, *Monthly Film Bulletin* vol. 56 no. 665 (1989), pp. 188–9.

9 Philip Strick, *Encounter at Raven's Gate*, *Monthly Film Bulletin* vol. 57 no. 675 (1990), p. 103.

10 Brian McFarlane and Geoff Mayer, *New Australian Cinema: Sources and Parallels in American and British Film* (Cambridge, Cambridge University Press, 1992), p. 61.

11 Ibid., p. 62.

12 O'Regan (1996), p. 104.

13 Ibid.

14 Brian McFarlane, The films of Peter Weir, *Cinema Papers* 26 (1980), Special Supplement: 1–24 (p. 7).

15 Adrian Martin, Fantasy, in Scott Murray (ed.), *The New Australian Cinema* (Melbourne, Thomas Nelson, 1980), p. 107.

16 Bruce Kawin, The Mummy's Pool, in Gerald Mast and Marshall Cohen (eds), *Film Theory and Criticism* (3rd edn) (Oxford, Oxford University Press, 1985), p. 474.

17 Robert Winer, Witnessing and Bearing Witness: The Ontogeny of Encounter in the Films of Peter Weir, in Joseph H. Smith and William Kerrigan (eds), *Images in Our Souls: Cavell, Psychoanalysis and Cinema* (London, Johns Hopkins, 1987), p. 92.

18 Brian McFarlane, Horror and Suspense, in Murray (ed.) (1980), p. 74.

19 Jack Clancy, *The Plumber*, *Cinema Papers* no. 23 (1979), pp. 569, 571 (p. 571).

20 Dermody and Jacka (1988), pp. 124–6.

21 Tim Pulleine, *Harlequin*, *Monthly Film Bulletin* vol. 47 no. 560 (1980), p. 176.

22 McFarlane and Mayer (1992), p. 64.

23 McFarlane and Mayer (1992), p. 63, note the factual basis for the narratives of *Heatwave* and *The Killing of Angel Street* (Donald Crombie, 1981).

24 Tim Pulleine, *Heatwave*, *Monthly Film Bulletin* vol. 49 no. 584 (1982), p. 200.

25 O'Regan (1996), p. 286.

3 The period film

The AFC genre

The role of these films as quasi-official representatives of, rather than representations of, the nation did endow the industry with cultural and political legitimacy during those early difficult years. The institutional commitment to the cultural flagship may well have cushioned film producers from some of the commercial consequences of their judgements at a time when the commercial consequences were particularly harsh ... [period films] possessed attributes which were the reverse of those commonly identified with the ocker films: they were

Picnic at Hanging Rock

tasteful and lyrical rather than brash and iconoclastic; reflective and artistic rather than physical and populist. While these attributes were just as misleading as those they replaced, they did create a 'brand name' for Australian films, without which there was no chance of being marketed at all.[1]

Graeme Turner's judgement of the place and significance of the period films produced during the revival re-emphasises several key issues already acknowledged in relation to the Ocker comedies and the Australian Gothic. Commercial and artistic aspirations are again seen to be in conflict both with each other and with the notion of a filmic national identity. The locally popular and commercially successful Ocker films had represented a double-edged sword as the first feature films to appear, since they generated a financial return at the expense of a reputable and respectable national image. The acceptance (if not the accuracy) of the portrait of national character contained within the Ocker comedies was of benefit to the commercial future of the revival in reaching the local audience, but was the bane of aesthetic ambitions harboured for the new national cinema, in its ability to define and broadcast a refined and mature Australian cultural identity. Consequently, a shift in emphasis away from the popular and exploitative materials of the Ocker films towards the treatment of historical and literary subject matter occurred in the latter half of the 1970s:

In a 1975 review of the industry the institutional rhetoric underwent a crucial change. According to the new rubric, what Australia needed was 'quality' films which could be the cultural flagships of the nation. Commercial success was no longer the primary object (few Australian films made since the revival have returned significant profits), but cultural capital was.[2]

The degree of control implied in this reorganisation of a national 'command economy' of film inspires the labelling of the cycle of period films as the 'AFC genre' by Susan Dermody and Elizabeth Jacka.[3] They contend that the Australian Film Commission (created by legislation in 1975 and assuming the role and responsibilities of the former Australian Film Development Corporation), favoured culturally respectable projects to the disadvantage of more commercial productions. This was achieved through the Commission's authority in the distribution of film finance and its advice to the individual State Government film boards on the apportionment of their developmental funding. The Commission's official obligations were simply to ensure the exhibition of home-produced films, to encourage and support production through loans and grants and to begin to record and preserve Australian filmmaking history through the establishment of a national film archive.[4]

Arguments for the persistence of the period film as the 'authorised' form of Australian film production are persuasive, given that the type came to dominate the output of features between 1975 and 1982. To a large extent the period drama and literary adaptation came to define the products of the Australian cinema abroad, providing the 'brand name' seen as necessary for the film industry.[5] The filmic depiction of the country's history, both distant and recent, stressed the nation's cultural heritage. This was portrayed as derived almost entirely from European (British) models, just as the simplified conception of the nation it supported was limited to the white settler population. This ideological positioning extended to the treatment of the landscape, which is appropriated as a formative national influence rather than being posited (as in the Gothic) as an alien environment inimical to the European mentality. In line with the political agenda suggested for the type's prominence, its formal and thematic aspects have been dismissed as characteristically conservative:

The closest thing to *mise-en-scène* are lyrical pans across picturesque landscapes or beautifully dressed interiors, giving brief rapturous play to cinematography's recognition of what is our own. This includes not only distinctly beautiful place, but space, history and cultural traditions.[6]

In their literary sources, meticulous period recreation and often anticlimactic or episodic narrative structure, films of the AFC genre were seen to draw inspiration from 'British "quality" dramatised literature on television'.[7] However, the period film represented a majority rather than the totality of production, and its importance as a citable cultural export may have been overstated in later years.[8] The years of the period film's dominance were also marked by the success at home and abroad of Australian Gothic films (particularly the *Mad Max* films, but also *The Last Wave* and *Summerfield* which received AFC support), which hardly conform to the rubric of discretion, positive discrimination and cultural respectability. There are also films with historical settings beyond the shores of Australia and openly critical of the British colonial influence (such as *Breaker Morant* (Bruce Beresford 1979) and *Gallipoli* (Peter Weir, 1981)). Additionally, as is suggested by the conservatism of its materials and styling, the period film cannot be described as strictly non-commercial in its approach. Scott Murray asserts that the box-office success of early period films, rather than the incentive of the AFC's blessing, provided the impetus for the continued production of heritage films.[9] This challenges the aesthetic bent and political motivation presumed to lie behind the period film cycle, and suggests that the type may actually have represented (briefly) a union of the revival's artistic and commercial poles. Rather than aiming for an aesthetic and cultural exclusivity, period films exploited a briefly popular nostalgia for an unchallenging cinema, expressing and encouraging pride in a constructed, communal past. In appealing to local and overseas audiences and fulfilling demands for a refined and representative film product, the period film could lay claim to being the first mature expression of Australian film culture. The film credited with inspiring the cycle of period films, and with endowing the new Australian cinema with an aesthetic maturity belying its age, was *Picnic at Hanging Rock* (Peter Weir, 1975).

Picnic at Hanging Rock and the literary adaptation

Picnic at Hanging Rock was Peter Weir's second feature film, following the critically acclaimed but commercially unsuccessful *The Cars That Ate Paris* (1974).[10] Among the group of new Australian directors working in television or independently at the end of the 1960s, Weir had come to prominence through his short films which preceded *Cars*. In addition to the independent production of *Homesdale* (1971), which was financed by the Experimental Film Fund, Weir contributed to the portmanteau film *Three to Go* (1971), which became a landmark success for the Commonwealth Film Unit. Weir joined the CFU after several years of television work, and was part of the vibrant, creative atmosphere at the Unit which nurtured the first generation of young Australian filmmakers:

Before the existence of the Australian Film and Television School, Film Australia (from 1973 the name of the former Commonwealth Film Unit) was one of the industry's few training grounds for aspiring filmmakers. Feature film producers and directors who worked there at various times in the 1960s and 1970s, included Peter Weir, Donald Crombie, Joan Long, Anthony Buckley, Michael Thornhill, Brian Hannant, Oliver Howes, Arch Nicholson and Richard Brennan ... All had come on to the staff when commercial film activity was negligible and the only serious rival for documentary work was ABC television. Many were involved in the industry-wide agitation for a reconstructed film industry, and this was to be reflected in the new types of films being made by Film Australia.[11]

Although the first feature films made by Thornhill (*Between Wars* (1974)) and Crombie (*Caddie* (1976)) shared a period film approach by depicting Australia during the era of the Depression, their differences from each other and from Weir's *Picnic at Hanging Rock* illustrate the variety of filmmaking styles being cultivated at the CFU at that time. Having concentrated on the production of documentary films in the years prior to the revival, the CFU inaugurated the new era with the production of *Three to Go*. Weir, Hannant and Howes each directed a segment of the film, which addressed the problems of contemporary Australian youth: Weir's *Michael* concentrated upon the frustrations of a young, middle-class male who is tempted to drop out and explore an alternative lifestyle; Hannant's film *Judy* details the difficulties a teenager from the country encounters when she tries to move to the city; and Howes' *Toula*, in examining the experiences of a young Greek immigrant, formed an early example of the Australian cinema's depiction of contemporary, multicultural society.[12] These early films helped to establish Weir's reputation as one of the foremost filmmakers of the revival, with both *Michael* and *Homesdale* winning the Grand Prix of the Australian Film Institute.

Weir was approached by producer Patricia Lovell to direct *Picnic at Hanging Rock* before the completion of *The Cars That Ate Paris*. Lovell had bought the rights to the source novel several years earlier, but the scale of the project prompted the involvement of the producers of *Cars* (Hal and Jim McElroy) and the seeking of funds from the Australian Film Development Corporation and the South Australian Film Corporation.[13] Although the period film may have enjoyed preference from the Australian Film Commission after the success of *Picnic*, establishment support was not immediately forthcoming. The producers' estimate of the film's budget was not accepted by the AFDC at the outset, but the institutional commitment to the film was maintained by the Australian Film Commission after its creation in 1975. Lovell has described the obstacles encountered in the development of the production in interview.[14] However, the partnership of Lovell and Weir met with approval from the novel's author Joan Lindsay. Despite setbacks, Patricia Lovell went on to produce another period film *Break of Day* (Ken Hannam, 1976), in collaboration with the screenwriter for *Picnic*, Cliff Green. The McElroy brothers, who also produced *The Cars That Ate Paris* with Weir, went on to produce the director's next feature film, *The Last Wave* (1977).

The eventual success of the film at home and abroad seems to have been apparent to those engaged on working on it, leading to some friction between the key creative personnel by the time of the opening in Adelaide.[15] *Picnic*'s formal sophistication (in its period recreation and the aesthetic quality of its cinematography and use of the landscape) was championed as a major break-through for the new Australian film industry, with Weir being considered its first potential auteur.[16] There were those, however, who criticised the film for its frustration of audience expectation, in failing to resolve its mystery, and for the elevation of style over argument or substance.[17] What Weir and his collaborators attempted was the adoption in an Australian film of the stylistic features, rhythms and preoccupations of the European art cinema of the 1960s. Joan Lindsay's novel, which sets up a mystery with-out a solution, was the ideal vehicle for the manipulation of *mise-en-scène* to allusive effect and the re-orientation of audience expectation away from the inconclusive narrative. Weir's con-ception of the film in this fashion was driven as much by neces-sity as invention:

Here was a movie which had no solution ... this in fact in America caused the film not to be a success, despite how I'd made it, but it did seem to me to be the only way to approach it was to work in the style of the European film with the slower rhythms, with the lack of exciting developments that lead you to an expectation of a solution, but to try and develop within this approach something approaching the hypnotic, that is the rhythm of the film would lull you into another state and you would begin to go with the film and drop your expectations.[18]

Contrary to commercial mimicry of the Hollywood format of nar-rative construction and conclusion, *Picnic at Hanging Rock* essayed a sophisticated art film treatment. Its use of the natural landscape, of light, colour and costuming and its perceived artistic quality (as an adaptation from literature, and through its inclusion of other art forms within its scripting and *mise-en-scène*) represented a major achievement in the furtherance of the emergent Australian film culture, and inspired many inferior imitations.

Picnic's derivation from literature established one of the trends within the period film cycle. Adaptations from novels (such as *The Mango Tree* (Kevin Dobson, 1977) from Ronald McKie's award-winning novel) and from autobiographies (*The Getting of Wisdom* (Bruce Beresford, 1977), *My Brilliant Career* (Gillian Armstrong, 1979) and *Caddie*) represented a significant proportion of the period films produced. Brian McFarlane has attributed this reliance upon literary texts as illustrative of two factors affecting the first decade of the renaissance. Firstly, the translation of novels into film has compensated for the lack of original screen-plays. Secondly, literary adaptation and the period film cycle have been interconnected because of the perceived cultural agenda set out for the Australian film industry in the wake of the revival's initial commercial successes:

> There has ... been a strong element of nostalgia, an almost deliberate anti-'ocker' element in many films of the period as if to establish a cinema at odds with prevailing myths of Australian life. Not surprisingly, this has led film-makers to novels of an earlier period, or at least novels set in an earlier period.[19]

Literary adaptation to film is seen to fulfil an educational as well as cultural function, with several of the Australian novels translated to the screen being part of school curricula. Brian McFarlane has attacked this dependence on literature as a root cause of the 'unadventurous carefulness'[20] which has characterised Australian film in general and the period film in particular.

Although it is credited with setting the period film cycle in motion, *Picnic at Hanging Rock* can be seen to vary significantly from most of its subsequent imitators. The novel was relatively unsuccessful prior to the appearance of the film adaptation, but gained a marked popularity after it because of the film's reception.[21] At the same time, the film manages to be both a faithful adaptation and a distinctive cinematic experience. In translating the interplay of mystery, destiny and coincidence at work in Lindsay's novel, the film uses a variety of filmic techniques. The novel's unpredictable shifts in tense and perspective are expressed through alterations in film speed. Time-lapse photography is used in the observation of ants consuming a celebration cake at the picnic grounds. The point of view of male characters watching the girls crossing the creek on their way up the Rock is relayed through eroticised slow motion. Weir also used a range of effects on the soundtrack to exaggerate the sense of disorientation which accompanies scenes on the Rock.[22] Many of these techniques were also used on *The Last Wave* to create a similarly nightmarish atmosphere. In mimicking the European art film, *Picnic* also incorporated or quoted other literary, musical and visual arts. Elizabethan love poetry and Shakespeare's sonnet number 18 are recited on the morning of the picnic, and the scenes around the Rock are composed and lit in emulation of the Australian Impressionist painters of the Heidelberg School. Graeme Turner has noted the visual and thematic resemblance between Frederick McCubbin's *Lost* (1886) and aspects of *Picnic*'s art direction,[23] and the works of Tom Roberts and Arthur Streeton provide the inspiration for the dissolving views of the bush and the Rock seen during the credit sequence. At a more fundamental level, the film's concentration on the passing or freezing of time bears a strong resemblance to the conceptual notions underpinning the Impressionists' work. The characters' frequent comments on mortality and time within the film accord with the artists' attempts to capture a personal experience or interpretation of the landscape:

An effect is only momentary: so an impressionist tries to find his place. Two half-hours are never alike, and he who tries to paint a sunset on two successive evenings must be more or less painting from memory. So, in these works, it has been the object of the artists to render faithfully, and thus attain first records of effects widely differing, and often of very fleeting character.[24]

The film's discussion of time is allusive and metaphorical, in tune with the existential concerns of the European films from which it draws its inspiration. The open-endedness of its narrative encourages the viewer to concentrate the interpretative effort upon the minutiae of *mise-en-scène* and scripting, when the predictability of plotting bound to cause and effect is removed. Despite its inconclusiveness, the film's narrative occupies a clearly defined time frame, from Valentine's Day, February 14th to March 27th 1900. The sense of expectancy is heightened by the watches stopping at noon exactly during the picnic on the Rock, and by Miranda's repeated statement that 'everything begins and ends at exactly the right time and place'. Miranda is, however, the only character who specifically renounces the rationalisation of time. She refuses to wear a watch since she cannot bear it 'ticking above her heart'. The loss of control over time within the diegesis parallels the frustration of plotting and audience expectation. Since no one is sure of the precise time on the Rock, it becomes impossible to determine when the girls and their mistress disappeared. This simple but insuperable obstacle defeats the subsequent investigation, just as the many searches of the area produce no more clues, even when one of the missing pupils is recovered unhurt. The stopping of the watches represents a pivotal moment in the film, as incomprehension and enigma succeed it just as apparent certainty and control precede it. Another, alternative time scale, suggestive of predestination or sexual maturation, takes over during the picnic, and the disruptive powers vested in the natural landscape and symbolised by the Rock extend their influence to the girls' college itself.

The connection between the Rock and the college which the picnic creates stresses their antagonistic positioning within the film and the landscape. The imposing, dominating volcanic landmark and its opponent, the proud, classically-styled edifice of the college, seem to be 'two monoliths set down incongruously in the

Australian bush'.[25] This opposition is also signalled by contrasting elements dominating the soundtrack. Scenes within the college and polite society are accompanied by classical pieces, specifically Beethoven's Fifth Piano Concerto ('The Emperor'). The other principal theme, heard alongside scenes at the Rock, is provided by Gheorge Zamphir's panpipes. The measured assurance of 'The Emperor' is contrasted with the primordial pipe music to illustrate the conflict between repressive but secure society and liberating but threatening nature. The film can be read as a criticism of the imposition of culture upon nature, with the school's suppressive powers (preparing its pupils for the class- and sex-based prejudices of the Victorian world) being defeated by the seductive, primeval forces of the landscape. Other aspects of the film's symbolism support such an interpretation. The pupils' pure white costuming is transformed in the cases of those who return from the Rock: the dowdy Edith is dressed in insignificant brown, while Irma wears a scarlet, adult costume redolent of an awakened sexuality when she comes to leave the school. The spreading influence of nature is suggested by the infestation of the college with flowers, which appear as decorations and blooms exchanged on Valentine's Day. This crescentic sexuality and its fascination with the landscape leads the party of 'chosen' pupils to their communion with the Rock, which is accompanied by a gradual disrobing (gloves removed once they have left town, and shoes and stockings taken off near the summit).

The film's extravagant detail in *mise-en-scène*, and its consequent openness to interpretation, enhance its art cinema reputation as much as its episodic and inconclusive narrative. Its reputability and marketability as an example of refined Australian culture (and *film* culture) have drawn attention away from its more disconcerting and less conservative elements. Unlike subsequent period films, *Picnic at Hanging Rock* does not regard the inheritance of British-based social, educational and cultural structures with pride or nostalgia. While admitting the symbolic nature of the Rock versus college pairing, and the caricatured portraits of the English aristocracy, middle-class schoolmistress and lower-class Australians which the film contains, it can be seen that the imposition of foreign (British) institutions upon the Australian natural and social landscape is unwise and unwanted. It is after contact (and conflict) with a specifically Australian landscape that the ideals of the college and the fabric of the society it represents begin to disintegrate. The failure to find the girls and solve the mystery defies the previously unshakeable, regulatory order of Victorian society. Lindsay's novel highlights the implicit vulnerability of the establishment, which appears in history shortly after the fictional events, by referring to the Boer War and Queen Victoria's approaching jubilee.[26] The ignominy of the twentieth century's first war and the imminent death of the monarch in 1901 underline the pessimism and fragility of imperial authority, which is also implied by the elegiac tone of the 'Emperor' Concerto. Its melancholic mood, heard alongside the final scenes of the fruitless searches of the Rock, emphasises the overthrow of an anachronistic social construct. Yet the same historical period also provides the setting for decisive movement towards a definition of Australian nationhood, with the federation of the colonised states in 1901. The call to and retreat into a distinctive natural landscape, away from a foreign and imposed authority, to which the girls respond represents a call to national as well as sexual liberation. Such a mobilisation of the landscape as a symbol of identity and source of distinctive Australian-ness recurs across the period film cycle, in support of the new national cinema's cultural agenda:

It is not by chance ... that a crop of extensively publicised and acclaimed films highlighting a unique Australian landscape have come to light during this decade of resurgent nationalism. The landscape cinema asserts an Australian difference ... the time setting allows the filmmakers to focus without obfuscation on the theme of individuals in confrontation with nature.[27]

The aesthetic and symbolic treatment of the landscape in period films reinforces one construct of national character, as seen for example in *The Man from Snowy River* (George Miller, 1982). However, *Picnic*'s treatment of the natural landscape is ambiguous, in contrasting its seductiveness and liberation with its inscrutability and menace. This feature, taken with the film's depiction of establishment authority and its place in the Weir canon between *The Cars That Ate Paris* (1974) and *The Last Wave* (1977), reveals its association with the Australian Gothic. Dermody and Jacka maintain that 'the unconscious, the subjective, the marvellous, the disturbing, [and] the cinematically literate' are 'off-limits' to the 'tasteful, rather old-fashioned film storytelling'[28] of the period film. The irony of *Picnic at Hanging Rock*, the period film's progenitor and inspiration foregrounding all these qualities in its handling of narrative, editing, composition and *mise-en-scène*, is furthered by the elevation of the film as revival's key text in cultural and artistic terms:

It was the first Australian film that was clearly a 'quality film'. Weir became the first Australian 'auteur' as *Picnic* legitimated Australian movies for the middle-class audience still ready to believe in the inferiority of Australian culture.[29]

The formal and ideological challenge of Weir's film would be transformed or muted in later period dramas in appealing to a mainstream, middle-class audience sympathetic to the period film's construction of cultural heritage, and susceptible to its image of national identity.

The period film cycle

The institutionalisation of the period film as the dominant mode of feature filmmaking in the wake of *Picnic at Hanging Rock*'s success led to the downplaying of many of the unconventional formal and thematic elements which had distinguished Weir's film. *Picnic*'s basis in the Gothic and its extension of its director's interest in alienating subjective experience underline the film's adoption of a period setting in order to offer a critique of authority within a fantasy-horror format. The period setting provides a suitably distant backdrop for the rumination on the nature of hierarchies of gender, class and race, along with Weir's abiding interest in the irruption of the uncanny within mundane and controlled environments. The representation of the past alters significantly in the cases of later period films, even though other characteristics of *Picnic at Hanging Rock* (the concentration on childhood and female experience, on institutions and forms of education, and the pictorial treatment of the landscape) were retained and developed.

Caddie (Donald Crombie, 1976), adapted from an autobiography detailing the experiences of a single mother working to bring up her family during the Depression, helped to centre the period film's interest on female protagonists. It also emphasised the period film's anodyne gentility in its refusal to address any unsettling social issues in its treatment of economic conditions in Sydney during the 1920s and 1930s. The heroine leaves her adulterous husband and takes on a series of lowly-paid jobs in bars and hotels in order to support her children. She enjoys romantic interludes with several rich men, who could rescue her from her penury, but she does not compromise on ideals of love and respectability. At the same time her situation and her reaction to it offer a critique of the double standards prevalent in employment and sexual relationships. In spite of her impoverished circumstances, her 'class' and attractiveness is always perceptible to men of means. Consequently she is desired as an ornament or possession by her suitors, one of whom gives her her titular nick-name by comparing her to his conspicuous American Cadillac car. Caddie's efforts to earn a living wage are undone by the national economic crisis as well as social and marital injustices, but while her predicament seems insoluble it never appears to be hopeless. The film shows a community, representative of a population and a given era, which responds to successive crises with good humour and philanthropy. Poverty and near-starvation are greeted with a jovial wistfulness: 'If it was raining gravy we'd be the ones holding forks!' The film's ending, in mid-stream with a explanatory title, is one of its few similarities to *Picnic*, but does not represent a debt to art film ambiguity. Instead the narrative simply stops rather than pursue its soap-operatic material any further, and the refusal to offer any climax or resolution accentuates its failure to create any momentum or tension. The respectable box office performance of *Caddie* helped to entrench the period film further as the preferred form of indigenous drama:

Caddie explores ... sexual harassment and breadline survival. But it is a fundamentally aesthetic poverty, with genteel suffering and a psychologically cushioned descent into working-class hell ... Certainly it is confidently written and made, with strong period production values that belie the film's relatively modest budget. The appetite for a respectable film industry was translated into general appreciation for a respectable film, especially one with a respectful, proto-feminist attitude towards its attractive central character, and charming period detail, authenticating our sense that we have a history of our own.[30]

The distancing and defusing of traumatic events in the past is also evident in the subjective but retrospective summation of experience in *Emma's War* (Clytie Jessop, 1985). As a relatively late example of the period film, *Emma's War* like *Caddie* reflects the trend towards the amalgamation of films set in the past with narratives articulating formative personal experiences or rites of passage. The adult Emma's voice-over accompanies the film's recreation of the Australian home front during the Second World War stressing a concordance between the country's physical isolation and the detachment of her childish self from national and parental concerns:

I was fourteen in that long summer of 1942. The summer of that war that had scarcely touched us. We didn't feel threatened in any way, and the land itself, lazy and slow under the dry, seductive sun, was indifferent to conflict. My father had been away for many months, but except for his absence the world he'd left behind remained unchanged.

Her mother's loneliness during her husband's absence receives the same innocuous treatment as Caddie's hardships, and Emma herself appears removed from the realities of contemporary events on the personal and global levels by the child's limited perspective. Her isolation is completed by the 'cocoon' of her school and her country.

Picnic's depiction of repressive schooling recurs in a different form in *The Getting of Wisdom* (Bruce Beresford, 1977). Beresford's film is based on the autobiographical novel of the same title by Ethel Florence Richardson, published in 1910 under the pseudonym Henry Handel Richardson. It follows the school career of Laura Tweedle Rambotham, who is sent from her remote rural home to an expensive Melbourne school. Her widowed mother works as the local postmistress and as a seamstress in order to support the family and pay Laura's fees. Laura is highly intelligent, energetic and talented musically, but her loquacity and immodesty lead to censure from her teachers and peers. Prejudice informs the hierarchy of pupils within the school, with Laura and another new girl nicknamed 'Chinky' bearing the brunt of the bullying because of their impoverished backgrounds. Laura's immediate lessons on entry to the school are in the virtues of reticence, economy with the truth and conformity within her group of bigoted and unambitious peers. As in *Picnic*, the colonial cultural debt in evidence in Australian religious and educational institutions represents a structural incongruity and obstacle to the development of relevant, indigenous social foundations: 'Such curricular wisdom as its schoolgirl heroine ... "gets" is essentially European, notably British, and it is dished out by a staff with little regard for either youthful needs or the freer social modes of Australia.'[31]

Laura is a non-conformist not simply because of her upbringing, though the suggestion of lower-middle class origins is enough to provoke derision from the offspring of aristocrats and entrepreneurs. She is distinguished from her peers by the desire for self-improvement through education, and for learning for its own sake which is linked to personal and artistic ambition. The channel for her creativity is changed from writing in the novel to music in the film, and Brian McFarlane has lamented the inconsistency or incoherence which results in the screenplay because of this alteration.[32] However, the change in Laura's artistic bent allows the film to illuminate other aspects of her development within the school, and in relation to the wider society whose mores it replicates and inculcates. Laura's first arrival at the school, dressed in a garish home-made dress establishes her inferior status within the community: she is seen to be dwarfed in her opulent surroundings of oak panelling, dark decorations and drapes. Her diminution in long shot against the college interiors registers as a graphic illustration of her minority, in age, class and knowledge (of the world) at this stage. The education she gains and subsequent activities she undertakes will lead towards an improvement in her social status (with her success in music ensuring acceptance and recognition), but her negotiation of compromise and non-conformity betrays the difficulty of realising personal desires within a restrictive environment.

On arrival at the school Laura is classified by the other pupils according to the class and wealth of her family. Her unease in the school's social milieu is reproduced in scholarly activities, either because her self-tuition (of French) leaves her open to ridicule or her eagerness to participate embarrasses her lazier fellow pupils. Ashamed of her own oddity, Laura prays for the strength to conform with expectations: 'I want to belong. I'll remember dates, and only play the right music and try to behave like a lady. I'll try and try.' In seeking to integrate, Laura is measured and measures herself against the other female characters (mother and siblings, pupils, teachers, wives and spinsters) she encounters. When Laura divulges the truth to the bully Lilith about her mother's work to support her, she realises quickly how frankness exposes one to a deceitful enemy. Consequently when under pressure she fabricates an equally humiliating story about Lilith, which proves the perfect deterrent to the bully's revelation of Laura's secret. Where Brian McFarlane sees the film's excision of Laura's writing ambitions in the novel in favour of the concentration on music as an ill-considered alteration, the film's equal stress upon Laura's proficiency in lying broadens the metaphor of 'fiction' in a pertinent commentary on the hypocrisies of social existence. The acknowledgement that skill in falsification is crucial to survival, let alone success, within genteel social circles ironises the notion of the 'wisdom' Laura needs to acquire. In lamenting the absence of the novelist's self-conscious irony in Beresford's film,[33] McFarlane passes over other examples of an ironic tone which are present: Laura being seen to cheat in a history examination shortly before her elevation as the college's star pupil, and her embarrassment of the principal Reverend Strachey by reciting verses from the Song of Solomon when asked to read from the Scriptures which pervade the school's timetable.

Fictional narration becomes most useful to Laura when she fabricates a romance between herself and the newly-appointed curate Reverend Shepherd in order to tantalise and gain acceptance with the older pupils. Her ability to accomplish this deception is implied from the first scenes in which she relates a romantic story of her own to her sister prior to her departure for Melbourne. Her description of 'verdant fronds' and 'sylvan glades' jars against the surroundings of arid land and parched, fallen trees, and connects with later comments made by the junior teachers. While they read and censor the pupils' correspondence (which consists of lurid love letters), some of the unmarried mistresses display envy of the affluent schoolgirls and desire for romantic entanglements for themselves. The same teachers are far from disapproving when Laura's intricate falsehoods are exposed: 'Reality's mostly damned unbearable. One has to escape into something.'

Laura's second ostracism from the community follows the revelation of her deception. When her attempts to rejoin the school community are rebuffed, she submerges herself first in her music and later in her intense relationship with an older girl, Evelyn. Ironically, when one avenue towards acceptance and conformity is blocked, the pursuit of personal expression and ambition through music leads eventually to integration and approbation from the establishment, when Laura wins the Woodfull Scholarship for Musicianship. Her friendship with Evelyn is also, ironically, an alienating but ennobling development, since Laura's peers aspire to keep the older girl company but she consorts only with the equally isolated Laura. The pair seem to be kindred spirits in their impatience with the curtailment of individuality imposed by the school and the limited opportunities for women within wider society. As a final irony, Evelyn and Laura are drawn to each other through music. Their first proper meeting comes about because of Evelyn's inability to play the required piece (a Schubert impromptu) for her examination, and because of Laura's frustration with being restricted to playing certain (easier) pieces rather than her own selections. The paradoxical amalgamation of alienation from pupils of her own age and opposition to the school's mind-set, with inadvertent social climbing and official support through her music and friendship with Evelyn provides evidence of the satiric potential within Beresford's film, which arises from the re-direction rather than removal of the novel's irony.

Musical accomplishment develops for Laura as a channel for expression, a manifestation of difference and a means of advancement. When she volunteers to play at the Reverend Strachey's afternoon of 'cultural offerings', she affronts Lilith (who is forced to sing) and her teachers, who disapprove of the tasteless 'theatricality' of the Thalberg variations she chooses. She is playing this piece again, in rebellion against the limitations on her practice imposed by Miss Hicks the music teacher, when Evelyn interrupts her and ask for help with her Schubert impromptu. The deepening of their relationship, and their increasing isolation from the rest of the college community, follow as a consequence of this scene. Laura's sexual development (in fantasising over the Reverend Shepherd, fabricating her romance with him and listening in trepidation to her peers' gory descriptions of childbirth) has been interwoven with her attempts to integrate. Her progress in music, which accompanies a withdrawal from the community into a solitary friendship, comes to dominate the latter half of the film.

The relationship with Evelyn is based, on Laura's side at least, on a belief that they share a similar dissatisfaction with their educational and social environment. The rejection of the mores of established society extends, in Laura's perception, to a refusal to submit to male authority in marriage. Laura's sense of betrayal when Evelyn becomes engaged and leaves the college arises from her reliance on their previous intimacy, and precipitates an intensification of mutual feeling when they share Evelyn's bed on the following night. Robin Wood interprets the Evelyn-Laura relationship, this scene and the film's climax with Laura's musical performance before the school, as an unequivocal representation of radical lesbian identity. This challenge to accepted patterns of behaviour is articulated covertly through Laura's piano:

She is supposed to perform a Beethoven sonata for the assembled dignitaries, parents and peers. We expect her to substitute, as an exhilarating if childish act of defiance, the vulgar Thalberg variations on 'Home Sweet Home' with which she earlier discomfited a Principal's tea-party. But what she actually performed is the Schubert impromptu associated with her lesbian affair – the piece the two girls practised together. That no one in her audience understands this is unimportant: nothing Laura does is going to affect the system radically. The function of the choice she makes is her private assertion, for herself, of her own integrity and the validity of her sexual commitment; after which, freed at last from the oppression and hypocrisy of a monstrous institution, she can express her inner freedom in her run through the park.[34]

Laura's ascendancy over the establishment is signalled at this point by a reversal in composition in comparison with the scenes of her arrival at the school. As she plays she is seen magnified in the foreground, with the hall and its occupants shrunk in the background. McFarlane dismisses Wood's interpretation of the relationship as a sexual one, but also criticises the climactic scene as obscure to the inattentive viewer.[35] Irrespective of the evaluation of Laura's and Evelyn's relationship, the playing of the Schubert piece implies a personal motivation behind Laura's non-conformist behaviour, which counters the Reverend Strachey's pompous remarks at the award ceremony (suggesting that Laura's success is as attributable to the school, her peers and teachers as to herself). The institution is seen here, as elsewhere, as not so much 'monstrous' (in the way Appleyard College in *Picnic at Hanging Rock* harbours sadism and suicide) as hypocritical, ridiculous and anachronistic. In this way it concurs precisely with the society it serves and mirrors, and this injects a note of pessimism into Laura's escape and victory. The chances for true independence, suggested by her exuberant run from the school gates, still appear sadly limited: 'there is no social alternative to the school; its structures are those of society'.[36] It is noticeable that Laura's scholarship will take her overseas and away from Australian influence, suggesting that creativity and freedom must flee the suffocation of British-based society. A similar desire for escape, articulated more forthrightly by the heroine and the film, is found in another contemporary literary adaptation, *My Brilliant Career* (Gillian Armstrong, 1979).

Where Beresford's film retains much of the reticence and respectability expected of period drama (despite its openness to oppositional readings), Armstrong's adaptation of Stella Franklin's semi-autobiographical novel grounds the representation of the past firmly in contemporary gender politics. The full development of the source material's feminist orientation is achieved not least because of the preponderance of female creative personnel (including screenwriter Eleanor Witcombe, also responsible for the screenplay of *The Getting of Wisdom*) on the production team.[37]

My Brilliant Career charts the journey to maturity and independence undertaken by Sybylla Melvyn, a young woman from an Outback family who, like Laura, aspires to fame as an artist. She seeks to avoid a life of drudgery and child-bearing in the desert, but is not disposed to submit to marriage and conformity within polite society either. Her progress from her parents' homestead at Possum Gully to her grandmother's country house at Caddagat epitomises both aspiration and repression. Like the school to which Laura is sent, the house represents the sort of circles Sybylla should move in, since she is distinctly out of place in the remote, rural environment. However, the contrast between the two locations is also redolent of the distinction drawn between imposed British social patterns and authentic Australian society. During Sybylla's stay she is expected to gain a suitable refinement and humility, which together should secure her a good match. A suitable candidate soon appears, in the person of the moneyed and handsome Harry Beecham, whose own luxurious estate exaggerates the contrast with the heroine's upbringing. Sybylla responds to his obvious attachment, but social circumstances and Sybylla's own choices intervene to preclude the conventional conclusion of their romance.

The unconventional nature of Sybylla's conduct runs parallel to the film's unexpected handling of her destiny. The transcription of her disruptive actions and outspoken opinions into the novel she is writing reflects the double challenge with which she confronts her social milieu. Her behaviour allows her to wrest control away from those who seek to contain and mould her, and at the same time provides material for her creative career which she hopes will represent a source of income sufficient to allow her to repudiate financial dependence in marriage. Her refusal to submerge herself in marriage (even to Harry, the man she admits she loves) epitomises her confrontational stance, and her insistence on equality and independence. Before the film's conclusion both Sybylla and Harry are humbled. She is forced into employment as a governess to a family living on a squalid outback farm, to whom her family are indebted, and he suffers financial ruin. Despite this reversal and the 'freedom' it offers for the characters to live subseqently as they please, Sybylla still rejects the idea of marriage and returns to Possum Gully to complete her manuscript. Her characteristic 'plainness', in both speech and looks, undergoes no last-minute moderation and the expected romantic resolution is forestalled. In stressing the similarity of the film's narrative to that of *Jane Eyre* (which extends to employment as a governess, the separation of the couple and the disabling of the hero), Jocelyn Robson and Beverley Zalcock note the overt statements in support of contemporary feminism to be found in Armstrong's film:

Jane Eyre settles for marriage, albeit a love marriage and highly unconventional. Bronte's heroine is of her time and there is no other choice except marriage or loneliness. Sybylla is a representation of the film's own time, addressing the issues of 1970s feminism; she is not to be so easily recuperated. In a sense, the film sacrifices verisimilitude to make a contemporary personal-political point: Why be a Wife?[38]

Like Laura Sybylla prefers a close friendship (even with a potential lover) to a socially acceptable marriage, but most desires creativity and escape. Paradoxically the literary work is completed by a return to her original seclusion. The novel, and not the writer escapes as a closing title informs us that Sybylla's book was finally published by Blackwoods in Edinburgh. While in theme and characterisation Armstrong's film exhibits a debt to the literary-based melodramas and women's pictures of Classical Hollywood,[39] its deliberate divergence from the anticipated narrative resolution underlines its national and political difference. The obduracy of Sybylla's stance and the endurance her chosen path demands offer no respite. Where *Picnic* uses period-fantasy for an unconventional depiction of national self-determination, *My Brilliant Career* (like *Journey Among Women* (Tom Cowan, 1977)) recruits the historical setting to offer a critique of previous and contemporary social circumstances from the female perspective, entailing a systematic re-arrangement of narrative structure and audience expectation.

Various motifs from all of these Australian period films concentrating on the expression of feminine experience can be seen to merge in the New Zealand/Australian/French co-production of *The Piano* (Jane Campion, 1993). Campion's film assumes the Gothic tone of Emily rather than Charlotte Bronte in its narrative of forced marriage, sexual repression and the colonial conquering of land and the female body. The heroine Ada is mute through a combination of her disempowered circumstances and her indomitable will to resist patriarchal control. Instead she expresses private emotion and public defiance in passionate and disconcerting playing of her piano. As with Laura and Sybylla, creativity in general and music in particular convey the heroine's implicit imperviousness to social, male-dominated authority. As in *Picnic*, landscape is also an important frame of symbolic reference within the narrative. Ownership of Maori lands, which Ada's husband Stewart and her lover Baines exchange, forms a currency of equal value with the piano and Ada's body. Progression from colonising to buying to bartering to sharing marks the development of preferable, though still imperfect, bases for sexual relationships within the prevailing social environment.

Fred Schepisi's period films

In the previous examples, the period film has centred on the experiences of children and females in positions of social inferiority. However, the gentility of the drama and aesthetic appeal of period recreation have often disarmed or obscured the criticism contained in examinations of restriction and prejudice. Fred Schepisi's films which use the period setting focus on male experience of intolerance and oppression, and refuse to temper their criticism of prevailing attitudes through simplification of issues or prettification of *mise-en-scène*. Schepisi's feature debut *The Devil's Playground* (1976) was another Australian film set in the past which detailed the difficult, formative experiences of youthful characters within rigorous educational institutions. What distinguished Schepisi's film was its semi-autobiographical nature. The director also assumed the roles of writer and producer in bringing aspects of his own youthful life to the screen. This resulted not only in an uncompromising portrayal of a secluded religious community, but also in an unusual slant on the treatment of different epochs in depicting the comparatively recent past:

> Its fictional 'period' – the mid-fifties – doesn't qualify for costume-drama lyricism, and it is semi-autobiographical rather than literary in origin. It is European in flavour only because it deals with Catholicism ... The seminary is closed in behind high walls and closed doors. Even the swimming pool visited downtown is an indoor pool. The echoes in its tiled enclosure are a lovely metaphor for unnatural repression. Like the *kammerspiel*, the film is an introspective look at the passions that arise and are forced by enclosure and systematic repression to find indirect expression. But the imagery is drawn more from the documentary than from expressionism.[40]

The Devil's Playground shares many of the thematic concerns of more mainstream period films such as *Picnic at Hanging Rock* and *The Getting of Wisdom*, but its near-contemporary critique of the religious educational system (and by extension the conservative establishment as a whole) sets it apart from other period films. The refusal of *The Devil's Playground* to soften its perspective or aestheticise its material set the agenda for Schepisi's subsequent work in Australia. Its uncompromising style and subject matter were developed more fully in Schepisi's next feature production.

Schepisi was again responsible for the screenplay of *The Chant of Jimmie Blacksmith* (1978), which was derived from historical, documentary sources. Working as producer-director-writer for the second time, Schepisi was able to realise a personal interpretation within a faithful adaptation of Thomas Keneally's source novel, retaining a large proportion of dialogue and incident. The narrative concerns the encounters with racial prejudice which the titular Aboriginal character experiences in turn-of-the-century Australia. Jimmie grows up on an outback mission station, where the minister and his wife take a special interest in him. He is 'chosen for higher things' in the eyes of the Reverend Neville, who encourages him to aspire to a life of equality with white

Australians, in work, marriage and property ownership. As an ambitious, educated man, the product of an interracial relationship who is out of step with traditional Aboriginal culture and seeks integration into white society, Jimmie falls foul of both communities. He becomes a symbol and symptom of the racial divide within Australian society, feeling the injustice of his treatment and reacting violently against it. While the film problematises the authenticity of Jimmie's Aboriginality, suggesting that the 'half-caste' is neither truly black or white, the unremitting prejudice exhibited by the non-Aboriginal characters forms an unflinching indictment of pervasive racial bigotry. Irrespective of his aspiration and differentiation of himself from his own people, Jimmie is perceived and treated as an Aborigine. Just as one white couple assert his difference in being 'half white' and instigate his hopeless ambition, the entirety of the white community confirm his blackness and inferiority.

The Chant of Jimmie Blacksmith emerges as an intense and bleak story of the inevitability of violent confrontation between segregated races.[41] Its obvious commitment to the recognition of institutionalised injustice causes the appearance of anachronistic, polemical lines in the mouths of the principal characters (such as Jimmie and McCready during the hostage episode) which reveals the director's use of the 'screen at certain key points as a platform'.[42] However, the majority of the film's impact is derived from its powerful manipulation of *mise-en-scène*, composition and editing, which serve to politicise the period film genre. These features are evident from the pre-title sequence which juxtaposes Jimmie's tribal initiation in the bush with the Reverend Neville's frustration at his unexplained absence. While he discusses his dissatisfaction with the indolence and apathy of the 'blasted blacks' and his dream of imbuing 'just one' with a 'decent ambition', the scenes in the interior of the Neville home are intercut with Jimmie's rituals and lessons in lore and survival. The avowal of distance between the races, enunciated in the distinction between culture and cluttered interiors on one side and nature and blank exteriors on the other, begins with the film. The combination of seduction towards and entrapment within the materiality of white society is signalled by Neville's invitation to his study on Jimmie's return. In the final scene before the appearance of the titles, Jimmie is caned for his truancy. The politeness of the welcome belies the inflexibility of the punishment, and this incident prefigures the rest of the drama. Jimmie is encouraged to integrate himself in white society, as symbolised by the home of the Nevilles. He is then sent forth into the world, where he is repeatedly refused hospitality and respect. The obvious constraint of the society Jimmie attempts to join is shown by the scene of the farewell meal in the Neville home. With Jimmie, the Reverend Neville and his wife seated around the dining table, the camera slows draws out to show the characters bounded on every side by the frame of a doorway. This illustrates both the insuperable obstacles confronting Jimmie's plan, and the limited comprehension of the Nevilles, whose liberal patronage is as grounded in the politics of prejudice as the unthinking bigotry their protégé encounters elsewhere. This graphic illustration of constraint occurs elsewhere in the film's *mise-en-scène*: in the shadows of prison bars marking Jimmie's body even when he is being released from jail, and in the restriction of the frame around him in the registry office when he marries Gilda, his working-class white bride.

In comparison with the constriction of the composition around its central protagonist, the use of exterior landscapes does not suggest an unequivocal freedom. After leaving the Nevilles, Jimmie is seen as a minuscule, insignificant figure against a featureless wall of rock when he applies for work at an opencast mine, and is immediately rejected. The same diminution of the protagonist against the landscape is seen when Jimmie brings Gilda across country to their home on Mr Newby's land. Jimmie's blank acceptance of the initiation rites seen at the film's opening contrasts with his impatience with the same rituals enacted by his brother Mort later during their flight from justice. The wide expanses of territory are not ennobling or liberating because, in direct contravention of Aboriginal custom, Jimmie seeks to own land individually like a white settler. In the natural landscape he is literally homeless, cut off by choice from the traditional Aboriginal cultural and spiritual relationship with the land, and constantly shut out of white society by working or trespassing on land belonging to others. Poignantly, the only work Jimmie can get is fencing off the land of Scottish and Irish immigrant farmers. This employment symbolises the imprisonment of the hero and the land itself under white rule. Jimmie's revenge against white injustices is also couched in these terms. With his uncle Tabidgi he comes to the threshold of the Newby house like a supplicant before bursting into the kitchen to kill the family. The violence is shown graphically in spilled blood but also metaphorically by scattered and broken crockery, the violent disruption of the propriety of period decoration. When on the run, Jimmie and Mort laugh as they use the farm fences as a means of travel, so that they leave no tracks on the ground. Jimmie has lost the traditional Aboriginal connection with the land, and the white proprietorial relationship with territory is also denied him. His only effective kinship with the landscape comes with his skillful campaign of living off and hiding in the land in the wake of the Newby murders.

The compositional contrasts within the film between interior and exterior settings are heightened by the use of disconcerting close-ups. These clash with the shrinking of the hero against the backdrop of the land, but produce a distorting and claustrophobic effect. Instead of magnifying and ennobling Jimmie, they reaffirm his entrapment. If the landscape is not given a simplistic, pictorial treatment, the native fauna is also included as an unnerving choric presence. Discomforting close-ups of reptiles and insects testify to the land's menace and alien-ness, and to its function as a stage for violent, predatory activity by animals and men. Shots of Tabidgi reflecting in court that it takes only 'a second' to decide to kill are succeeded by close-ups of insects. A close-up of a nest of fledgelings, which emphasises their noise and vulnerability, immediately precedes the scenes of Mort and Jimmie, armed with rifles, observing children leaving the Tambourine Public School. At the same time, Jimmie's white oppressors are equally associated with slaughter. The Scottish farmer Lewis has a dead rabbit dangling from his saddle. Jimmie's first employer Healy beheads chickens and butchers pigs, and seals his crooked contract with Jimmie with a bloodied handshake.

In comparison with such overt brutality, other aspects of white intolerance are revealed as examples of sophisticated hypocrisy. The upholders of law and order, seen discussing the Blacksmith brothers' crimes and likelihood of their capture in a darkened, luxurious drawing room, reflect that their execution must be timed carefully in order not to upset the debate on the federation of the states and the apportionment of the monarch's honours. When Jimmie's son is born and found to be white, Miss Graf's words to Jimmie are redolent of insulting equivocation: 'This is the boy child your wife has given birth to.' Ironically Jimmie, shut out of the Newby house where the child is delivered, is seen to engage in a traditional dance instinctively when he hears the baby cry for the first time. His fleeting reconnection with his original culture, perhaps inspired by the thought of initiating his own son in future years, is undercut by his seclusion from the (again symbolic) house and his subsequent bitter realisation that his 'son' will never want to recognise him. Having been betrayed and humiliated by the white women he was encouraged to court and aspire to wed, Jimmie exacts his savage revenge upon them. As in *Picnic*,

The Piano and *The Getting of Wisdom*, women are portrayed as both the victims and defenders of the established order, reinforcing the structures of control even as they are restrained and defined by them. Where *The Piano* draws a pertinent comparison between the subjugation of women, the colonisation of land and the suppression of indigenous peoples, and *Picnic* identifies differences between youth and age, culture and nature and Britishness and Australian-ness, *The Chant of Jimmie Blacksmith* accentuates an unexpected, unpleasant and contradictory congruence between male attitudes towards the women who symbolise refinement and gentility. Jimmie's greatest rancour is directed at Miss Graf, the supercilious and pretentious school teacher whose comments about his marriage and child represent a decisive provocation. Her bereaved fiancé tracks her killer remorselessly, but is upbraided by his companion who asserts that he would never have married her. Her refinement has represented an aspiration for her farmer fiancé as much as for Jimmie, but her pretentiousness is incompatible with the lack of refinement of Aboriginal and non-Aboriginal men. Jimmie himself is the product of a counter current to the aspiration towards white gentility: the unacknowledged truth of white men visiting black camps for sex. Within the film's organisation of meaning, the women's refinement and white men's racism both produce Jimmie and provoke his bloody reaction to their shared prejudice. While he is viewed as unequivocally black by his white tormentors, to his Aboriginal relatives he is a 'mongrel man' who is altered by association with the Nevilles and distance from his tribe. In seeking equality with the white men and then in revenge killing white women and children, Jimmie becomes in Mort's words a 'devil man', incarnating the worst of both worlds and shunned by both communities.

Having been enunciated in symbolic terms, the narrative of Jimmie's resistance is also concluded with a concise visual expression. Wounded in the jaw and thereafter unable to speak in his own defence, Jimmie is tracked down by the authorities. He is caught when he takes refuge in a nunnery, ending where he began in a constrained, devotional space. His childhood punishment at the hands of Reverend Neville is magnified to become his execution at the hands of the state. In the condemned cell Jimmie is seen shrunken and encircled through the observation port in the door in a final and definitive depiction of confinement. The reverse shot, of the watching hangman's grossly enlarged eye looking inwards, confronts the viewer with a lasting image of the film's unflinching gaze upon its subject.

Newsfront: the nation on record

The assault on institutional racism embodied in *The Chant of Jimmie Blacksmith* also incorporates a pessimistic tone, derived from the inevitability of the outrages committed by both sides. Jimmie is certainly portrayed as a victim, but his comprehension of his own circumstances and responsibility for his own actions eschew the mantel of heroism. His defeat appears inevitable not simply because his goals are unattainable, but because he is like other Australian characters shown to be out of place within the human and natural landscape. Circumstances and environment often appear to be antipathetic to the presence and efforts of the Australian (male and female) within the period film cycle. Such a recognisable and ubiquitous tone to the films of the period cycle undermines their status as positive, authorised portrayals of national culture and character unless, as the representation of Australian subjugation under colonial authority in films depicting educational, military and religious control suggests, defeatism and the surrendering of self-determination is itself a communal characteristic. This pessimistic estimation of human potential flows over from films set in the past to narratives portraying the endeavours of male individuals and groups (the 'male ensemble' films), many of which also adopt the characteristics of the AFC genre. Poised between the qualified heroics of the male ensemble pictures and the depictions of social constraint contained within the period cycle, *Newsfront* (Phillip Noyce, 1978) anticipates the later films detailing collective male defeat in its narrative of vain, individual resistance.

Noyce's film, like his later Gothic thriller *Heatwave* (1981), positions its hero within a specific 'historical' background (the immoral enterprise culture of the 1980s in *Heatwave*, the social and political changes in post-war Australia in *Newsfront*). As in the case of the literary adaptations and artistic period recreations of its contemporaries, *Newsfront*'s reconstruction of recent history is posited as a object of national pride. This conservative approach again suggests the reduction of the record to a single, deproblematised entity:

Newsfront starts in 1948 with the beginning of intensive post-war European immigration under Chifley's Labor Government, through the 1949 defeat of Labor as an early casualty in the Cold War; the establishment of the Menzies Government that would last a generation; the clear start of consumerism, the suburbanisation and Americanisation of Australian life, to 1956, TV, and the Melbourne Olympic Games.[43]

The collective and factual story of the country is related to and by the career of a newsreel maker, intertwining national and filmic history in the feature narrative. The character of Len Maguire, played by Bill Hunter, is supposedly based on the real-life filmmaker Ken G. Hall.[44] Len incarnates a resilient orthodox Australian male, who resists the temptation to sell out to American money and mores (unlike his brother), supports the enduringly conservative political regime and takes pride in the cottage industry in which he works:

Hunter's role is a beautifully understated advertisement ... that Australia is habitable as a culture, inoculated against the American disease by a maverick larrikinism that cannot be bought or sold. Of course, this view is intensely nostalgic, reinforced by the iconic power of the newsreel footage to summon a quainter, simpler and purer past. Len Maguire is of the generation which parented the post-war 'baby boom' and is invested with the power of 'the time from which our time has come'.[45]

The characterisation of Len's stoicism reflects an old-fashioned amalgamation of British propriety and Australian individuality, equating public and private honour and cherishing self-respect. His determination to complete his work and stick to his principles appears to be a vain (in every sense) undertaking in the face of more pragmatic opposition. Such quiet glory in the certainty of honourable defeat becomes an Australian preserve in the representation of Australians at war in the male ensemble films.

Set beside the film's conservative perspective, founded on the assumption of an unambiguous shared past traversed by an iconic character, *Newsfront* employs a formally challenging technique in the integration of black-and-white and colour, documentary and fictive footage. Yet this apparently unconventional feature serves to reinforce the film's affirmation of orthodoxy. The use of actual historical footage alongside the film's period reconstructions validates both the events and those (re)experiencing them on and off screen:

The collapsing of the main character's history into that of the nation is accomplished by the simple method of moving slowly from one film stock to the other; that is, when the film is moving out of the monochrome newsreel footage and into the coloured narrative, the black and white is only gradually replaced by colour – as if the two histories were dissolving into each other.[46]

Film history and the construction of an officially sanctioned version of national character are more closely connected in Noyce's film than in the putative AFC genre texts forwarded as Australian aesthetic and cultural ambassadors. More pointedly than in those period dramas set at the turn of the century, *Newsfront* constructs an authorised, orthodox picture of national history and national character, and proposes causal links between them (colonial experience, individuality and victimhood).

Sirens: the parody of the period film

Sirens (John Duigan, 1994) achieves a belated revival of many of the key features of the period film cycle, while developing the themes of its writer-director. Frequently, Duigan has been associated with film narratives detailing formative experiences and rites of passage (acting as writer-director for *The Year My Voice Broke* (1987), *Flirting* (1991) and the adaptation to the screen of Jean Rhys' novel *Wide Sargasso Sea* (1992)). *Sirens* moves away from the examination of adolescent experience to focus on unenvisaged (sexual) development in the relationship between a young English couple, Anthony and Estella Campion, visiting Australia after the First World War. Certain aspects of casting, narrative and *mise-en-scène* are indicative of the film's varied debts, emphases and influences. The English couple's transformation through contact with liberal Australians and the liberating landscape recalls the treatment of class, nationality and sexual repression found in *Picnic at Hanging Rock*.

The disingenuous documentary atmosphere of Weir's film is also implied by the film's fictionalisation of the Campions' stay with the historical figure of Norman Lindsay. The behaviour of the Lindsay household (comprising the painter's wife, daughters and female models) is the antithesis of the Campions' marital existence. The stereotypical reticence and modesty of the English vicar and his wife are opposed by an equally caricatured commune espousing free expression and free love. The inclusion of Lindsay and his shocking work also provides a pictorial motif which influences aspects of composition, in a fashion comparable to *Picnic's* quotation of Australian Impressionism. That such a narrative of symbolic national and sexual values cannot be delivered with a straight face twenty years after *Picnic at Hanging Rock* is reflected in the casting. Hugh Grant's portrayal of Anthony Campion's repressed but curious Englishman builds on the persona established by his role in *Bitter Moon* (Roman Polanski, 1992) and underscored by his performance in *Four Weddings and a Funeral* (Mike Newell, 1995). The comic potential of Anthony's awkwardness is strengthened by Sam Neill's provocative performance as Norman Lindsay. The casting of Australian supermodel Elle MacPherson, and the film's many nude scenes emphasise its appeal as a self-conscious comedy, which parodies national stereo-types and the period film model simultaneously.

Prior to the exposition of plot (the Bishop of Sydney dispatch-ing the Campions to the Lindsay estate to persuade the artist to withdraw a blasphemous painting from an upcoming exhibition) a short dumb show in black and white outlines the focus of the narrative. Estella is seen in evening dress on the deck of a four-funnelled liner. A roughly dressed sailor tries to catch her eye and she turns away haughtily, but then looks after him tentatively, over her shoulder. The lyrics of the song which accompanies this sequence ('The finest ship that sailed the sea / Is still a prison to the likes of me') reveal the ironic relevance of these scenes to the following narrative. The passenger ship which carries the Campi-ons to Australia is likened to a craft carrying convicts to the colony in previous centuries. The English couple, and especially Estella will become 'Australian' rather than British when they shed their inhibitions. Paradoxically the ship carries them from restraint to liberation. The monochrome styling of the sequence reinforces its retrospective or even dreamlike atmosphere, linking it with Estella's subsequent reveries. A tiny model of the liner is seen beset by miniature storms in the fountain at the Lindsay home, suggestive of the travellers' peril in venturing from the old world to the new.

The danger of sexual temptation to travellers resurfaces in Lindsay's current work, the depiction of the Sirens seducing Ulysses. The artist's invitation to his guests to pose with his models (and his eventual inclusion of Estella in the painting with-out permission) indicates their increasing susceptibility to the lure of the household and the land. The characterisation of the Australian landscape as an Edenic, liberating environment is also implied in the presence of coiling snakes outside the room in which the Campions stay. Lindsay's obsession with the lost continent of Atlantis, home to a enlightened and libertarian civil-isation, also mythologises the Australian island continent as an emancipated and uninhibited paradise. The licence Lindsay indulges in his paintings provokes criticism because of their association with a distinctive nationality. Newspapers worry that on seeing his pictures, English viewers will imagine that Aus-tralia's people are afflicted with 'sex mania'. Lindsay argues that if this is this case, it will validate the original deportation of con-victs to the colony.

The conception of Englishness as a shorthand for repression is outlined in the Campions' meeting with the Bishop of Sydney. In time with the soundtrack music, the vicar's and the bishop's feet march along corridors of parquet floor past the pictures in the exhibition. The paintings themselves are seen aligned squarely in the centre of the filmic frame, with conventionalised content to match their unchallenging presentation. The images of romanticised shearers, cattlemen and Australian landscapes are uncontroversial, but a dog bark heard on the soundtrack when Campion walks past a painting of picturesque South Sea islanders in a canoe causes him to return for a second look. The startling life which the picture exhibits anticipates how Estella's growth will be traced and incorporated into Lindsay's and the film's pictorial compositions. Similarly, the works by Lindsay which cause the Bishop most worry bear a marked significance to later events. The Bishop labels as 'merely vulgar' a painting of voluptuous, naked, female spirits confounding well-dressed young couples. The couples confronted by the female spirits appear shocked despite their obvious amorous attachment, and the mythic figures therefore seem to represent a temptation or incitement to erotic pleasure. (This painting connects with another of a naked sylvan goddess and a picture showing satyrs approaching a sleeping couple which hang in the Campions' room.) The final picture, seen in close-up and condemned by the Bishop as 'blasphemous', shows a naked Venus crucified before a crowd of lawyers and churchmen. The figure's attitude and aura of martyrdom is echoed on two later occasions by Estella in her attraction to Devlin, Lindsay's male model.

The serious discussion on the impact of the paintings in which Norman and Anthony engage is relevant to the influence the painter's home environment has upon his guests. Rather than corrupting his potential audience, the artist simply records the untroubled sexuality of his models. Similarly he notes the transformation or acquisition of self-knowledge which Estella undergoes and assimilates her (as does the film's final image) as a fifth Siren in his latest work. Viewing and admitting the temptation to view nakedness runs through the film in another evocation of the Eden myth. Estella's spying on Sheela and Pru with local men and watching Devlin bathing are matched by Anthony's secret observation of the models as they pose, and by the artist's scrutiny of them both. The blurring of distinctions between watching and dreaming, wishing and experiencing hinted at by the opening scenes becomes increasingly relevant to Estella's growth. In church with Anthony at evensong at the end of a day disturbed by the realisation of her attraction to Devlin, Estella imagines herself naked and humiliated in public. That night, she rises from her bed after passionless sex with Anthony and walks to the studio to meet Devlin, standing in the pose of the crucified Venus as they make love. Like her night visit to the stables to watch Pru and Sheela with their men, this journey is preceded by a flower petal falling on her cheek in slow motion as she lies in bed, with the repetition of the image again suggesting the merging of conscious and oneiric experience. Her last twilight journey, to the pond where Pru, Giddy and Sheela rise from the water like mermaids to caress her while she floats in the crucified pose, is ended by Estella intoning 'I want to wake up now'. Like a sojourn in a Shakespearian arcadia, Estella's dreams reveal the potential for alternative relationships and fulfilment, which can be realised on return to a transformed everyday existence.

The other controversial subjects of conversation (industrialisation and trade unionism, the Russian revolution and female emancipation) provide a simplified contemporary socio-historical framework for the evolution of Estella's and Anthony's marriage. Lindsay's scandalous, wry humour and the archness of the sexually predatory models do not represent a genuine threat to the inhibited couple. The physical peril of the natural landscape is made ridiculous by the repeated newspaper headlines and anecdotes reporting snakes 'running amok' in kindergartens and war-veterans eaten by sharks. The film's symbolism, its humour grounded in lewd farce and stereotypical characterisation and its sedate treatment of Estella's evolving sexual nature betray a range of apparently contradictory elements: 'These could help to work this either into a lavish fantasy, or into a camply outrageous romp. But the film does not quite have the courage to go for one or the other'.[47]

The comedic elements in the narrative and characterisation do not jar against the earnest treatment of Estella's maturation and empowerment. Instead, the caricaturing of Anthony's inhibition disarms the patriarchal control which Estella, through her experiences and acting on her desires, succeeds in evading or negating. The repressive establishment seen in previous period films melts away in *Sirens*, as the Bishop backs down over Lindsay's paintings and Anthony is scandalised but humanised when Estella initiates sex in their train carriage at the film's conclusion. The Bishop's unlikely categorisation of Anthony as a 'progressive' is finally vindicated. Estella's self-confidence is reaffirmed by the awareness that the other 'sleeping' occupants of their compartment are really observing them. Estella gradually gaining the courage to look is followed by her enjoyment of being watched, as her acceptance of her inclusion in the picture of the Sirens has already confirmed. Remembrance of her past self, and the

distance travelled to self-fulfilment, is included in the train compartment in a black and white photograph of a four-funnelled
liner, the *Titanic*, shown in close-up. In recalling the opening
sequence, this detail demonstrates how Estella has jumped ship to
escape the fate of an outdated and repressed Edwardian society.
The martyrdom of women within a patriarchal society (the sub-
text of several period literary adaptations and emphasised by
Lindsay's Venus) is reversed by the freedom gained by Estella. The
nightmare prison-ship of the opening is thus consigned to history,
before the final image of the Australian Sirens (including Estella)
dancing on the peaks of the Blue Mountains. Despite the injection
of humour and parody, Duigan's film advances a positive national
image without the denigration of Britishness, and also manages
to complete a narrative of personal maturation under the
influence of the landscape which follows the the patterns of
previous period films.

Conclusion

The period film offered a peculiarly equivocal nationalism; while it did
produce and reproduce Australian myths and images it tended to
locate these in the colonial past. The Australia most of these films
mythologised was defined by its landscape and by its colonial history
rather than the complex contemporary realities of an urban, middle-
class, post-colonial 'multicultural' society.[48]

The period film cycle has endured criticism because of its perceived conservatism, in supposed political ratification, the partiality of funding and the pedalling of a anodyne, selective,
authorised version of Australian culture. In support of nascent
nationalism, the portrayal of a historical, artistic, literary and
geographical heritage in the cinema was considered to represent
an unholy alliance between political centrism and formulaic filmmaking. The limitation of the period film to the depiction of the
British basis to white settler culture denied the diversity of Australian society in its past and contemporary incarnations. This
initiative served political and cultural agendas at home and
abroad, asserting and broadcasting contemporary Australian cultural and filmic maturity through deference to the unassailable
past. The timing of this cycle of costume dramas and literary
adaptations in Australia is compared by McFarlane and Mayer
with the production of British 'quality' films based on classic
novels and plays during a similar boom period of national film
production in the 1940s and 1950s.[49] The two phases of production also share a popular connection with their local audiences,

their recognition and favourable reception overseas, and their concomitant elevation to the status of representative cultural artefacts. The British and Australian films are seen to begin to formulate a national subject matter and to draft an appropriate filmic style and idiom in which to express it.

As in the case of the male ensemble films, the treatment of the past is not synonymous with conformist, conservative or conventionalised filmmaking. The dichotomies of popularity versus aestheticism, and contemporary nationalism against historical criticism informing the decade of Australian period film productions are summarised in the emulative but parodic treatment of the past, nationality and sexuality in *Sirens*. The style and subject matter of Duigan's film are predicated on those of *Picnic at Hanging Rock*. As the Australian Gothic creates an indigenous film style from numerous generic sources, so the period film produces a Australian genre out of disparate elements, drawn from British-based culture, British-inspired drama and modernist European cinema.

Whereas the Australian Gothic films seemed to side-step the art vs. commerce divide (foregrounding problematic analysis of nationality within a hybridised popular generic format), the period films initially appear to confirm the polarisation in their claim upon the aesthetic and respectable high ground within the revival. Their popularity with audiences complicates rather than contradicts this categorisation, but examination of the texts themselves brings their reputation for unchallenging good taste into question. *Picnic at Hanging Rock* may have received praise at the Cannes Film Festival in 1976, but it was *The Chant of Jimmie Blacksmith*, which exploited 'the power of the period film in addressing continuing social and political problems',[50] which was screened in competition two years later. The uncompromising stance of Schepisi's film underlines the relative dissent (against alien authority and the colonial heritage, as in the Gothic) and contemporary emphasis (in gender and race politics) to be found in examples of the period film, belying their conservative reputation. Where the female protagonists in *Picnic*, *The Getting of Wisdom* and *My Brilliant Career* rebel to greater and lesser extents against establishment control, the conservatism of the central male character in *Newsfront* parallels the elegiac elevation of nationality and masculinity in the male ensemble films. The separation between the incorporation of positive, empowered, white male perspectives on the past and the negative, disempowered experiences of women, childen and Aborigines reflects the distinction between superficial harmlessness of the period films and the apologetic national agenda of the male ensemble films.

Notes

1 Graeme Turner, Art Directing History: The Period Film, in Albert Moran and Tom O'Regan (eds), *The Australian Screen* (Harmondsworth, Penguin, 1989), pp. 113–14.

2 Ibid., p. 103.

3 See Susan Dermody and Elizabeth Jacka, *The Screening of Australia Vol. I: Anatomy of a Film Industry* (Sydney, Currency, 1987), p. 132, and *The Screening of Australia Vol. II: Anatomy of a National Cinema* (Sydney, Currency, 1988a), p. 31.

4 Graham Shirley and Brian Adams, *Australian Cinema: The First Eighty Years* (revised edn), (Sydney, Currency, 1989), p. 271.

5 See Pauline Kael in interview in 1982 in Peter Hamilton and Sue Mathews, *American Dreams, Australian Movies* (Sydney, Currency, 1986), p. 34.

6 Dermody and Jacka (1988a), p. 34.

7 Ibid., pp. 32–3

8 Elizabeth Jacka, Critical Positions, in Susan Dermody and Elizabeth Jacka, *The Imaginary Industry: Australian Film in the Late '80s* (North Ryde, AFTRS Publications, 1988b), p. 69.

9 Scott Murray, Australian Cinema in the 1970s and 1980s, in Scott Murray (ed.), *Australian Cinema* (St Leonards, Allen & Unwin, 1994), p. 92.

10 Andrew Pike and Ross Cooper, *Australian Film 1900–1977: A Guide to Feature Film Production* (Melbourne, Oxford University Press, 1980), p. 354.

11 Shirley and Adams (1989), pp. 264–5.

12 Ibid., pp. 265–6.

13 David Stratton, *The Last New Wave: The Australian Film Revival* (London, Angus and Robertson, 1980), pp. 68–9.

14 Scott Murray and Antony I. Ginnane, Producing *Picnic*: Pat Lovell, *Cinema Papers* 8 (1976), pp. 298–301, 377.

15 Stratton (1980), p. 71.

16 Pierre Greenfield, *Picnic at Hanging Rock*, *Movietone News* nos. 62–3 (1979), pp. 8–10.

17 Richard Combs, *Picnic at Hanging Rock*, *Monthly Film Bulletin* vol. 43 no. 512 (1976), pp. 196–7.

18 Remarks made in interview with the author in 1993.

19 Brian McFarlane, *Words and Images: Australian Novels into Film* (Richmond, Heinemann, 1983), p. 19.

20 Ibid., p. 20.

21 Ibid., p. 39.

22 Sue Mathews, *35mm Dreams: Conversations with Five Directors About the Australian Film Revival* (Melbourne, Penguin, 1984), p. 95.

23 Graeme Turner, *National Fictions: Literature, Film and the Construction of Australian Narrative* (London, Allen & Unwin, 1986), p. 27.

24 Bernard Smith, *Australian Painting 1788–1970* (Melbourne, Oxford University Press, 1971), p. 81.

25 Brian McFarlane, *Australian Cinema 1970–1985* (London, Secker & Warburg, 1987), p. 72.

26 Joan Lindsay, *Picnic at Hanging Rock* (London, Penguin, 1970), p. 60.

27 Ross Gibson, Camera Natura: Landscape in Australian Feature Films, *Framework* nos. 22–3 (1983), pp. 47–51 (p. 50).

28 Dermody and Jacka (1988a), p. 34.

29 Mathews (1984), p. 69.

30 Dermody and Jacka (1988a), pp. 111–12.

31 Brian McFarlane and Geoff Mayer, *New Australian Cinema: Sources and Parallels in American and British Film* (Cambridge, Cambridge University Press, 1992), pp. 187–8.

32 McFarlane (1983), pp. 63–8.

33 Ibid., p. 58.

34 Robin Wood, Quo Vadis Bruce Beresford?, in Albert Moran and Tom O'Regan (eds), *An Australian Film Reader* (Sydney, Currency, 1985), p. 202.

35 McFarlane (1983), p. 68.

36 Turner (1986), p. 74.

37 Jocelyn Robinson and Beverley Zalcock, *Girls' Own Stories: Australian and New Zealand Women's Films* (London, Scarlet Press, 1997), p. 10.

38 Ibid., p. 11.

39 Ibid., p. 12.

40 Dermody and Jacka (1988a), p. 110.

41 By contrast, the portrayal of interracial conflict during the nineteenth century Maori land wars in *Utu* (Geoff Murphy, 1983) provides a shocking and destabilising experience because of its juxtaposition of tragedy and black humour, and its transplantation of the generic Hollywood Western to New Zealand.

42 McFarlane (1983), p. 103.

43 Dermody and Jacka (1988a), pp. 129–31.

44 Diane Jacobs, Australian Originals, *American Film* vol. 4 no. 7 (1979), pp. 52–6 (p. 53).

45 Dermody and Jacka (1988a), p. 131.

46 Turner (1989), p. 107.

47 Amanda Lipman, *Sirens*, Sight and Sound vol. 4 no. 8 (1994), pp. 53–4 (p. 54).

48 Turner (1989), p. 115.

49 McFarlane and Mayer (1992), pp. 114–16.

50 Turner (1989), p. 112.

4   The male ensemble film

Australian-ness and masculinity

The male ensemble film, in its first phase up to *Breaker Morant* (1980), is also strongly influenced by the posture of the ocker; blunt, loud, hedonistic and conservative in the populist manner. Its working class or lower middle-class male figure is not an appeal for class solidarity, but a gesture towards the classless common man as last bastion of 'real' Australian virtues and vices ... the assertive use of vernacular is empowered by the feeling it is breaking with old taboos and the old, staid past; with a sense of freeing the irreverent larrikin

spirit. The irony, by no means wholly unconscious, is that influential writers like David Williamson pitted this spirit against the conformities of male group behaviour, in which even male 'freedoms' were prescribed and ritualised.[1]

The male ensemble films represent another delimited generic category of the revival identified by Susan Dermody and Elizabeth Jacka. They trace the type's evolution across more than a decade, from its inception in features at the beginning of the revival to its migration to television and further development in the mini-series in the early to mid-eighties. The examination of the particular manifestations and characteristics of Australian masculinity is undertaken against contemporary and historical backgrounds. Male institutions, professions and obsessions (farming and shearing, the military, and sport) provide the basis for illustrating aspects of national character. The origin and expected audience for these representations of masculinity and nationality is significant, and comparable to those of the near-contemporary Ocker comedies. As in the cases of *The Overlanders*, *They're A Weird Mob* and *Crocodile Dundee*, the portraits of male Australian-ness correspond to local and international expectation, and reinforce myths, inaccuracies and prejudices in relation to the ethnic composition, cultural immaturity and sexual inequality they locate within the nation. The depictions of Australia, whether historical or contemporary, rural or urban, conservative or radical are dominated by the majority masculine presence. By reiteration of the stereotype and exclusion of an alternative, the national character becomes circumscribed in social, sexual, moral and political terms:

the essential Australian is male, working-class, sardonic, laconic, loyal to his mates, unimpressed by rank, an improvisor, non-conformist, and so on. These virtues are defined and refined under the hard conditions of the bush, workplace, war or sport, in which women, and the feminine qualities, are considered to be beside the point.[2]

Films foregrounding the amusing and harmless, scandalising and offensive or momentous and tragic activities of male Australian groups clearly have a nationalist potential when read in line with or against their intention. Ensemble acting (portraying a national individuality within a context of integration and conformity) leads to communal recognition (submerging personal interpretation in collective comprehension) and consensual acceptance (consenting to the group identity) of the images of nationality conveyed. However, within this apparent homogeneity of representation and interpretation, certain significant divergences are discernible. As with the period films, the perception of orthodoxy and conservatism is belied by the texts' formal challenges or ironic tone. Distinctions emerge between the treatments of past and contemporary events and societies, and between the beliefs associated with different generations of which the male groups are composed. Not only are the lines between period films and male ensemble pieces frequently blurred, but also the perspectives and emphases inevitably vary between examples of each category. As such the classifications adopted for Australian genres (the Gothic, the period film and the male ensemble) provide little more than indications of the atmosphere of one, or thematic or design elements present in another.

Whether read positively or negatively, the Australian male characteristics most often represented within the Ocker and male ensemble films remain consistent. The pastimes of drinking, gambling and womanising encapsulate the social activities which bond men to each other as 'mates'. Male-to-male relationships, though strained by rivalries and competition, are pre-eminent, and male-to-female relationships never assume equal importance. Paradoxically, while sexual curiosity and competitiveness are given principles and subjects for debate between males, relationships with women are hamstrung by deference and allegiance to other men. Other paradoxes traverse the consistencies of male bonding: the championing of individuality and opportunism connected with the pioneer spirit conflicts with the humility and interdependence of teamwork; the competitiveness associated with personal ambition contradicts the obedience required in undertakings of national importance; and the desire for marriage is undermined by the precondition of mateship, which subordinates the familial existence to the social or professional:

The sentimental ideal of mateship may well be Australia's chief contribution to the history of human relationship. Like most images which together constitute a national identity, the image of men as mates derives from that blurred territory between myth and reality. The concern here is less with the origins of mateship – whether or not it is rooted in the early days of the country when men considerably outnumbered women, or in the pre-eminence of male-dominated activities like agriculture and mining, and in the sheer loneliness of the settings in which these took place – than with how it has made itself felt in the new Australian cinema.[3]

The working environment

The proximity in the timing of production between the first male ensemble films and the Ocker comedies prompts a comparison between the treatment of the stereotypical male Australian across

Contemporary Australian cinema

both types. The convergence is strongest in *Don's Party* (Bruce Beresford, 1976). Beresford, as the director and co-writer of *The Adventures of Barry McKenzie* (1972), and David Williamson, the playwright responsible for the play on which *Don's Party* was based, are key figures in the development of the male ensemble film. They collaborated again on *The Club* (1980), adapted from Williamson's play set inside a struggling football team. Beresford went on to direct *Breaker Morant* (1980), while Williamson worked with Peter Weir on the screenplays of *Gallipoli* (1981) and *The Year of Living Dangerously* (1982). However, a more low-key production predating these films gained critical acclaim for its portrayal of masculinity under pressure in the rural environment.

The first revival film to foreground the male milieu and masculine ethics was *Sunday Too Far Away* (Ken Hannam, 1974). While identifying some characteristics of the male ensemble in the forerunning Ocker films, Dermody and Jacka see Hannam's film as the earliest and purest embodiment of the characterisation and thematic interests associated with the male-centred drama.[4] *Sunday Too Far Away* follows the progress of Foley, a proud gun shearer who is past his prime but unable to accept the decline of his skills. The shearer's itinerant lifestyle, short-term perspective and the melancholia they provoke are examined within the setting of competitive seasonal employment. Foley (played by Jack Thompson) and his colleagues travel between the sheds of stock farmers, enduring hard work for a minimal wage which is quickly squandered in beer and betting. The film's fictional events occur against the background of an industrial dispute over pay and conditions which took place in 1956. The film's precise historical context and its documentary-drama aesthetic have prompted some commentators to construe it as an early manifestation of the period film tendency.[5] *Sunday Too Far Away* received a positive reception at Cannes during the Director's Fortnight in 1975, a year before *Picnic at Hanging Rock* attracted attention at the Festival and set in motion the cycle of period film production.

The film's cultural legitimacy, suggested by the period setting and its critical recognition, resides more pertinently in its depiction of the isolated male group. The examination of individual characters occurs only in relation to their abiding social existence. The males are bonded by communal experience and mutual respect, just as they are divided by instinctive competitiveness. Foley returns to shearing after he fails to integrate himself into city life in Brisbane. Having boasted in the past of his escape from the drudgery of shearing, subsequently Foley has lost the money he had saved from his work and has lost face among his peers. His goal is to save money for the future, working without 'busting a gut' and re-establishing himself as top shearer. When an outsider questions his record of 'ringing' the local sheds, Foley's reputation is defended at once by his old acquaintances, despite their ambivalence towards his pipe dreams and his ignominious return.

The portents for Foley's future are, however, dispiriting. During the opening sequence as he drives back into the country, he unaccountably crashes his car. Stoically he climbs out of the wreck and continues on foot. For the rest of the exposition he is seen consistently constrained within the frame, being seen through the window of the overturned car, through the doorway of a ruined cottage as he walks across country, and being framed by ranks of beer glasses on shelves when he arrives at the town pub. Restriction of the frame around him, and the dissolution symbolised by the wreck, the ruins and the glasses, encapsulate the circumscription of Foley's environment and prospects.

As well as these images of limitation and defeat, Foley is surrounded by contemporaries with whom he is compared. The other characters within the group offer an unspoken emotional support, if only in recalling Foley's former pre-eminence, but also embody the 'seven ages' of the shearer's life. In incarnating his limited alternatives, they concretise Foley's entrapment. Old Garth, the best shearer in Foley's youth, is now a solitary, terminal alcoholic. Seeing him fighting over a bottle with another drunk, Foley remarks that 'someone should shoot the old bastard' to end his indignity. At the opposite end of the profession, young Michael Simpson lies his way into his first job as a 'learner', just as Foley had done years earlier. Between these extremes are Foley's peers, Basher Grant and Tommy West, who welcome Foley back to the fold but privately brand him 'a weak bastard' for returning to shearing. Another of Foley's friends, Tim King (played by Max Cullen), has crossed the line between worker and manager during his absence, and has become a shearing contractor to the estate owners. His employment of Foley, Michael and the others increases the stresses within the group, since they help him to fulfil his contract as mates but resent his assumption of authority over them. However, Foley's pre-eminence remains uncontested until the arrival of Arthur Black (a solitary and disliked man nicknamed 'Black Arthur'), who threatens to supplant him as the best shearer. The limitation and conciseness of the film's narrative, in its time-frame (defined by the six-week contract), its characters, their specific social milieu and the factual background of the dispute, do not preclude a mythic treatment of masculinity and national character:

Black Arthur is a black knight figure, the one who cannot be beaten. His arrival effects a painful self-evaluation for the protagonist, and signifies, in a sense, Foley's inevitable death. His character, and the tripartite configuration Garth-Foley-Simpson, are signs of the narrative archetype and symbolic register present in the work.[6]

The circumscription of the characters' activities and opportunities connects with the narrowness of their experience and ambition. Hectic weekday work is followed by drinking and sleep, and weekend rest-days appear intolerably empty. Garth laments sacrificing time with his wife to his work and travel between sheds, but the shearer who writes frequently to his wife is attacked verbally by Foley. Communally the shearers suffer humiliation, in the reduction of their pay by the farmers, and individually Foley and Garth endure defeat (in the former's competition with Black Arthur) and death (after the latter's itinerant and under-payed working life), yet escaping from the inevitabilities of their life style or changing their behaviour within it appear unthinkable or unattainable. The hardships are accepted stoically, since the articulation of grief or self-pity equates with the admission of weakness, and is seen to precede or even precipitate one's downfall. Garth's death follows soon after his confession to Foley. Foley's breakdown before Sylvia Dawson the shed owner's daughter is succeeded by his humiliation at the hands of Black Arthur. Foley's acquiescence to his fate is confirmed by losing his earnings in gambling once the work is completed and by leading the vain and violent resistance to scab labour during the subsequent strike. The film's admiration for the shearer's resignation to their lot and preservation of principles is tempered by acknowledgement of their stubborn self-destructiveness. The film's portrait of national character, both in its documentary aesthetic and the circumstances of its central character helped to make Jack Thompson into 'the first icon of essential Australianness'.[7] The nobility of an inevitable defeat, or the tragedy of an avoidable one, are wedded to the representation of Australian masculinity in Hannam's film and subsequent ensemble features.

Sexual politics

The absence of female characters in *Sunday Too Far Away* highlights the exclusivity of the male group and professional affiliations. Sylvia Dawson is only allowed to view the mens' work by special dispensation, but is soon sickened by the speed and violence of the shearing. The sanctity of the working environment is maintained, through the employment of male cooks and the prohibition of writing to wives. *Don's Party* examines the tensions inherent in heterosexual relationships within this sexually-partitioned society. The elevation of male-to-male connections incorporates a degradation of marriage and family ties. Play and film assert the predominance of gender-based affiliations over sexual, political or class-based ones.

The party at the home of Don and Kath is arranged to follow the developments in the 1969 Federal Government elections, and the assorted couples that attend cover a range of social classes, generations and professions. Don's intention of celebrating the end of 'twenty years of Conservative rule' is dismissed as 'an excuse for a booze up' by his wife. Furthermore, Don's supposed radicalism is undermined by the chauvinistic treatment of wives and girlfriends exhibited by the host and his male guests. The party's concern with sexual as well as national politics is emphasised by Don's insistence that his guests each bring along a 'pornographic object'. Mal arrives with a nude drawing copied from *PlayBoy*, and Mac brings a nude photo of his ex-wife. Both pictures are paraded to the dismay of Kath and Mal's wife Jennie. When asked for his contribution, Coolie claims that his current girlfriend Suzie is his 'pornographic object', and she is similarly displayed to the group when the men strip her and throw her into a neighbour's swimming pool. In the course of the evening, the female artist Kerry and Simon's wife Jodie are also pursued by different members of the male group. Despite the stated interest in the evening's political proceedings, the only debate of the pertinent issues in which the guests engage is provoked by Mal's attack on Simon's and Jodie's loyalty to the Liberal party. The abiding physicality of the party, dominated by drinking, eating and dancing, carries over into the guests' response to news from the polls. When the Labour party appears to be winning, the males' lechery is at its height, but the late swing back towards the Liberals sees them urinating together in the vegetable garden. As with the near-contemporary Ocker comedies, the film's portrait of Australian masculinity is both stereotyped and representative, with the males' characteristic behaviour being both satirised and celebrated. Bawdy humour assists the recognition of the caricature's basis in fact. Don tells Kerry that Coolie once screwed a woman with a tin leg 'out of sheer pity'. Later Kerry asks Coolie if he thinks sex is 'an organic part of a relationship', to which he replies 'organ first, relationship second'. Although the males' attitudes and authority are deplored, their single-mindedness is also open to satire and ridicule:

Mac	Certain men are going to offer themselves to you tonight.
Kerry	Certain men are going to be disappointed.
Mac	Which ones?

At the end of the party Mal and Don discuss wife-swapping, only half-jokingly. As such, the unremitting competition for the women, between the married and unmarried men, culminates in the hospitable and deferential offering of wives to best friends.

As with the shearers in *Sunday Too Far Away*, a composite picture of Australian masculinity within heterosexual relationships emerges from the range of party guests. While they lament their husbands' vulgarity and selfishness, Jennie and Kath find the quiet and self-effacing Simon too boring to bear. Simon cannot resist watching the other husbands stripping Suzie, but is humiliated and forced to leave on his own when Jodie becomes attracted to Mac. Coolie embodies the unbridled sexuality to which Don and Mal aspire, but which marriage, the 'most boring way that any society could regulate sex', denies them. At the same time sex within marriage is dissatisfying for both sexes. Mal's and Jennie's sex life is tarnished by Mal's own feelings of inadequacy. Mac confesses to Don that he encouraged his wife to sleep with his friends to see if she would respond more to them than she did to him. While the men appear obsessed with observation of the 'pornographic object', through magazines, photographs, drawings and conversations, their possession of it is limited or fleeting. Suzie leaves Coolie after a row, Kerry leaves her jealous husband and Don's and Mal's marriages are seen as ties rather than connections or partnerships. The women's grievances are expressed in one brief scene, in which they discuss their experiences of marriage and relationships. The suggestion of a sexual life without men (advocated by Kerry and Suzie) is never explored as a valid alternative, as Simon's prurient eavesdropping interrupts the conversation. However, the men's failures as partners are complicated by their interconnection with their personal inadequacies. Coolie recalls his first meeting with Mal the academic and his acolyte Don, when the former's political ambitions and the latter's hopes of publishing his 'magnificent but never completed novel' were first voiced. Fourteen years later they are still pontificating about their pretensions without pursuing them. Bitterness towards their mates as well as their spouses is as indicative of disappointment with themselves as dissatisfaction with others. In the final scenes, Kath breaks her silence to condemn Don's self-absorption. His unfinished novel delayed her having children for seven years, and his peevish disappointment prevented his full commitment to their marriage. Chastened by her vituperation, Don is last seen walking through the detritus of the party in the early morning. Kath tells him to go to bed, and he obeys without replying. Their resignation to the continuance of a loveless union coincides with the electorate waking up to an unchanged government, returned to power despite the desire for change. The entrapment seen in *Sunday Too Far Away* is repeated for both sexes. In placing their small-scale dramas within the context of national events, both films suggest the inescapability of social conditions and cultural determinants, despite the characters' contribution to their fates:

> The film's distinction lies partly in its refusal (despite the fact that it clearly favours the women above the men) either to endorse as 'correct' any of the positions it dramatises or to attribute blame to particular individuals: it is the fundamental structures of patriarchal capitalist society that are called into question, the ways in which our culture constructs notions of male and female, determines gender-roles and organises sexual difference.[8]

The sporting life

The Club's depiction of sporting and business rivalries within a football club offers a further example of a male-dominated milieu within Australian society. The disharmony within the team and management are shown to be influential in their failures, just as communal effort and commitment assure success on and off the field. The unifying activity of a male group (working, sporting or military life rather than shared emotional or familial experience) furnish the conditions for the establishment of mateship or the instigation of jealous rivalries. The film's similarity to *Sunday Too Far Away* extends to the amalgamation of working-class culture and national representation. Both the shearers and the footballers incarnate the heroic qualities and melancholy victimhood which define Australian-ness within the male ensemble films, and both also engage in class-based struggles against unjust authority:

> *The Club* ... deals with anti-authority bickerings at various levels, from the dressing rooms to the boardroom of a Melbourne football club. There are suspicions about a highly paid newcomer to the club which lead to attempts to make him look foolish at training, aggro about the possible replacement of Laurie (Jack Thompson) as coach, and a mixture of sentimentality and opportunism in the club president's appeals to tradition to try to enforce his point of view; the film develops into a very Australian conflict between players (=workers) and committee (=management).[9]

Animosity arises between the team coach and club president, and the players and the new signing Geoff Hayward, because of doubts over commitment to the club's traditions and future. However, personal ambitions intervene to complicate relationships within the organisation. The president Ted Parker recruits Geoff in order to win the championship, but Laurie resents his interference in team selection. Geoff's selfishness in demanding a greater fee is balanced by Ted's payment of $10,000 of his own money to ensure that he signs. Laurie is supported by a players' strike, but his dispute with Ted is settled when the president makes an emotional appeal in the terms of personal and communal history. Their common ground is the club, where Ted, despite being useless at the game in his youth, watched the seventeen-year-old Laurie start his career. Laurie subsequently re-uses the manipulative aspects of Ted's speech to upbraid Geoff's lack of commitment to the club. The real mouthpiece for tradition within the club is Jock, a former player and coach who now holds a place on the board. He recalls the myths of the club's history ('during the Depression they practically played for nothing'), but is rendered ridiculous by his racial and sexual prejudices. When Geoff says he 'felt like Achilles' during a match, Jock reflects that Greeks and other new Australians 'could be real champions if they could forget about soccer and just learn to assimilate'. He also warns Ted against criticising the performance of Danny, the twenty-nine-year-old captain:

You've got to be bloody tactful when a player's getting on in years ... I remember Tommy Robbins took me apart in the '39 Grand Final. When I got home Dulcie says to me 'I think you met your match today', so I thumped her one. She apologised later but by then the damage was done.

However, his deference to tradition hides a self-serving ambition which runs counter to the club's interests. He values his own career ahead of club history, as his record number of appearances as a player and his premierships as a coach have not been equalled. He plots with other board members to remove Ted, fabricating a scandal to force him to resign. Once installed as the new president, Jock woos wealthy investors, plans to sack Laurie and to sell Hayward and other obstructive players. However, this misdirection of club traditions is countered by Laurie's realisation of Ted's love of the club and the game. When Ted is deposed he and Laurie again reminisce about past games, from the opposite perspectives of spectator and player, and Laurie learns of Ted's use of his own money to sign Geoff to the team. Subsequently

Laurie confronts Jock with his memories of club history. Jock is accused of sabotaging player acquisitions to prevent Laurie succeeding as a coach, and of seeking to sell Danny so that his record of appearances for the club would not be broken. Geoff learns commitment to the club, returns Ted's personal cheque and helps the team to a championship win. The team's championship win is both a victory over the past (tradition tainted by personal vendettas) and future (the club's history under threat from the 'business logic' of profiteers). The balletic, slow-motion sequence of the championship final serves as an illustration of individual skill and communal effort in harmony, with the present team's performance inspired by and comparable with the glories of the past. The due acknowledgement of tradition, and the integration of personal strengths in communal endeavours, are the conservative morals to be derived from this triumphal ending.

The personal factor: *Between Wars*

Michael Thornhill's first feature *Between Wars* (1974), which predates *Picnic at Hanging Rock* and *Sunday Too Far Away*, has been forwarded as the first example of both the period film cycle and the male ensemble film. In fact, its emphases are distinct from the aestheticism of the AFC genre and the conservative ideological position of later male-centred dramas. Like *Picnic*, *Between Wars* offers a critique of the pervasive, reactionary authority exercised by an Australian establishment based on the British model. Like Weir's film, Thornhill's debut takes an unconventional, art cinema approach to narrative construction, but unlike *Picnic* its representation of the interwar period is grounded in a social realist tradition, and as such incorporates a cogent social commentary:

The supposed incapacity of the 'nostalgia film' to speak to contemporary reality makes it forget the critiques of cultural, intellectual conformity, parochialism and a society inimical to new ideas that are central to Thornhill's *Between Wars*.[10]

The film follows Edward Trenbow from his service as a medical officer at the end of the First World War, through his career as a psychiatrist and general practitioner during the 1920s and 1930s to the beginning of the Second World War. The film's time period and its concentration on the discrepancies between personal experience and perennial structures of social control is signalled by the series of musical pieces heard over the titles. The succession of ragtime and jazz tunes, interspersed with military marches, encapsulates Trenbow's gradual recognition of the continuities of authoritarian control which lie behind the surface changes and elusive freedoms of each decade. Trenbow's lack of success in opposing the forces of conservatism in military and civilian life makes him an equivocal hero at best. Frequently he is forced to yield to official pressure simply to preserve his livelihood. The film is divided into four acts located in personal and national history by titles ('1918'; '1920'; '1932'; '1941'). This episodic construction emphasises the extent and irrelevance of change: much alters in Trenbow's personal life (marriage, family and career), but little changes in his unpopularity with the military, medical and political authorities.

In 1918, Trenbow earns official distrust because of his treatment of 'shell-shock' victims on the Western Front. His suggestion that some men may simply 'be unsuited to warfare' causes alarm. General Headquarters disallows the use of the term 'shell-shock', and insists on tougher treatment of 'malingerers'. At a convalescent home in England Trenbow meets Dr Avante, another failed surgeon who espouses gentler, 'commonsense' therapy, and also begins a friendship with a German POW. Dr Schneider's military experience mirrors Trenbow's: rather than being allowed to offer psychiatric care to mental cases, he treated dysentery at the front. Trenbow courts controversy in his association with the prisoner and his 'alienist' therapies, and their discussions are broken up by xenophobic colleagues. According to Trenbow, mental illness and the works of Australian psychiatrist Havelock Ellis are 'never mentioned in polite society'. Schneider reflects, 'Are any important ideas ever mentioned in polite society? And can there be a polite medicine?' The ironies of Trenbow's situation are multiplied on the day of the armistice, when he takes Schneider for a picnic in the hospital grounds, and is forced to shoot a guard who fires on the 'escaping' prisoner.

In 1920, Trenbow courts and marries Deborah, but her relatives are dismissive of his psychiatric ideas. When a malarial treatment for syphilitic cases instigated by Avante leaves three patients dead, Trenbow is forced to write a whitewashing report to clear the asylum of any culpability. The resulting Royal Commission Enquiry, learning that Trenbow is a 'follower of Dr Freud', interrogates him on his professional conduct, and he denies being a Freudian in order to avoid being deregistered. Inconveniently, students from the University of Sydney then deliver a written resolution supporting his pioneering work in Freudian psychiatry in Australia. By 1932, Trenbow is working as an inconspicuous general practitioner in a quiet rural town.

He is encouraged to offer therapy to Marguerite Saunders, who wishes to control her 'unstable' sexual behaviour. They both become supporters of a farmer's co-operative, which organises food storage and sales to the local community. Anti-communist graffiti appears on his house, and a fair at the municipal showground is broken up by reactionary forces. Under pressure from the BMA and frightened for the safety of his family, Trenbow resigns from the co-operative.

With the coming of the next war, the friendship between Trenbow and Schneider again causes problems. The German doctor is interned and against Avante's advice, Trenbow appeals to Marguerite, who now works in the office of the attorney general, for help. Now a pillar of the establishment, she refuses to assist. When he is invited to speak on ABC radio, Trenbow uses the opportunity to protest about his friend's treatment, but the broadcast is censored. Again Trenbow joins an outlawed organisation, the anti-war Australia First Movement. Even though they play the national anthem at their meetings, they are raided and questioned by the police. While Deborah defends her husband's championing of friendship, his son Rodney considers him a traitor. Subsequently, the Trenbow family home is ransacked during a search by security officers. In the final scenes Trenbow and his wife sit brooding silently as Rodney, in uniform, gets ready to depart for service overseas.

The strength of *Between Wars* lies in the weakness of its central character. Trenbow is not heroic in any conventional sense, as his outspoken stance is often wilful, naive and readily surrendered. He gains nothing from resistance or friendship, as his acquaintances Marguerite and Avante prove able to integrate and advance themselves within the establishment despite past misdeeds. However, his lapses of commitment and his inability to affect history and society do not excuse the injustices and protectionism of establishment authority. (The existence of a covert, controlling brotherhood within the Australian establishment is portrayed in Thornhill's later film, also adapted from Frank Moorhouse's writings, *The Everlasting Secret Family* (1987).) The inconsequentiality of the man, and the comparative irrelevance of his struggles against the background of national and international history, provide a more telling criticism of persistent institutional inertia and conservatism than a symbolic victory against the establishment and a classically concluded narrative might otherwise offer. In perspective, rather than setting or structure, it remains distinct from the majority of period films:

Where *Newsfront* generates energy and intensely affectionate moments of recognition through its old newsreel footage, *Between Wars* has an existential distaste for much of what was Australia in those respectability-ridden decades ... Trenbow is a mildly disaffected, disengaged, drifting sensibility. Whole scenes are given over to philosophical conversation between men at loose ends. The point is that they do not connect, do not act, and only sometimes suffer the world acting on them.[11]

The portrait of the defeated and defeatist Australian male in Thornhill's film does not differ greatly from that seen in later male ensemble dramas. However, Trenbow's intellectual status sets him apart from the definitions of Australian masculinity based on terms of physicality and working-class victimisation. His gradual isolation from peers, colleagues and family also distinguishes the film from others concentrating on the male group. It is not simply that Trenbow is excluded from every group because of his controversial attitudes: conformity to the group is shown to be surrender, and the power of the group is revealed to be tyrannical. Trenbow is as self-destructive in his resistance to the group as Foley is in his loyalty to it. That the protagonists' inaction could be as fatal as their action was, in Thornhill's opinion, more evidence of the film's relevance to the portrayal of national character: 'I think it is about repressive people who don't face up to things and who, though basically decent, tend to avoid conflict. I think that's very Australian'.[12]

Sons of Anzac: *The Odd Angry Shot*

The sense of Australian male characters being prey to the forces of history which appears in *Between Wars* is developed into a persistent theme within the ensemble films which address Australian war experience. Before the wars fought under colonial rule were examined in *Breaker Morant* (1980) and *Gallipoli* (Peter Weir, 1981), Australia's involvement in the Vietnam War provided the subject matter for Tom Jeffrey's adaptation of William Nagle's novel, *The Odd Angry Shot* (1979). In following the tour of duty of a squad from the Australian Special Air Service, the film shares much of its humour (and most of its cast members) with earlier ensemble films. Its critique of the war and Australia's subordination to the American military effort is muted in some sequences, limiting the film to a study of camaraderie and the undifferentiated horrors of war similar to *The Boys in Company C* (Sidney J. Furie, 1977). Elsewhere the pronouncements against the conflict appear anachronistic in the mouths of characters (especially the squad leader Harry, played by Graham Kennedy) in the diegetic period. In some respects the futility of the Vietnam conflict over-flows into the depiction of Australian involvement in the Second World War in *Attack Force Z* (Tim Burstall, 1980). The Anzac and Dutch special forces mission behind enemy lines ends in dispirit-ing failure, with the death of all but one of the team.

The Odd Angry Shot opens with a young recruit, Bill, enjoying a leaving party with family and friends before departing for Vietnam. His thoughts rest squarely on sex with his girlfriend before his departure, and on guaranteeing that she will write while he is away. The realities of war, and especially the partic-ularities of the conflict in South East Asia, remain distant as the platoon embark on a Qantas airliner and drink Fosters beer *en route* for Vietnam. The American influence behind their deploy-ment is implied in airline trolleys emblazoned with the slogan 'Things go better with a Coke', but it takes a mortar attack on a drunken card game to underline the invisible dangers of their duty. The deaths of two of their number in this incident, and the fatal wounding of another on their next patrol begin the inex-orable depletion of the squad in line with the conventions of other war films.

Generic expectations are met in Harry's assumption of the role of surrogate father to the other recruits, the absence of letters to Bill from his girlfriend, and the arrival of bad news from home for Bung. In others scenes the specific frustrations of fighting in Viet-nam are fully explored: a tense sequence follows the squad's lengthy and stealthy approach to a Vietcong hideout, which is revealed to be empty; Bung's breakdown at hearing of the death of his mother and girlfriend in a car accident is juxtaposed imme-diately with the grief of a Vietnamese woman after a patrol kills her son; when Rogers (Bryan Brown) is crippled by a landmine, the group's shock and despondency are communicated by the depiction of only the aftermath of the incident; and when Bung is killed within days of the end of their tour, Harry and Bill merely turn their backs on his body and smoke.

These illustrations of the squad's operations serve to punctu-ate the portrayal of their day-to-day existence. The majority of the film is composed of scenes which detail the group's drinking, gambling and competing (amongst themselves and with Ameri-can soldiers) in exactly the same ways as civilians. Australian-ness, as well as masculinity in adversity, are articulated in such exchanges. Harry spars verbally with the camp cook as Foley did on the sheep station. Sardonic humour emerges when they joke that the leeches that bite the sergeant will 'all get pissed', and when, after another fruitless reconnaissance, Rogers reckons the score as 'Home Team 8, Visitors 1'. Harry discloses, and laments, another national characteristic: the willingness of Australians to participate in foreign, colonial wars:

It's the poor man, the shit shoveller with the arse out of his pants and two bob in his pocket that makes Australia. Every time trouble starts, there he is, standing like a fool at the recruiting office with his hand out for a rifle ...

The difference he identifies, between this and previous wars in which Australia has participated, is that this conflict and all who serve in it will be a political and national embarrassment when it is over. As inheritors of the traditions of Australian military, the 'fearless sons of Anzac' in Vietnam will endure disinterest or contempt. When Harry and Bill return to Sydney as the only uninjured survivors of the group, they deny that they have been in Vietnam when they enter a club for a drink. They end as victims as much of their own survival as of the immature political establishment which consigned them to the war:

The Odd Angry Shot ... indirectly and slightly apologetically celebrated an Australianness, deflected through representative, less-than-heroic men. Furthermore, of course, the Vietnam War did not inspire a national sense of heroism; shame, guilt and failure were plainly associated with it, long before it was declared to be over. It cannot be taken as just any war and used to illustrate the effects of war on the men.[13]

While Jeffrey's film maintains the humorous portrayal of the Australian male seen in the Ocker films and Don's Party, it also stresses the particular Australian perspective on an infamous war. It may succeed in expressing the unusual and ignominious circumstances of the Vietnam War, but subsequent films detailing Australian involvement in Britain's colonial wars sustain and extend its characterisation of the martyred Australian soldier.

Parabolic history

Earlier stages of the male-ensemble group of films were marked by double-edged icons of Australianness in the form of Jack Thompson's Foley ... Breaker Morant marks the change; from Gallipoli onwards, we find protagonists who are increasingly purified cyphers of mythic intention ... The merging of the AFC genre and the male ensemble films, starting with Breaker and completed with Gallipoli, is indicated by this shift from a mode of irony to one of calculated innocence, from a more equivocal, indirect and definite assertion of Australianness, to an earnestness robbed of all lively contradiction.[14]

The amalgamation of the period and male-centred narrative strains in Australian film production during the 1980s propounds the expression of national character through images of masculinity, by concentrating on historical examples of male martyrdom. In place of the fictional characters seen in earlier social realist narratives, mythic archetypes and heroic national symbols inhabit dramas based on historical incident. Rather than emphasising documentary authenticity, *Breaker Morant* and *Gallipoli* offer re-enactments of events already invested with national significance. They constitute new renditions rather than radical re-interpretations of established national myths.

Bruce Beresford adapted the screenplay for *Breaker Morant* from a play by Kenneth Ross.[15] The director's successive drafts reduced the theatricalities of the original script and added details to authenticate its characterisation of Lt. Harry Morant (played by Edward Woodward) and depiction of the Boer War.[16] Where Beresford had planned to film a large part of Morant's career, the play's concentration on his court martial, with the Australian lieutenants Handcock (Bryan Brown) and Witton, allowed for both an economic and dramatic narrative. By centring the film on the trial process and showing the trio's actions in flashback, the film evokes comparisons with other narratives of military injustice, such as *Paths of Glory* (Stanley Kubrick, 1957) and *Sergeant Rutledge* (John Ford, 1960).[17]

Towards the end of the Boer War, Morant and his fellow officers in the Bushveldt Carbineers (an Australian unit formed especially to combat the roving groups of Boer commandos) are tried for the execution of Boer prisoners and the murder of a German missionary. In their defence they contend that the British High Command, led by Lord Kitchener, has ordered that no Boer prisoners are to be taken. The unit's mobility and the difficulty of logistic support on the veldt preclude the humane treatment of POWs, and in any case Morant's friend Captain Hunt has told his subordinates that British commanders expect no Boers to be taken alive. The circumstances of Morant's ordering the execution of seven prisoners are also inflammatory. After Hunt has been killed and mutilated in an ambush, Harry insists that his troops form a firing squad to kill the Boer found wearing the captain's uniform. This act of vengeance is, however, still within the terms of Kitchener's unofficially acknowledged directive. Within the context of prosecuting this morally ambiguous war against roaming guerilla groups, Handcock's shooting of the Reverend Hesse is justified privately on the grounds that he was acting as a Boer spy.

Alongside the heroic, mercurial Morant and the laconic and pragmatic Handcock, the third defendant George Witton embodies an untarnished Australian innocence, symbolic of colonial obedience to the Mother Country. He states his belief in the British Empire as the reason for joining up, but such naivety differentiates him from the other, more worldy accused and the manipulative British authorities. The trio's inexperienced defence lawyer Major Thomas (played by Jack Thompson), has been selected carefully by the British command. Fellow officers who might be able to corroborate Morant's assertions or act as witnesses for the defence have either been sent to India or are themselves under investigation. The only other British officer of the Carbineers (the intelligence officer Taylor, who in flashbacks is seen orchestrating firing squads and urging Morant to avenge Hunt's death) is a defendant in another murder case. The British command, up to and including Kitchener's aide Col. Hamilton, deny the orders to shoot prisoners and insist on the death penalty for the Australians. As a result, the court martial becomes a show-case trial, leading to the public condemnation of Morant and his comrades but ultimately revealing the disparities between the nations, and distinctions between the preservation of honour and persistence of honesty.

The issue at hand is not the defendants' guilt, since Morant does not deny the shooting of the prisoners. The allegations of murder in wartime evoke comparisons with the kaleidoscopic journey through a battlefield bereft of rational authority seen in *Apocalypse Now* (Francis Ford Coppola, 1979). Morant's ironic quotation of 'Rule .303' reflects the pressures of his circumstances and his understanding of the hypocrisy he and the others face. The similarity of the case to incidents in Vietnam (such as the My Lai massacre) was not lost on the director, and as such no condonation of their conduct is offered.[18] Rather it is the equivocation of the British authorities which is highlighted for condemnation. They complain of ill discipline in a colonial unit raised by Kitchener himself to conduct unconventional operations in an increasingly ruthless war. They prosecute the colonial officers for obeying orders which contravene the articles of war. The convenience of using the Australians to subdue the Boers is succeeded by the diplomatic expedient of sacrificing them in order to maintain peace with Germany. Evidence of the illegitimacy of the authority the British exercise over the Australians is not limited to the court's partiality. Thomas's objection on the first day of the trial, that it is unconstitutional for the defendants to be tried in a British rather than Australian military court, is brushed aside, since the Australian government has relinquished mastery of its own citizens to the colonial power. Confidentially, Thomas is told that a quick conviction would be welcomed back home 'to remove any lingering impression of a frontier colony and frontier behaviour'.

As a final irony, the accused are acquitted of the crime Handcock did commit – the murder of a non-combatant – but are convicted of executing prisoners and sentenced to death. Thomas' demand for Kitchener to be called as a witness, which would put the entirety of the British Army and Empire on trial for its conduct, goes unheeded. The illegitimacy of the colonial absentee authority which condemns the men is illustrated when Thomas forces his way into Kitchener's office to demand an appeal, only to find the room deserted. As a test of national character, the court martial draws important distinctions between birth and identity. The forthright 'colonial' temperament, and the actions it entails, are censured in the cases of Morant and Handcock, even though Morant is British by birth. He admits wryly that his impetuosity is 'most unBritish', and his similarity to Handcock is illustrated in their shared sense of humour. Early in the trial Handcock observes that Thomas' experience in writing wills 'might come in handy'. By the time of their sentencing Morant has assumed the same mordant wit: when Handcock complains that the carpenters haven't measured them for the coffins which they can hear being made, Morant remarks 'I don't suppose they've had many complaints'. This sardonic drollery, in addition to the emotional bond the men clearly share, marks Morant as an honorary Australian in the eyes of the accused and accusers. His (British) bond with Hunt at the film's opening is replaced by his (Australian) mateship with Handcock at its end, when they both reject solace from the padre and walk to their execution hand in hand. Their evident mutual respect, reliance and love provides the climactic contrast to British detachment and deceit:

the execution of Morant and Handcock is seen as a racist act; the features which define the characters as Australian (... the three central characters encapsulate the various positive formations of the Australian – the larrikin, the worldly misfit from Europe, and the innocent) are precisely those which incite the British to destroy them. They are presented to us as individualistic, independent, resistant to authority and determinedly iconoclastic.[19]

In contradiction of Dermody and Jacka's analysis of representations of the (male) national character, *Breaker Morant* maintains the equivocal and self-destructive aspects of Australian masculinity seen in earlier ensemble features. Beresford's film went on to critical acclaim at home and praise at Cannes where it represented Australia in competition in 1980.[20]

Peter Weir's *Gallipoli* combines several trends and thematic features from the period film's portrayal of Australian cultural history and the male ensemble's characterisation of masculinity and mateship. The pairing of Peter Weir and David Williamson is reflected in the varying tone of certain sequences. Broad humour and idiomatic authenticity characterise the scenes of recruitment and the antics of Anzac troops in Cairo, while the pre-ordainment and necessity of their sacrifice to a greater good evokes the mysticism of *Picnic at Hanging Rock*. The film's importance, in cultural and industrial terms, can be gauged from its budget (the largest for an Australian film to date[21]), the involvement of notable Australian entrepreneurs (Rupert Murdoch and Robert Stigwood) as producers, and its concentration on the historic baptism of fire for Australian soldiers in the First World War:

The combination of perhaps Australia's best known director, Peter Weir, with its most successful playwright, David Williamson, therefore seemed appropriate for an assault on what is, with the possible exception of the Ned Kelly legend, the biggest Australian story, standing at the heart of Australian mythology.[22]

The central characters and their circumstances in Weir's and Williamson's narrative bear a resemblance to those of *Breaker Morant*, but the positioning of mateship is altered to emphasise the national significance of their sacrificial role. Morant and Handcock fight in a British war and die at the hands of British authority, and their death is attributable to the distinctive Australian character and behaviour they exhibit. The younger, purer Witton survives, and as a result of his and the others' treatment he is enlightened as to the harsh realities of colonial subordination. The injustice of the court martial and execution provides a political education, rather than an uncomplicated national symbol. In *Gallipoli*, the death of the innocent, blond and unflinching Archie (Mark Lee) redeems the life of his close companion, the darker, worldly and cowardly Frank (Mel Gibson). He is destined to personify the loss of innocence in colonial service which will lead to a nascent national consciousness. Unlike the 'character' of Morant and the 'type' represented by Handcock, Archie and Frank are symbolic personae embodying perceptions and interpretations of the Anzac myth. Witton's innocence and naivety are components of these, but in Weir's film these facets coexist with a 'sense of predestination ... totally out of place in a film which purports to be historical'.[23]

Gallipoli begins in the Western Australian desert, with the young Archie training as a sprinter under the tutelage of his uncle Jack. His apparent destiny to represent his country at Olympic level is undone by his desire to join up, despite being under age. Archie's wish to emulate his uncle's youthful adventures is deflated by Jack who states, without elaboration, that 'war is different'. The individuality of Jack's voyages and the personal danger he courted are distinct from the loss of personal control (not only in uniform but under British command) Archie will undergo. At a symbolic level, however, this loss of control is precisely what Archie seeks. In his urge to join the war adventure, he offers himself willingly to the imperial purpose. While the British military authority which abuses the men is lambasted in the same fashion as in *Breaker Morant*, the tragedy of loss (multiplied manifold but exemplified by Archie) is leavened by acknowledgement of death as a national rather than colonial duty. Archie runs to death, and 'death meets him as fast', within a national and spiritual ritual. The men die for England, but the myth lives on in and gives identity to their homeland.

The national identity born from the tragic campaign is first suggested by the union of men and landscape at the film's opening. Archie's rural origins, his skill as a stockman and athlete and his recruitment to the 10th Light Horse mark him as the archetype of Australian masculinity and emblem of Anzac:

> The projection of a national identity in *Gallipoli* involves the use of established cultural symbols which have come to signify an overarching national ideology, whether or not they reflect the actual conditions of national life. The nationalistic motif of outback, inhospitable but rendered grand by a visual trope which *celebrates* the deprivations of rural life, is a symbol to establish a distinctly Australian identity, while in fact it was no reflection of the metropolitan experience of the majority of the home audience ... The desert is woven into the narrative structure as motif for the heartland which bred the 'best' type of Australian. The death of the boy from the outback signifies the destruction of all that is youthful perfection and potential in a battle mismanaged.[24]

Notably, progression through the film's three-act structure is based on movement between three geographically separate but physically identical environments: the deserts of Western Australia, Egypt and the Dardanelles peninsula. The identification of these different locations by titles underlines their similarity. The fitness of the Australians for their role is heightened by their familiarity with and inseparability from the landscapes around them. Overseas, they are 'at home' (and fighting 'for' home) in each desert.

The contrast to Archie is provided by Frank, the city boy, whose stated motive for joining up is not patriotism or the dream of adventure but the chance of advancement in the post-war world. The pair have little in common except their running, which originates in close competition but becomes a bond of common endeavour. Frank is linked initially with a group of mates (Barney, Snowy and Billy), but this association is broken, like Archie's connection with his mentor Jack. Ostensibly, their separation is precipitated by Frank's refusal to enlist while his mates join the infantry, but this is reinforced later by his preference for the 'class' of the Light Horse. On Frank's bitter departure, Snowy remarks that it is bad luck for mates to break up. In due course, the trio of mates suffer representative fates (one shell-shocked, one wounded and one killed) in a battle preceding Archie's fatal charge. The close affinity with Archie (through competition and shared trials) dissociates Frank from the conventional group of mates, and prepares for the elegiac tone of the film's final act.

Rather than 'mates', Archie and Frank are the embodiments of attitudes and perspectives. Their oppositional characteristics (fair–dark, rural–urban, unafraid–afraid, victim–survivor) illustrate their limited dramatic existence. If Archie personifies the archetypal Outback youth sacrificed in the war, Frank embodies a post-war cynicism, which is politically removed from but emotionally affected by the earlier national incarnation that Archie represents. At one level, Archie and Frank exemplify the 'greater love' (of laying down one's life for a friend) experienced between men of all nationalities in the First World War. Yet at the symbolic level at which the film also operates, the death of colonial obedience on the battlefield grants life to a new Australian consciousness, endowed with a modern, sceptical perspective upon the duties of the past.

This contemporary viewpoint within a period film, incarnated by Frank the witness and survivor, is also present in other aspects of the production. As with *Picnic*, the soundtrack music is polarised between classical and other pieces. Albinoni's 'Adagio for Strings and Organ' is heard over the titles and during the night landings on the Turkish coast. Its foreboding melody provides the first suggestion of the characters' impending fate. In contrast, Jean-Michel Jarre's 'Oxygene' accompanies the running races and gives a startling modernity to the period recreation. Its inclusion, alongside the predetermined tragedy on the battlefield (already known to the Australian audience from the film's title and signalled by the funereal tones of the Albinoni piece), stresses that Weir's film offers a modern perspective on past events. The sense of a completed and acknowledged history also appears in the newspaper cuttings of the campaign, already apparently yellowed with age and frequent reading, which Archie studies. When the young soldiers swim off the Gallipoli beaches, and examine quizzically the detritus of war (bottles, broken rifles) found underwater, the scene again has an atmosphere of archaeological discovery. Such a parallelism of perspectives (a period recreation inhabited by a contemporary witness or interpreter) reveals the film as more complex and less conservative than some readings have suggested:

[*Gallipoli*] is an attempt at a visionary recall of the 'original' moment of entry into myth. It is in fact more revisionist than visionary ... The legend must be projected positively. *Gallipoli* identifies a responsibility to re-mythologise, as if the moment can be emptied of all but contemporary myth and meaning. It rejects the stale glory of the myth that these young men went knowingly to self-extinction on behalf of country, King and Empire. It also rejects the long backlash of cynicism. It is oblivious to all the intervening generations of myth and counter-myth, view and reaction, right- and left-wing appropriations of the legend, as though the sentiments at the time the legend was wrought were right, simple and pure, unsullied by contradiction and conflicting political purpose.[26]

Despite the film's enthusiastic reception on release as an important product of the new national cinema,[27] and its depiction of the massacre of Australians orchestrated by bigoted British officers, its perspective on history, and on the cultural significance of historical interpretation, reveal it to be a more sophisticated treatment than this criticism suggests.

The inevitability of fate in *Gallipoli* is comparable with the inexorable socio-political forces exerting their influence over the characters of *Between Wars*. As in the earlier film, the protagonists' incapability to intervene meaningfully in the events deciding their fates reflects an Australian subordination to and victimisation by external, colonial authority. In this respect, a crucial thematic continuity in the director's work supports the film's nationalistic interpretation:

Against intentions, against all will, there is some force, vaguely that of 'History' in *Gallipoli* (less mystical, less mysterious than the happenings in *Picnic at Hanging Rock* or *The Last Wave* though similar to these), which not only conjoins and disjoins Archy [*sic*] and Frank throughout the film, but sweeps them both (and other Australians) to Gallipoli and to actions and courses they cannot understand, not control, not alter.[25]

In this respect, Weir's films exhibit a more generalised distrust of authority and lamentation for individual disempowerment than is implied by *Gallipoli*'s caricaturing of the British military command. The historical specificity of Australian victimisation seen in *The Odd Angry Shot* and *Breaker Morant*, is not replicated in Weir's film despite its painstaking recreation of the period and its reliance on accepted documentary sources.[28] Its sense of naive ignorance in the past, and painful knowledge in the present, ironically precludes the occurrence of the overtly nationalistic and anachronistic commentary found in Jeffrey's and Beresford's films:

Morant's suggestion that they are fighting on the wrong side – against 'farmers' like themselves – is a critique of the system itself. To see a greater brotherhood between the Boers and the Australians than between the Australians and the English is to go beyond nationalism to a more political understanding of the social structure, and it is a perception that *Gallipoli*, in contrast, is unable to reproduce.[29]

Landscape cinema

The use of the landscape as an index of nationality in *Gallipoli* epitomises a trend within Australian filmmaking since the revival. The unique Australian environment is foregrounded in numerous productions as the landscape shaping the (masculine) national type, as the primary influence upon the development of national character, and as a distinctive resource or selling point to be used to an aesthetic and commercial advantage. Clearly, the natural setting is ever present in location shooting across all the genres of current production within the Australian film industry, and the landscape has been used to ambiguous or negative effect in Gothic and some period films. However, the celebration of a distinctive landscape, as an integral part of filmic and cultural identity, is undertaken primarily in male-centred dramas (including those with past settings) because of the definition of nationality and masculinity through a respectful and/or competitive relationship with the land. This connection is formative and definitive even when the landscape is apparently disguised or de-nationalised. South Australian locations, standing in for South African veldt in *Breaker Morant*,[30] in effect accentuate further the Australians' familiarity and correspondence with the land, in contrast to their British masters. Even with its overseas location shooting, the same congruity between men and land is achieved in *Gallipoli*. If the Western Australian desert engenders national virtues in Archie, his travel to (and death in) other desert lands reveals this richer dust to ally and foe alike. In depicting the relationship between territory and nationality within the emergent film industry, Australian film both drew upon and supported existing forms of conservative national ideology. Ross Gibson has coined the term 'landscape cinema' to classify this phenomenon within revival filmmaking:

The idea of the intractability of Australian nature is essential to the national ethos. It is a notion that was instigated by commentators like William Dampier long before European settlement; a notion promoted by the First Fleet journalists who detailed the anguish of a harrowed and perverse society struggling to understand and survive in a bizarre environment ... In discussion of Australian cinema specifically, this notion appears enigmatic and convincing enough to shelter a seductive implication which marshalls so much lyrical panoramic cinematography to persuade us that, because human beings haven't cluttered the ground with their artefacts and connotations, the continent still stretches out as the text of some divine and immanent (as opposed to social and arbitrary) system of native, *Australian* meaning.[31]

In addition to films specifically incorporating pioneering and pastoral myths (such as *Sunday Too Far Away*, *Gallipoli*, and *The Man from Snowy River*), Gibson asserts the constant, interpretable presence of the landscape in a significant proportion of Australian features since 1970. Films as diverse as *Journey Among Women*, *Picnic at Hanging Rock*, *My Brilliant Career* and *The Chant of Jimmie Blacksmith* are as much 'about the Australian landscape'[32] as about human societies, protagonists and predicaments. The landscape's varying characterisation in these films (as a menacing wilderness, a site of racial conflict and an allegorical mirror to personal and societal turmoil) reflects the utility of the natural environment in filmmaking for national and international audiences. However, it is the predominance of the stereotyped rural male and his formative experience with the land (emblematic of the emergent nation's relationship with the continent) which best illustrates this trend in filmic national representation:

Given the basic inappropriateness of the bush legend and the iconography of the bush to contemporary Australian existential realities, the congruence of interest and focus on these pastoral myths requires explanation. The longevity of the pastoral ideal, surviving as it does Australia's urbanisation and suburbanisation, suggests that its survival is due to ideological and mythic functions rather than its close relation to historical conditions at any point or series of points in Australia's past or present.[33]

Within conservative landscape films, the beckoning space of the natural environment seldom contains a threat to masculine success or survival. Rather it is the constrained *human* environment that becomes the site of conflict and disempowerment. Morant's and Handcock's professional duties are displayed on the expanse of the veldt, but their recollection in the claustrophobic court room robs the men of freedom and authority. Having begun with Archie's apprenticeship in the immensity of the desert, *Gallipoli* ends in the restriction of a slit trench. The restriction of this space allows the troops' physical entrapment to double for their colonial subjugation. Faced with the unfettered spaces of farming country, Foley and the shearers have their lives shrunk to the dimensions of crowded bars and sheep stalls. The majesty of athletic prowess expressed on the football pitch is hampered by (and reacts against) the machinations of the locker and board rooms. The antitheses of space and restriction, freedom in activity and defeat in compulsion, concur with the ambivalence of the male national characters traversing the social and natural landscape:

The image of the paradoxical region can be used to 'explain' so many of the inconsistencies of a colonial society. If the land can be represented as grand yet 'unreasonable', the society which has been grafted on to it can also be accepted as marvellous though flawed. Indeed, it can portray itself as marvellous because it has subsisted, with all its flaws, in this grand yet unreasonable habitat.[34]

Even as, in its conservative and male-dominate forms, the landscape cinema promotes the natural environment as a positive feature and reflection of an idealised and simplified national identity, it provides an ironic and unexpected illumination of the ambiguities, insecurities and ephemerality of Australian settler culture.

Male drama and the mini-series

A later film which sought to replicate the success of Beresford's and Weir's films, by again centring on Australian war experience and forwarding heroic examples as sources of national pride, was *The Lighthorsemen* (Simon Wincer, 1987). Unlike the earlier hybridised male ensemble-period films, Wincer's film essayed a unashamedly commercial approach to its First World War narrative of a new Australian recruit unable to kill. This feature of characterisation, and the film's loose, discursive progression evoke comparison with *The Big Red One* (Samuel Fuller, 1980). Elizabeth Jacka viewed *The Lighthorsemen* as a 'shameless rerun of *Gallipoli*',[35] with which it shares its period setting, its desert locations and its themes of cowardice and mateship, but noted its similarity to Charles Chauvel's *Forty Thousand Horsemen* (1940), a Second World War propaganda film recounting the heroism of Australians in the earlier conflict.

. By contrast to the conspicuous structure and sedate pacing of *Gallipoli*, Wincer's film is characterised by an economical, melodramatic narrative style, unambiguous in its development. The film portrays events based in fact (the Light Horse's charge at Beersheba during the later stages of the war in the Middle East), placing its fictional characters within an historical setting. The unconventional character of the Australians is again crucial to their victory: the success of the surprise attack relies on the assumption by the German and Turkish defenders that the Light Horse will dismount to fight. Dave, the wounded but redeemed hero, survives and the casualties, though miraculously light, are honoured. Coming several years after Weir's film, *The Lighthorsemen* was 'widely panned as a well-produced, momentarily exciting anachronism',[36] but its commercial crafting reveals its affinity with a different media form then appropriating the subject matter and popular appeal of the male ensemble film:

[The film] neatly dovetails the logistics and tactics of the campaign, treated in what might be termed the mini-series fashion, with an episodic structure and frequent recourse to explanatory captions, with the 'human interest' of Dave, adjusting to his more experienced comrades and the realities of war.[37]

The television mini-series had already treated the Australian contribution to the First World War in the form of *ANZACS* (John Dixon, Dr George Miller, Pino Armenta, 1985) described by O'Regan as 'Paul Hogan's vehicle to "serious acting"'.[38] Mini-series became attractive undertakings when they were included in eligibility for tax concessions under the '10BA' taxation legislation, in operation between 1981 and 1988. In adopting the historical, military and sporting narratives of the male ensemble films, the mini-series exploited the 'commercial possibilities of declared nationalism'[39] which had previously benefited the Australian cinema. While production of the male ensemble and period films declined in the mid-eighties, the mini-series embraced their thematic and stylistic features in addressing sporting history (the *Bodyline* series (1984) recreating the controversial 1930s cricket tour), political events (*The Dismissal* (1983)) and war (*The Last Bastion* (1984)). The popularity of mini-series with producers and audiences is attributable to its negotiation of the same commercial and cultural imperatives spanned by *Sunday Too Far Away*, *Newsfront* and *Breaker Morant*:

Contemporary Australian cinema

The central strategy of the Australian historical mini-series is to portray the development of national consciousness inside emergence of an individual consciousness. The series in question examine the origin of a nation or of a national maturity. Great public moments become turning points in the lives of characters.[40]

Pre-eminent in creation of the mini-series in this period was the partnership of Byron Kennedy and Dr George Miller. Kennedy-Miller Productions, responsible for the *Mad Max* film trilogy, also produced a succession of successful television series which adhered to and developed the features of the male ensemble drama. Their unerring commercial sense was reflected in their employment of writer-directors such as John Duigan, Phillip Noyce and Chris Noonan, who benefited from the company's strong collaborative ethos, and the relationship built up with Warner Brothers, who were involved in the *Mad Max* cycle and Miller's later films made in America.[41]

The treatment of the hero and history within Kennedy-Miller mini-series is not always as straightforwardly commercial and conservative as the combination of medium and material might suggest. While national heroes and sports are forwarded uncritically in some cases (Jardine and Bradman in *Bodyline*, the company's most successful series), the recreation and interpretation of recent political history in *The Dismissal* skirted controversy but achieved considerable popularity.[42] The nationalistic stance of the former series, venerating the Australians' struggle against English brutality during the 1932 Test Series, contrasts with the criticism of political processes contained within *The Dismissal*, and underlines the contemporary cultural relevance of the mini-series. Cunningham asserts that such programmes perform a 'bardic function', confirming their status as '"social text" through their transparent use of history *for* the present'.[43] The diegetic connections established within these series, between historical and fictional characters and an accepted version of social history shared with their audience (accomplished with such stylistic devices as the cross-fading of images from black-and-white to colour seen in *Newsfront*) reveals them to be the inheritors of the period film's and male ensemble's agenda of cultural representation.

Males and mateship in '90s cinema

Portrayals of male mates in later Australian film have outstripped the ambiguities, recessiveness or conservatism characterising the earlier cycle of male-centred dramas. In recognition of the accelerating racial and cultural diversity of Australia, the racism implied in the positive depiction and unchallenged representativeness of the white male in earlier films has been opened for scrutiny. Two teenage boys are seduced by the adventure and empowerment offered by association with a group of white supremacists (for whom 'Hate is a fair dinkum emotion') in *Holidays on the River Yarra* (Leo Berkeley, 1990). Their youthful fecklessness and lack of commitment to any principle or profession make them ineffectual but susceptible recruits. Racial, sexual and family tensions overwhelm the members of a Neo-Nazi gang in *Romper Stomper* (Geoffrey Wright, 1992). The controversial subject matter in Wright's film belies its tight focus on the male-to-male relationship between Hando, the leader of the gang (played by Russell Crowe) and his lieutenant Davey (Daniel Pollock).

Hando organises the gang's relatively minor criminal activities in the Melbourne suburb of Footscray. In the course of orchestrating a disastrous campaign against Vietnamese immigrants moving into their area, Hando and Davey meet Gabe, who has left the home of her rich father after enduring years of sexual abuse. Although both men are attracted to her, she begins a sexual relationship with Hando and helps the gang to burgle her father's house. Incensed by Hando's failure to pull off this robbery, Gabe leaves the gang with Davey and betrays their hideout to the police. After a police ambush, Hando tracks down Davey and Gabe and the inevitable show-down between the three characters ensues.

Despite its concentration on the underworld of the extreme Right, the film offers little explanation of the attraction towards xenophobia and violence which motivates the gang members. Hando's recourse to *Mein Kampf*, the assorted Nazi memorabilia in his hideout, and the predictable iconography of British bulldogs, Union Jacks and swastikas imply a nostalgic romanticism rather than a contemporary political vision reacting against multiculturalism. The meeting with the 'Canberra Boys' becomes an excuse for a party, during which Flea (who has joined the Navy for no reason other than to fire torpedoes from a submarine) is denounced by Hando for becoming 'cannon fodder for the system'. Flea's unthinking enlistment parallels the desultory decision-making and random associations highlighted in this portrait of contemporary youth. Despite their aggressive demeanour, the skinheads are shown to be ineffectual in their battle with the Vietnamese youths, and in their botched robbery of Gabe's father's house. The male is also humiliated elsewhere within the film: Gabe betrays the gang to the authorities, and punishes her father for his abusive past; in staying with Hando's gang, Sonny rejects his girlfriend, but is humbled by a policewoman who incapacitates and arrests him. As well as being emasculated by the female characters, the gang are defeated conclusively by their racial enemies. The Vietnamese are well organised and prove successful in their pursuit of the skinheads. The economic mobility of the immigrants contrasts with the vagrancy and joblessness of the skinheads. Close-ups of the dying Hando, motionless on the beach, are intercut with shots of Japanese tourists, looking on curiously. Their economic and physical mobility contrasts with the stasis, failure and misplaced nostalgia of Hando.

Instead of defending racial purity, Hando seems concerned with preserving his clique in general and his status and relationships within it in particular. As such, his relationship with Gabe is at once a challenge and an irrelevance to his relationship with Davey. Davey does not vie with Gabe for Hando's attention, but Hando feels forced to contest Davey's attention with Gabe. The relative importance of the emotional links between the three characters is shown by their first meeting. Both Hando and Davey see Gabe across a bar, and Hando's attraction to her is expressed (or repressed) by his immediate robust embrace of Davey. Consequently Gabe and Hando engage in a competitive tussle to tend a wound on Davey's hand. When Gabe and Hando have sex upstairs during the party, Davey is seen attempting to obliterate the thought of them together through an explosion of fighting and drinking, related through frenetic montage. The frustrations of the white youths' socio-economic circumstances, dynamised by racist propaganda and aggravated by their own emotional insecurities, motivate the aggressiveness of this sequence:

A slam-dancing party sequence, where Wright intercuts from the mayhem on the floor to Hando and Gabe having rough sex and again to Davey pummelling a punchbag, serves to underline the thesis that the gang's violent behaviour is, in part, a pleasurable outlet for physical frustrations, while Davey's use of a Hitler Youth knife to fatally dispatch Hando in the final reel is an obvious injection of symbolism to ram home the notion that violence breeds only more violence.[44]

At the film's climax, Hando insists that Davey must abandon Gabe to re-establish their relationship. Hando's love of Davey is thus translated into a violent hatred of Gabe, to which Davey is forced to respond. The symbolism of this scene may suggest the duplication of racism and violence from one era and country to another, but the specific Australian notions of masculinity imply instead that repressed male-to-male bonds and expressed male-to-female emnity entail destructive consequences for mateship. The consistent orientation of such relationships, and their conclusions in death (even in celebrations of nationhood such as *Gallipoli* and *Breaker Morant*) evince continuities of masculinity and nationality within the output of the Australian film industry:

> The teenage passions that permeate the American cinema, and often end in a triumphant union of the young couple despite parental and peer pressure, in Australian films ... end in the disintegration of the couple ... Passion is often seen as obsessive and destructive, as in *Monkey Grip* (Ken Cameron, 1982) and *Dogs in Space* (Richard Lowenstein, 1987).[45]

The absence of consensual, consummated heterosexual relationships in Australian cinema can be linked to the stress, culturally and therefore cinematically, on male-to-male relationships. The downbeat or inconclusive resolutions to narrative seen throughout the revival can also be connected with this view of relationships and the conception of masculinity. Disempowered heroes (in the Gothic, Australian thrillers and the ensemble/historical male dramas) are unable to command and conclude narrative action positively, and as a consequence the upbeat ending which a climactic romantic union would represent is consistently unattainable. In *Romper Stomper*, emphasis on the male and exclusion of the female (both explicit and sublimated in xenophobia) tend towards a hyper-nationality and destructive masculinity. The concentration on white male experience within the Australian cinema, and its mobilisation in the portrayal and definition of national identity, are subjected to withering criticism in Wright's film.

Conclusion

The bush as a repository of moral virtue has been a continuing strain in Australian fiction, since the last century. It has been seen as a testing-ground for manhood, as a site for the forging of the relationships between man and man and between man and nature – and 'man' is important here for the myths are essentially male-oriented ... Australia's two most popular films, *The Man from Snowy River* and *Crocodile Dundee*, both seem to subscribe to older notions of the bush as the crucible in which real Australians are forged. The fact that so many Australians (and others) have helped to make these two reactionary pieces so successful no doubt points to the extent to which the agrarian vision still forms a powerful strain in Australia's thinking about itself – and the way others still like to think of Australia.[46]

The conservative image of white Australian masculinity championed in *The Man from Snowy River* is perpetuated, however ironically, by the Paul Hogan persona promoted in the *Crocodile Dundee* films. Notably, given the television mini-series' espousal of the male ensemble-period film rubric of cultural definition and promulgation of identity, Hogan's comic popularisation of the laconic, capable male originated in the same medium. Dermody and Jacka point out that the success of Hogan's film roles is rooted in his public image as:

a star famous for being a personality in TV commercials and as a TV performer with his own show [and] Hogan as a public figure, 'personality', and barefoot philosopher ... Hogan is preternaturally Australian with a genuinely popular appeal.[47]

The degree to which this conception of the adept, unaffected but naive Australian male can be exaggerated, ironised and popularised can be seen in *Young Einstein* (Yahoo Serious, 1988), which on release rivalled *Crocodile Dundee*'s success with the home audience. The reconstitution of Albert Einstein as the son of a Tasmanian farmer, whose greatest discoveries and inventions (gravity, atomic energy) are devoted to pleasurable pursuits (surfing, rock and roll and putting bubbles in beer), celebrates the stereotyped national qualities of pragmatism, hedonism and anti-intellectualism. Academic activity which appears antithetical to the national character is indigenised by its application to innocuous ends. At the film's conclusion, Albert dismisses Marie's worry that national governments might exploit atomic power in dangerous forms, and her exasperation at his naivety is swamped by love of his ingenuousness. The film suggests that if such discoveries had been made by an Australian, the world would be a better place; at the same time, an ending title (quoting Einstein's surprise that others took his theories so much more seriously than he did) naturalises history's greatest scientist ('a rebel, a pacifist, an eccentric with a clowning sense of humour') as an honorary Australian.

Both unambiguous and ironised individual heroes are celebrated and commercially successful within these popular products of the Australian cinema. The adept, unsophisticated and solitary hero is permitted the status and power of the Hollywood film's central protagonist, in winning a heterosexual partner and concluding narrative action. Conversely, the communal, composite heroes of ensemble dramas are weakened, thwarted, victimised and martyred – in the cause of defining and celebrating national character traits. The disempowerment of the males is all the more striking when compared with the self-determination of female characters in the analogous period films:

Australians harbour a special affection for those who take up the good fight, whether they win or not. The willingness to meet life's challenges or injustices head-on, unflinchingly and with resolve, is so admired and deeply ingrained that the popular vernacular has coined a description to define the type: the Aussie battler ... Generally, characters who break free of social shackles are female ... but characters who refuse to acknowledge societal constraints are generally male.[48]

Again, the disparity between commercial success and cultural authenticity in the national cinema engenders the distinction between popular, empowered heroes inhabiting texts conforming to classical narrative form and the powerless group heroes in downbeat, polemical, tragic or nationalistic dramas. Where the latter type is evident in the first decade of the revival, the former comes to prominence at the end of the second, in the run-up to the country's bicentennial in 1988. Barry McKenzie is repackaged and rehabilitated as Mick Dundee in a period of heightened national self-examination, with the most conservative, positive and popular elements being foregrounded and celebrated. In contrast to the period films of the 1970s (characterised by unconventional narrative form, oppressed female characters and anti-authoritarian themes) which supposedly enjoyed establishment support, the male-centred dramas and popular successes of the 1980s disseminated an exclusive and conservative form of national character, focused on the white Australian male. As hero or victim, or victim-as-hero, his pervasiveness represents a key feature of the Australian cinema's cultural credibility, commercial success, and national and international appeal.

Notes

1 Susan Dermody and Elizabeth Jacka, *The Screening of Australia Vol. II: Anatomy of a National Cinema* (Sydney, Currency, 1988a), p. 59.

2 Ibid., p. 62.

3 Brian McFarlane, *Australian Cinema 1970–1985* (London, Secker & Warburg, 1987), p. 54.

4 Dermody and Jacka (1988a), p. 61.

5 Graeme Turner, Art Directing History: The Period Film, in Albert Moran and Tom O'Regan (eds), *The Australian Screen* (Sydney, Currency, 1989), pp. 104–7.

6 Dermody and Jacka (1988a), p. 101.

7 Ibid., p. 98.

8 Robin Wood, Quo Vadis Bruce Beresford?, in Albert Moran and Tom O'Regan (eds), *An Australian Film Reader* (Sydney, Currency, 1985), pp. 200–1.

9 McFarlane (1987), pp. 59–60.

10 Tom O'Regan, *Australian National Cinema* (London, Routledge, 1996), p. 197.

11 Dermody and Jacka (1988a), p. 93.

12 Verina Glaessner, In the Picture: Australia, *Sight and Sound* vol. 46 no. 3 (1977), p. 150.

13 Dermody and Jacka (1988a), p. 149.

14 Ibid., p. 63.

15 David Stratton, *The Last New Wave: The Australian Film Revival* (London, Angus and Robertson, 1980), p. 54.

16 Gary Crowdus and Udayan Gupta, An Aussie in Hollywood: An Interview with Bruce Beresford, *Cineaste* vol. 12 no. 4 (1983), pp. 20–5 (pp. 20–1)

17 Tim Pulleine, *Breaker Morant*, *Monthly Film Bulletin* vol. 47 no. 559 (1980), p. 153.

18 Crowdus and Gupta (1983), p. 22.

19 Graeme Turner, Representing the nation, in Tony Bennett (ed.), *Popular Fiction: Technology, Ideology, Production, Reading* (London, Routledge, 1990), p. 120.

20 Stratton (1980), p. 56.

21 Susan Dermody and Elizabeth Jacka, *The Screening of Australia Vol. I: Anatomy of a Film Industry* (Sydney, Currency, 1987),. p. 182.

22 Jack Clancy, The triumph of mateship – the failure of the Australian war film since 1970, *Overland* no. 105 (1986), pp. 4–10 (p. 7).

23 Dermody and Jacka (1988a), p. 163.

24 Jane Freebury, Screening Australia: *Gallipoli* – a study of nationalism on film, *Media Information Australia* no. 43 (1987), pp. 5–8 (p. 8).

25 Sam Rohdie, *Gallipoli*, Peter Weir and an Australian Art Cinema, in Moran and O'Regan (eds) (1985), p. 195.

26 Dermody and Jacka (1988a), pp. 157–8.

27 See Freebury (1987), pp. 6–7.

28 See T.H.E. Travers, *Gallipoli* – film and the tradition of Australian history, *Film and History* vol. 14 no. 1 (1984), pp. 14–20 (pp. 16–17).

29 Turner (1990), pp. 121–2.

30 Dermody and Jacka (1988a), p. 155.

31 Ross Gibson, Camera Natura: Landscape in Australian Feature Films, *Framework* no. 22–3 (1983), pp. 47–51 (p. 48).

32 Ibid., p. 47.

33 Graeme Turner, *National Fictions: literature, film and the construction of Australian narrative* (London, Allen & Unwin, 1986), p. 32.

34 Ross Gibson, Formative Landscapes, in Scott Murray (ed.), *Australian Cinema* (St Leonards, Allen & Unwin, 1994), p. 49.

35 Elizabeth Jacka, The AFC-Genre and the Social Realist Film in the '80s, in Susan Dermody and Elizabeth Jacka (eds), *The Imaginary Industry: Australian Film in the Late '80s* (North Ryde, AFTRS Publications, 1988b), p. 88.

36 Turner (1989), p. 113.

37 Tim Pulleine, *The Lighthorsemen*, *Monthly Film Bulletin* vol. 55 no. 658 (1988), pp. 335–6 (p. 335).

38 O'Regan (1996), p. 199.

The male ensemble film

39 Dermody and Jacka (1988a), p. 32.

40 Albert Moran, Crime, Romance, History: Television in Drama, in Moran and O'Regan (eds) (1989), p. 252.

41 Stuart Cunningham, Kennedy-Miller: 'House Style' in Australian Television, in Dermody and Jacka (eds) (1988b), pp. 180–1.

42 Ibid., pp. 184–5.

43 Ibid., p. 186.

44 Trevor Johnston, *Romper Stomper*, *Sight and Sound* vol. 3 no. 4 (1993), pp. 55–6 (p. 56).

45 Debi Enker, Australia and the Australians, in Murray (ed.) (1994), p. 222.

46 Brian McFarlane and Geoff Mayer, *New Australian Cinema: Sources and Parallels in American and British Film* (Cambridge, Cambridge University Press, 1992), pp. 194–5.

47 Tom O'Regan, Fair Dinkum Fillums: The *Crocodile Dundee* Phenomenon, in Dermody and Jacka (eds) (1988b), pp. 157–8, 164.

48 Enker in Murray (ed.) (1994), pp. 216–18.

New glamour, new Gothic: Australian films in the 1990s

The quota quirky

There are only one or two, at most five, Australian feature films in any one year that a wide cross section of the public sees and that get taken up in subsidiary general public circulation – on radio, on television and in newspaper features. In 1992, it was *Strictly Ballroom* and *Romper Stomper*; in 1994, it was *The Adventures of Priscilla, Queen of the Desert*, *The Sum of Us*, *Muriel's Wedding*, *Sirens* and *Bad Boy Bubby*. Consequently these come to represent the Australian output and trends in it. This may not be withstanding the fact that they may be untypical of the films released ... But the successes inevitably present themselves as 'touchstone successes' and so find the horizon line of public explanation.[1]

Following the appearance and development of generic and stylistic trends in Australian film production during the first two decades of the revival, a different unifying feature has been perceived in the more recent critical and commercial successes. The eccentricity of the humour and narrative situations and the 'quirkiness' of characters are foregrounded as the appealing attributes of individual films (particularly *Strictly Ballroom* (Baz Luhrmann, 1992), *Muriel's Wedding* (P.J. Hogan, 1994) and *The Adventures of Priscilla, Queen of the Desert* (Stephan Elliott, 1994)) and by extension of the Australian industry's product as a whole. Significantly, these three films also examine problematic aspects of ethnic, familial, social and national identity, and resolve them optimistically within their comedic narratives. This concentration, and the films' contemporary settings and relevance, are characteristics shared by other Australian films of the last ten years. The

5

new label applied to Australian film in the 1990s underlines the link between its representation of new types of Australian-ness and the popular, commercial approach to filmmaking engendered by government legislation at the end of the 1980s:

> The prospect of a quirky, eccentric cinema to one side of the international norm [exists] as a means of establishing international attractiveness. In *Sweetie* and *Strictly Ballroom*, *Muriel's Wedding* and *The Adventures of Priscilla, Queen of the Desert* a space is created for what has become an international expectation of Australian 'quirkiness', 'eccentricity' and 'individuality'.[2]

The Australian Film Finance Corporation

An alteration to the ways in which feature films were funded was suggested in the late 1980s, in an effort to counteract the worst effects of the 1OBA legislation. Under the system of attractive tax benefits, productions had been overbudgeted or made without the likelihood (or expectation) of returning a profit on investment. Escalating costs in feature production had, ironically, favoured television work. The television mini-series flourished under 1OBA because of the reliance on finance derived from network presales. At the same time, the trend towards commercialism which the benefits system had encouraged had had a disadvantageous effect on other types of film production. In response to these problems, the AFC circulated a discussion document calling for the establishment of a national film bank, which would be responsible for nurturing cultural as well as commercial enterprises:

This bank would make investments in Australian films (as certified by the minister) on a purely commercial basis, but it would be able to scrutinise budgets and control costs in a way not possible under 1OBA. After much industry debate and negotiation among the various factions and interests, the government accepted the recommendation of the AFC and established the Film Finance Corporation (FFC) in 1988. Its initial budget was around $70 million (considerably less than the $150 million 1OBA was estimated to cost the taxpayer annually) and this is to be progressively reduced as its investments begin to generate returns and it becomes self-sufficient.[3]

Initially, the Film Finance Corporation's rubric was to act in support of, rather than replace, the funding structures existing under 1OBA. Feature films, television films, mini-series and documentaries would receive financial assistance provided they had earned a provisional certificate from the Department of the Arts, Sport, the Environment and Territories. However, productions were only eligible for support if they fulfilled certain cultural and financial criteria. A film was deemed eligible if it was 'made wholly or substantially in Australia with significant Australian content; or an official co-production made under a treaty or similar arrangement'.[4] Unlike the funding handled by the Australian Film Development Corporation (AFDC) earlier in the revival, the assistance offered by the AFFC was dependent on a favourable estimation of likely returns from the production. Therefore the AFFC's scrutiny of budgets and scripts was crucial to the assessment of viable presales and distribution deals.[5] Ostensibly, the Corporation's operations would rein in the excesses of the preceding era of tax relief and ensure balance in terms of budgets, content and commercial orientation. In practice, its (entirely appropriate) emphasis on popular appeal and guaranteed returns has resulted in economies of an unexpected sort:

In the last five years it has become increasingly difficult to produce and distribute films and programs that do not have what is called a 'robust' market character. This means a presale in an overseas market. The FFC insists on all projects having a presale of between 35 and 50 per cent of production budgets which tends to mean riskier and more experimental projects have less chance of support. The theatrical market for documentary film is practically non-existent and the television destination for documentary invariably affects the style, theme and length of the project. There is generally less money for the sort of film that used to be funded by the Creative Development Branch of the AFC – short fiction, documentary, experimental film and women's films.[6]

While attempting to maintain the diversity and representativeness of Australian filmmaking, the AFFC was tasked with fostering responsible and responsive economic and commercial approaches to production. Generically based productions promised the likelihood of popular success, but a close, contemporary cultural relevance, securing the recognition of the local audience, might also contribute to healthy returns from the Australian box office. Such representations of modern Australia, distinct from the gentility of platitudinous period-based dramas, might also provoke a re-orientation of perceptions of Australianness at home and overseas in the years following the 1988 Bicentennial. Many of the films produced in the 1990s, including those not financed by the AFFC, are derived from generic bases, but these conventionalised forms are chosen to be breached as often as observed. In developing, transforming or hybridising existing generic forms (the Australian Gothic and the rite of passage, and the American road movie and musical), recent Australian films have constructed a new image for the industry and the country, propagated through commercially successful, but nonetheless self-conscious and self-reflexive products.

New Gothic

Several Australian films of the 1990s incorporate Gothic elements, and often exaggerate the irony, black humour and reflexive characteristics exhibited by Gothic films of the 1970s and 1980s. They share a similar concentration on an isolated and unusual central protagonist, and examine the gradual and/or traumatic revelation of their true circumstances. In the course of this analysis, the modern urban environment is comprehensively deconstructed and defamiliarised. The antecedent of 1990s Gothic films in this respect is *Bliss* (Ray Lawrence, 1985), adapted from the novel by Peter Carey.

Bliss follows the experiences of Harry Joy (played by Barry Otto), a husband, father and salesman who returns to life after a fatal heart attack. He discovers that his belief in his world and family has been misplaced, and that his previous, secure existence was an illusion. The vision of heaven and hell which comes to him at his death is transferred into the everyday world, and he tests his friends and relatives to ascertain whether they are demons, or he is mad. His experiences and discoveries range from the comic to the banal to the horrific, as he learns that his wife is unfaithful with the junior partner in his advertising agency, his son is a drug dealer and his daughter an addict, and that his client companies are responsible for life-threatening pollution. Harry's revelation causes him to reject his responsibilities to family and business and wage a moral crusade against consumerism, and he falls in love with Honey Barbara, a redemptive earth-mother figure who offers him a new life in a pastoral idyll. His relatives counter this by having him committed to an insane asylum (evocative of a concentration camp), and he is forced to buy his freedom with acquiescence to his wife's plan to create an advertising campaign for a petroleum company. Barbara leaves him after this second fall and Harry spends eight years in the forest wilderness, learning humility within the natural world and winning back her love.

The transcendental conclusion of the film, with Harry dying again in a blissful old age and diffusing into the trees he has planted, strikes a note of spiritual optimism which seems out of tune with the occasionally horrific and depressive realisations which have preceded Harry's salvation. His traversing of 'heaven and hell, bliss and punishment' is suggestive of a modern pilgrim's progress rather than a contemporary social criticism, despite the environmental message it contains (with characters and the landscape burned and poisoned with petrol). The film's disconcerting shifts in tone and perspective endow its depiction of contemporary life with both black humour and potent criticism. Dismissing the hospital chaplain's reassurances that the idea of hell is 'old-fashioned', Harry recognises that individuals carry their personal hells within themselves. As such, Harry's mental and the family's moral disintegration correspond with the subversion of diegetic verisimilitude and the divergence from conventional narrative form. The buzz of flies accompanies Harry's fears of bodily corruption in hospital, but is also heard over scenes of moral collapse, as when Harry's daughter offers her brother oral sex in exchange for free drugs. Similarly, the faithlessness of Harry's wife Bettina is registered by a joking reference to, and then the physical appearance of, live sardines. The destabilisation of the diegetic world, and the erosion of a reliable perspective on narrative events (despite the voice-over narration given by Harry at the end of his life), reflects *Bliss*'s status as a fantasy text under Todorov's definitions. The inclusion of additional, alternative narratives (such as the opening recitation of the story of 'the vision splendid', and Harry's story of Little Titch told to the police officers) underlines the fluidity of the film's progression and its refusal to be fettered to a single organising perspective. So we can watch Bettina's death (at which Harry is not present), Davey's symbolic assumption of Nazi uniform in his (secret) meeting with his sister, and listen to the restaurant owner's opinions delivered direct to camera (before Harry arrives), in spite of the narrative perspective supposedly being centred on Harry in old age.

Bliss's ability to comment on the perception of social realities is dependent on its dissimilarity to social realism. Old Harry's voice-over first intrudes to inform us that 'this is a story about a fellow who told stories'. Such circumlocution (along with the repetition and appropriation of Harry's monologues in the film) highlights the self-consciousness of the narration within *Bliss*. Alex Duvall, Harry's colleague who rewrites the conference reports to produce official and honest versions of the week's business, is in effect undertaking the same exercise as Harry: reworking experience and perspective in order to create a better second life, in which immorality and dishonesty are redeemed as spirituality and truth.

Nirvana Street Murder (Aleksi Vellis, 1990) employs similar shifts in tone in its tongue-in-cheek narrative of petty crime and relationships across ethnic divisions. The deliberate mockery of the thriller format is broadcast by the film's disclaiming title: 'The characters, events ... in this motion picture are entirely fictitious. Any similarity to actual persons ... or actual events either past or present is purely a bonus.' The film evokes the long-running Australian television crime series *Homicide* in its title sequence, and also quotes the programme by showing certain characters watching an episode. The titles are accompanied by thriller music, and consist of a sequence of monochromatic images, gradually stained red with blood. Any dramatic tension is, however, defused by the realisation that the images portray the Poowong Abattoirs where brothers Boady (Mark Little) and Luke (Ben Mendelsohn) O'Hagan work. In spite of its lurid title, the crimes the film depicts are haphazard, accidental or mismanaged. Boady holds up a chemist shop, but only to get the $73 he needs for making speed, and the tablets he needs to control his sleepwalking. The speed he makes for sale is at first comically ineffective, then dreadfully potent. Other characteristics of the horror genre are included to bathetic effect. The Gothic mansion on Nirvana Street is home not to a Norman Bates, but an elderly lady Luke is required to visit as part of his community service while on probation.

While illustrating the brothers' incompetent criminal activities, the film also addresses the issue of relationships between different ethnic groups within modern multicultural Australia. Luke's Greek girlfriend Helen is blackmailed by another Greek girl, who threatens to tell Helen's parents of their relationship. Helen is already under pressure to accept a suitor of her parents' choosing, but Luke's and Boady's intervention merely starts a feud with the blackmailer's male cousins. The difficulties experienced by immigrant communities, in finding employment and integrating into society, are aired in a comic conversation between the brothers. In response to Boady's incomprehension of the issues, Luke makes an analogy to a group of shearers suddenly transported to Tokyo and unable to find work. Their dialogue recalls the prosaic wisdom and unwitting comedy of the male ocker character:

Luke   They can't speak the lingo, and they get the bum jobs.
Boady   Why don't they get a job as shearers?
Luke   'Cos they can't, mate, 'cos there's no bloody sheep in Japan!
Boady   Why go there if there's no sheep, you dick?

In a further example of the film's deliberate, comic deflation of masculine stereotypes and thriller expectations, the Greek males prove as inept as the Australian brothers in taking their revenge. The chaotic activities of all the characters build towards a climax of unpremeditated, tragi-comic violence. The fake documentary ending title represents the final example of the film's unpredictable handling of tone, convention and audience expectation.

Cappuccino (Anthony Bowman, 1989) also uses the thriller format and the vagaries of voice-over narration in a self-reflexive form. The experiences of a group of actor friends are related by Max, a cab driver by day and would-be stand-up comedian by night. Throughout the film he is seen in close-up as he delivers his narration in a spotlight to an appreciative but unseen audience. Only near the film's conclusion is it revealed that Max has been telling his story not to a club audience, but to listeners in prison cells surrounding his own. Initially Max's world weary voice-over satirises the insecurities and rivalries amongst his friends, as they compete in auditions, win or lose coveted roles on stage or television, and become involved in romantic entanglements. Maggie (Jeanie Drynan) laments losing custody of 'Sebastian' to her ex-husband in their divorce, and her last afternoon with him is given a clichéd, melodramatic treatment. However, the flashback episode concludes with the revelation that Sebastian is an Alsatian rather than a child.

The actors' circle is expanded by Max's young girlfriend Celia, and by the attentions of a corrupt detective Bollinger, who has left video tapes incriminating the police commissioner in Max's cab. Contact between the characters results in Bollinger and his partner (who 'could be Redford') behaving increasingly like actors and television cops, and in Max's imprisonment, which gives him the opportunity to write his own screenplay. Max is discussing his screenplay, entitled 'Cappuccino', and the parts he has written for his friends (which follow their characters and recent experiences exactly), when Bollinger confronts the group and is shot by Celia. As he dies Maggie walks into the shot, the director calls 'Cut!', and the scene is reshot. Subsequently the camera pulls back to reveal the paraphernalia of set, lights, tracks and technicians. The artificiality of the comedy thriller is parodied in this example in several interrelated ways. Max's voice-over to an audience mocks the laconic retrospective narration of the Film Noir detective, though the revelation of Max's imprisonment recalls the ending of *The Postman Always Rings Twice* (Tay Garnett, 1946). The stereotypical vanity of Max's actor acquaintances is reconfirmed by the ending revealing them to be actors playing actors. The improbabilities of the plot are emphasised by Max's voice-over, only for them to be excused by the admission of artificiality at the film's end. *Cappuccino* toys with the Gothic themes of official corruption and the protagonist's powerlessness, but softens its Gothic thriller sources through its self-conscious, comedic subversion of violence, suspense and stereotyping.

Death in Brunswick (John Ruane, 1990) adopts the Gothic sensibility wholeheartedly in its blackly humorous portrait of individual inadequacy, family authority and racial tension. Carl (Sam Neill) takes a job as a chef in a nightclub run by a Greek family, and is attracted to Sophie (Zoe Carides), who works behind the bar. She is betrothed to Yanni the manager against her wishes, and she begins a secret relationship with Carl. The club bouncer Laurie victimises Carl, and precipitates a fight between Carl and his Turkish kitchen helper Mustafa. Mustafa is killed accidentally, and Carl asks his friend Dave to help him hide the body. Subsequently Sophie and Carl find themselves caught between the feuding Greek and Turkish factions, and between their families (her traditional father and his pretentious mother), but they survive to be united in marriage.

The squalor in which Carl exists (in his own house and in the club's filthy kitchen) reflect his lack of status and self-esteem. His inability to defend himself deepens his degradation, when it becomes necessary to wallow in putrescence in order to secrete Mustafa's corpse in an already occupied grave. He may seem to deserve being a victim of the circumstances which he does not or cannot alter. Yet his active (but immoral) attempts to improve his lot are rewarded without incrimination. His determination to murder his hectoring mother is reinforced by the discovery that she has been withholding a legacy which would relieve his poverty, but she is incapacitated by a stroke before he can administer the poisoned drink he has made. However, the deadening parental authority cannot be evaded completely: the conclusion shows Carl's wheelchair bound mother present at Sophie and Carl's wedding, with the groom in a neckbrace after being punched by the bride's father.

Ruane's film is less exaggerated than but similar to examples of contemporary comic-horror films emanating from New Zealand. In *Braindead* (Peter Jackson, 1992), the introverted hero's attraction to his Spanish girlfriend provokes an all-consuming jealousy in his mother, who attempts to literally re-absorb him rather than allow him an adult, sexual existence. As Jackson's protagonist emerges from the containment of womb-like rooms, so Ruane's escapes squalor and inaction into a belated adulthood and relative independence:

This imagines a class of Australian males as fortyish adolescents, bullied either by their mothers or their wives, content to wallow in filth, and consistently engaging despite their burned-out life styles ... with Carl and Dave and Sophie signalling their strength of character by not overreacting to awful situations, instead greeting each appalling plot turn with a resigned shrug.[7]

Characteristics of the Gothic (in the portrayal of pervasive parental authority, the sudden irruption of doom-laden events, and the disempowered hero) are treated humorously in writer-director Ruane's debut feature. The black comedy and splatstick elements incorporated alongside the contemporary, multicultural context make *Death in Brunswick* a key example of the modernisation and modification of the Gothic aesthetic in later popularised forms. Having been made with the assistance of the AFFC, *Death in Brunswick* went on to become the second highest grossing Australian film at the home box office in 1991.

The third highest grossing film in Australian cinemas in the same year was *Proof* (Jocelyn Moorhouse, 1991), another writer-directorial debut. The narrative of *Proof* is built on paradoxes of truth and appearance, sight and perception, emanating from the central character Martin, a blind photographer played by Hugo Weaving. Having believed as a child that his mother lied in her descriptions of the world around him, Martin now takes pictures to create a body of incontrovertible evidence substantiating his existence and perception. He asks his friend Andy (Russell Crowe) to describe the pictures he has taken, so that they can be annotated to prove that 'what's in the photograph is what was there'. Martin is pleased by Andy's 'simple, direct and honest' way of describing the pictures, and asks him to continue in this task on a permanent, paid basis. The fragility of communication and comprehension between individuals is exposed when Martin interprets Andy's reply of 'No way' to mean that he refuses to help him, rather than that he refuses to accept payment. Although Martin wants to trust Andy, he is secretive and manipulative in his own relationship with his housekeeper Celia, whose cruelty towards Martin springs from his spurning of her love. When she becomes aware of Martin's preference for and reliance on Andy, Celia plans to ruin their friendship by seducing Andy and forcing him to lie to Martin about the content of a photograph. Her appropriation of Martin's pictures to identify and manipulate Andy provides another example of the partiality of visual perception and interpretation.

The paradoxical exercise of blind photography operates as the film's metaphorical core, since it comments upon the subjective haphazard and potentially damaging activity of interpreting a personally created, existential world. This is suggested from the title sequence, which consists of a series of Martin's oddly composed, off-centre and unfocused pictures:

> Martin's life is anything but the truth. The objective world he claims to record is one that he actively constructs. It is his own composite fiction, and there is a parallel in the way that Celia subverts his photos by building them into her own composite of Andy – not an Andy she objectively sees, but one she creates to use against Martin.[8]

Martin's insistence on the accurate annotation of his pictures over-values the gift of sight, which the heightening of his other senses has seemed to supersede. His reliance on the vision of others, in addition to doubt in his own sensory perceptions, undermines the solitary independence he seems to want, but cannot endure. His disbelief of his mother's description of the garden is based on his inability to hear the 'man with the rake' she assures him is there, and this doubt extends to the suspicion that his mother did not die but abandoned him. As a child we see him knocking on her coffin to determine whether it is empty, and as an adult being led to her headstone which is insufficient to convince him of her death.

Martin's bitterness at his isolation fuels his rejection of others, just as his testing of Andy's loyalty is fulfilled by the latter's failure. His desire for the truth contains a concomitant inability to tolerate it, and also reveals the paradoxical behaviour of those closest to him (in his refusal to acknowledge the love which motivates Celia's hate, and the friendship behind Andy's betrayal). While acknowledging the similarities between Moorhouse's film and the treatment of blindness in *Cactus* (Paul Cox, 1986), Jonathan Romney recognises that Martin's engagement with an illusive world and elusive relationships, and his status as a disadvantaged, questing individual, are evocative of the earliest narrative of existential investigation:

Martin's Oedipal drama (what could be more Oedipal than the story of a blind man and his mother?) is presented as the missing piece that 'explains' his relationship to the world, and as such, might seem unsatisfactorily pat. But it too is highly questionable. If we cannot trust photos, how can we trust Martin's remembered past with an idealised mother, in which he himself appears as an idealised child? And within that story is further gap – the absence of Martin's father.[9]

In attempting to confirm the facts of his past and determine the circumstances of his present, Martin appears as another emblematic, questing Australian protagonist. His physical and emotional vulnerabilities are inseparable from his needs and aspirations, as he seeks to prove himself in spite of his own and others' failings. His scrutiny and judgement of the world compare with those of Bernard (Chris Haywood) in *Golden Braid* (Paul Cox, 1990). The subjective recollection of human history and the mechanical recording of time are suggested by the opening Greenawayesque sequence composed of close-ups of clock faces, pendulums and movements, varying from the ornate and decorative to the dirty and functional. The eccentric music heard over the titles (Johann Albrechtsberger's Concerto for Jew's Harp, Mandora and Orchestra) furthers this contrast, as it provides the counterpoint to the varied and discordant clock chimes. Cox's protagonist repairs watches and clocks, but his obsession with timepieces, their previous owners and their reliability extends to a morbid fascination with fidelity within relationships, especially his affair with the married Theresa. The predictable, mechanical activity of clock movements is contrasted with the hero's incessant absorption in the past, and its inspiration of his florid fantasy life. Dwelling on past events (the death of a previous lover, the sanctity of earlier financial agreements not honoured by his brother who 'doesn't want to remember', and fantasising over a braid of golden hair he has found secreted in an antique Venetian cabinet) develops from a passion into a sickness, and threatens his present existence. His relationship with the severed but 'complete' braid (compared to other emotional bonds in which 'people only love bits of each other, never the whole person') must be revoked in order for the risky but rewarding connection with Theresa to be realised.

The Oedipal antecedent in sexual and investigative terms appears in *Bad Boy Bubby* (Rolf de Heer, 1993) in a more exaggerated form than that found in *Proof*, but there are other close comparisons to be drawn between Moorhouse's and de Heer's films. In both cases the central protagonist is comparatively unformed and inhabits a defamiliarised world, but Bubby enjoys a prophetic or messianic status similar to that of Harry Joy in *Bliss*. The presence of the Christ-like figure of the naive, unworldly but transcendent thirty-year-old can be traced across *Death in Brunswick* (in which Carl undergoes a redemptive epiphany during an ironic church visit) to *Proof* (with Martin's apparently immaculate conception and his scourging of flesh and dishonesty) to *Bad Boy Bubby* (with its man-child released upon an unknown world in which he offers unwitting hope and salvation to the fallen).

From birth Bubby has been kept imprisoned by his ageing mother Flo, who abuses him mentally, physically and sexually while controlling him with tales of the air laden with 'poison' existing beyond their basement room. His future is determined by the unexpected return of his father, a priest referred to only as 'Pop'. The emotional and spiritual world disowned or negated by his parents is opened to Bubby when he asphyxiates Flo and Pop with clingwrap (to save them from the poison), and wanders off into the city previously hidden from him. His subsequent encounters reveal the perversity and unpredictability of the modern urban environment. His education in immediate survival also incorporates a gradual revelation of the social forces and biological needs which drive the individual and the community. From his first double murder onwards, Bubby is both the innocent victim and heedless perpetrator of mundane yet horrific crimes. He passes through the company of a young couple with their own child, a single upper-class woman and a struggling rock band (who recognise him as the 'Clingwrap Killer') before being arrested and 'rehabilitated' by the police. In this odyssey he sees or talks to the woman called Angel on three occasions before they meet properly. Her frequent appearances and her physical resemblance to Bubby's mother seem to endow her with an 'everywoman' aura, but she also represents an aspiration for him in terms of his emotional development and socialisation.

Bubby mimics his earliest experiences of cruelty at the hands of his parents in his own treatment of his cat. He learns to handle his second kitten with kindness, and even though this animal is killed by youths this stage of his emotional growth is important as it immediately precedes his association with Angel and her clinic for patients with cerebral palsy. Here he learns love for Angel, and sympathy for Rachel's unrequited love of himself. The other vagaries of existence and love which are revealed to him (the merging of physical and spiritual ecstasy with 'Cherie the Salvo', the call to espouse atheistic humanism from the Scientist, the potted history of religious genocide provided by Paul, the group's lead singer) exemplify the ideological extremes from which Bubby must extrapolate a moderate path.

The eclecticism of Bubby's experience is paralleled by the heterogeneity of the film's reference (symbolic floor paintings for the exposition of religious history, described to Bubby as a series of institutionalised 'clingwrappings', and allusion to Bernini's sculpture *The Vision of St Theresa* (1647) in the episode with Cherie). This intertextual approach runs over into Bubby's performance with the band, in which his stream of consciousness recycles the words and phrases he has heard in an unwitting commentary. Just as the heightening of noises on the soundtrack and the occasional distortion of the film's images have served to articulate Bubby's defamiliarising perspective on the world, so the verbal fossils of his foreshortened childhood strike an epigrammatic cord with his audience:

Bubby fronts the band with a rant strung together from fragments of the abuse he's undergone. These replays are seized on as catch phrases by the audience, who happily chorus them back waving suitable fetish objects: gas masks, dog-collars and clingfilm.[10]

Bubby's assumption of Pop's dress and name is, however, a false elevation to adulthood. Angel and Paul force Bubby to acknowledge his true name and his past actions, before Bubby and Angel can create their idyllic family life. That they and their children live in the shadow of factories still pouring forth poisons reflects the fragile or illusory nature of any individual's bliss in the contemporary world.

The re-orientation of Gothic elements (such as the iniquity of authority, the fallibility of the hero, and the inconstancy of the given or constructed human world) in films of the 1990s maintains the black humour characteristic of Gothic films of the 1970s. Alongside the defamiliarising Gothic gaze, different examples of individual emphasis and national significance emerge. The thriller and the horror film are parodied in *Nirvana Street Murder* and *Death in Brunswick*, but are given a contemporary pertinence through their portrayal of multicultural tensions. *Proof* and *Bad Boy Bubby* extend the commentary of *Bliss* into an examination of identity readable in specifically Australian terms. The central Oedipal relationships and the problematic journeys of both films' heroes towards the establishment of independent existence provide an analogy to the emergence of a national, rather than colonial, identity for Australia. The hiding of the truth or the denial of the world, or the revelation of the truth of the world, which the protagonists of Lawrence's, Moorhouse's and De Heer's films experience symbolise the arduous task of constructing selfhood in the absence of parental authority figures. In a related biographical drama, David Helfgott, the hero of *Shine* (Scott Hicks, 1996) suffers under a violent parental authority which leads ultimately to his withdrawal from the world into a mental institution. The father who seeks to withhold the world from his son succeeds only in denying his son's talent to the world. The consistency of this theme and characterisation is borne out by their replication in Peter Weir's latest American film. In the media satire *The Truman Show* (1998), the hero's entire existence and environment are studio fabrications. Recognition of their artificiality is only the first step towards the establishment of an alternative space and mode of behaviour outside the control of self-elected authority. The world for Truman lies beyond the confines of the ersatz island, which as in the case of *Summerfield* (1977) may be taken to represent the Australian continent itself. Realising a new definition of national identity may depend on abandoning the territory plotted and the culture contrived by another (colonial) authority, subjecting the received political and cultural environment to a defamiliarising gaze and the world beyond to an unfamiliar scrutiny.

The rite of passage film

The protagonist undergoing fundamental, formative and traumatic experience, travelling and questing within a country supposedly his own but over which he can exert little control, emerges as a key characteristic of Australian film narratives across the Gothic, period film and male ensemble cycles of the 1970s and '80s. From the 1980s into the '90s, features foregrounding the rite of passage have forsaken the parabolic, historic settings of the First World War and the aestheticism of the period film to concentrate on the prosaic or unremarkable dilemmas of adolescents and immature adults.

John Duigan's films *The Year My Voice Broke* (1987) and *Flirting* (1989) follow the emotional, sexual and educational development of Danny Embling (Noah Taylor), first in his home town on the Southern Tablelands of New South Wales in 1962 and subsequently at boarding school in 1965. His position as an outsider is complicated by his attraction to girls who are also ostracised by the parochial communities of town and school. (The town itself seems to have become even more secluded than its physical isolation suggests by the building of a bypass which depletes the scant through traffic). In comparison with the bullying Danny suffers, Freya Olson, the adopted child of the 'town bike' in the first film, and Thandiwe Adjewa, a Ugandan refugee in the second, are alienated because of the pervasive, adult prejudices of sexism and racism. Their painful experiences contrast with Danny's more mundane sexual curiosity and disappointment, but contribute crucially to his development to adulthood in exposing the injustices unrecognised in childhood. Freya's hidden parentage is a common but unspoken knowledge within the town: laughter in the pub about visiting Sarah Amery at the house on the hill is tainted by the men's admission of their part in Freya's conception and their abandonment of her teenage mother in childbirth. The community's concoction of a ghost story to hide the secret and explain the derelict house misleads the offspring (Danny, Freya and local tearaway Trevor) into re-enacting the town's tragedy. The revelation of the truth is confirmed by the repetition of previous actions by a younger generation. This lends the narrative an air of both predestination and social authenticity, as the next group of adolescents repeat their parents' mistakes in pursuing the same desires. The inconsequentiality of the activity suggested by the title of *Flirting* hides the importance of Danny's and Thandiwe's friendship. Within repressive single-sex boarding schools, they maintain an individual and communal resistance against conservative, adult authority and cliques of their peers:

As in Duigan's earlier film, the narrow parochialisms of the time and place that oppress the outsider are neatly caught, and provide much of the wry humour. Danny, bending over to be beaten, finds himself gazing at a book entitled *The Great Australian Loneliness*, and a young debater solemnly calls up a supportive list of 'great thinkers': Aristotle, Kant, the Duke of Edinburgh, Sir Robert Menzies ...[11]

The challenge to conservatism is suggested on the soundtrack by the inclusion of contemporary pop songs, yet Danny's voice-over, despite its retrospectiveness, preserves the immediacy of his youthful ignorance and never imbues the past with forgiving nostalgia. Again, Danny's directionless rebellion is focused by Thandiwe's interest in politics of personal and national significance (the American intervention in Vietnam, and Idi Amin's rise to power in Uganda), as his growing love for her encourages a commitment to the issues arising in a 'much bigger world'. The couple's under-age sexual liaison, coincidentally across racial lines, provokes establishment censure, but the intellectual maturation Thandiwe offers Danny is both more important and potentially disruptive to parochial authority in later decades.

The specific positioning of generations and eras by popular music is foregrounded in *Secrets* (Michael Pattinson, 1992), an Australia-New Zealand co-production. Like Pattinson's earlier thriller success *Ground Zero* (1987), *Secrets* positions its quintet of teenage characters in a enunciated moment of cultural history, framing their experiences with the visit of the Beatles to Melbourne in 1964. Contemporary black and white footage of the crowds outside the group's hotel documents the general 'social misbehaviour' of the younger generation inspired by their arrival. The three girls and two boys are confined together in the hotel basement, after they have broken through the police cordon but failed to find the group's suite. Extrapolating from the official, censorious record of the event, the film's fictional narrative particularises the problems and pressures the teenagers endure, and relates them (as do the characters) to the euphoria or escapism the 'new' music offers. Randolph (Noah Taylor) essays a cool Liverpudlian persona through mimicry of the accent, wardrobe and 'mop top' haircut of his idols, and Didi (Danni Minogue) conflates her Catholic education and fandom by secreting a portrait of Paul McCartney in her Bible. However, the music contains as much disappointment as inspiration. Randolph resents the songs' oversimplification of love, and they offer only temporary release from the dilemmas facing Vicki (Willa O'Neill) and Emily (Beth Champion). Although the group and their music represent the motivation for the teenagers' unplanned rendezvous, this putative shared attachment is superseded by their common (universal) adolescent experiences and the emotional support they can offer to and receive from each other. Danny's illegitimacy and abandonment, Randolph's shyness, Vicki's unplanned pregnancy and Emily's change of heart about her imminent marriage can be disclosed and discussed within this impromptu peer group. The serendipity and importance of their meeting is underlined by the film's ending. Having failed to see their idols or even attend their concert, the five find themselves transformed into celebrities by their ordeal and are interviewed on television. In order to hide their identities from any watching parents, and in recognition of the benefits they have derived from each other through the night, they swap names before the cameras.

The particular emphasis on female adolescence in *Secrets* is duplicated across numerous other formative dramas in the late 1980s and 1990s. Sexual maturation and social deprivation are linked inextricably in the depiction of the life of the contemporary Aboriginal under-class in *The Fringe Dwellers* (Bruce Beresford, 1986), adapted from the novel by Nene Gar. The efforts of the young heroine Trilby (Kristina Nehm) to escape the inevitabilities of unemployment and teenage pregnancy are undone by the vicissitudes of small-town prejudice and her own and her family's fallibilities. While it imbues Trilby's circumstances with an exemplary and tragic significance, Beresford's film lacks the rancourous and aggressive tone of the comparable portrait of the existence of economically depressed Maoris in *Once Were Warriors* (Lee Tamahori, 1994). Trilby's paralysis echoes that of Mitch (played by Jo Kennedy), who drifts into a relationship with Rex, a petty criminal in *Tender Hooks* (Mary Callaghan, 1988). Her difficulties and disappointments are echoed in the abuse suffered by her friend Gaye at the hands of her fiancé and pimp Tony. Although the pain of the young women's relationships is rendered without sentimentality, their capacity to transcend them is also inferred, by Gaye's departure for a pecuniary marriage in America, and Mitch's humorous rebuttal of the unwelcome attentions of a 'maturer' man. By the film's end she can help to disguise Rex after his prison escape, and smile philosophically at his departure from the city and her life.

A superior rendition of formative experience, which combines the rite of passage with the Gothic and the period film, is found in *Celia* (Ann Turner, 1988). Growing up in the late 1950s, Celia Carmichael (Rebecca Smart) comprehends school rivalries, childhood fantasies and political realities as coexistent and covalent elements of her life, and does not recognise distinctions between them. She likes her next-door neighbours and their children irrespective of their communist affiliations, and similarly hates her uncle John and her cousin Stephanie because of the unjust power they exert. The centre of her world at the film's opening is her grandmother, and after the latter's death she focuses her affection on her pet rabbit Murgatroyd. Both these attachments have unenvisaged significance, in Granny's secret Left-wing sympathies and the analogy in the film's representation and Celia's mind between the Communist infiltration and rabbit infestation of Cold War Australia.

In assuming the subjective perspective of its central character, *Celia* utilises a variety of visual idioms to relate her conflation of imagination and actuality: the nightmares fueled by the reading of James H. Fassett's *The Hobyahs* overrun her feud with her father and relatives; public information films about the plague of rabbits are viewed by both conservative and radical families and their offspring during communal cinema trips; and the monochrome and the characters of film thrillers invade the aftermath of the climactic killing:

Celia's world is one of fantasy, the cinema and gang warfare ... Meanwhile the adults in her life are engaged in their own rituals of illicit affairs, hypocrisy, accusation and counter-accusation. These two worlds converge in the cinema ... As well as constructing a strong image, which conveys the mood and texture of small town, 1950s Australia, [Turner] is able to convey how, from a child's point of view, anything appearing on the big screen is as authentic (or fantastic) as anything else. Being unable to distinguish facts from fantasy is part of childhood (and in a reflexive way is also part of cinema). Adults, on the other hand, often fail to distinguish between ideology and reality (for example, Celia's mother) and some even deliberately indulge in mystification (for example, Celia's father and Uncle Bob), often to further their own interests.[11]

Concentration on Celia's perspective validates her version of events and undermines the parental (specifically male) authority which seeks to browbeat her. As such, the film's representation of the formal and experiential education which Celia receives, leading to a wisdom (and power) belying her years, becomes an inverted reflection of the rite of passage and period film models. Her obduracy in the face of injustice is rewarded with the opportunity for revenge. Killing her uncle is by extension revenge against the government he served and her vindictive father, and also encompasses revenge taken on behalf of her mother, who colludes with her daughter in concealing the crime. The narrative functions credibly as a childhood reverie carried to a logical extreme, and as an allegorical and polemical treatise outstripping the fundamentalism of *My Brilliant Career*:

Is it legitimate to talk of women revolting against the state? Celia is a cute kid with her blonde plaits and her freckles, but she is a rebel, a radical and a leader. [She] turns her dreams into realities yet Turner does not portray her as an over-imaginative child or a psychopath. Instead we are led to believe that murdering her uncle is an entirely natural outcome of the sequence of events and her mother thinks so too.[12]

The privileging of a subjective narrator, within a idiosyncratic and dysfunctional familial and social milieu, is also apparent within *Sweetie* (1989), Jane Campion's debut feature film. The voice-over narration provided by Kay begins with a childhood recollection of the favouritism her sister Dawn ('Sweetie') enjoyed, and of the morbid fear of trees which continues to afflict her in adulthood. When Dawn appears at the house Kay shares with her boyfriend Louis, her influence is condemned as disruptive by her sister. Her vivacity attracts Louis, even though she is clearly mentally unstable, but her infantile excess seems no more deranged than Kay's baleful and obsessive reserve. Kay's and Louis' relationship is stalled by her portents of doom before Dawn intrudes, and her pessimism appears no less isolating and immature than Dawn's lively puerility. Campion extends the relationships (and the responsibility) by including the sisters' parents, who are undergoing a trial separation because of the mother Flo's exasperation with the father Gordon's overindulgence of Dawn.

The peripheralisation of the characters from each other and their physical environment is relayed by the use of time-lapse photography and unbalanced and eccentric compositions. Hiding from the child next door, Kay conceals herself behind kitchen cupboards, with only her head showing above the bottom of the frame at the extreme right-hand side. Similarly Kay's and Louis' sexual impasse is illustrated by their motionless feet, on opposite sides of the bed and pushed to the extreme right of the frame. The aberration of Dawn's and Gordon's intimacy is also rendered visually. Flo's importance to Gordon is shown by the shrinking of her face, reflected in a oval hall mirror seen in the middle distance, when she leaves her husband. The self-absorption Gordon has encouraged in Dawn is seen in the exaggeration of her hands in close-up, and the associated diminution of her face in a make-up mirror, as she applies nail varnish. In noting such features alongside the weirdness of the characters and their situation, Steve Jenkins presupposes a stylistic debt to David Lynch's films.[13] However, in contrast to Lynch's depiction of violent abnormality fermenting beneath mundanity, Campion as writer-director offers an examination of oblique jealousies made manifest, private convictions grown to public embarrassments, and unremarkable family pressures exaggerated to a fatal conclusion:

> [Sweetie] is still 'Dad's real girl' and his 'princess' but he is as lost as she is in self-delusion and denial. Kay has to face her exclusion from their 'special relationship' and also her own collusion with the family's silence around it. We see her catch sight of Sweetie sponging down her father's body in the bath and we see her moment of recognition, the realisation of the family's dirty secret to which she has been privy and of which she is part.[14]

The possible interpretation of Sweetie as the symbol of Kay's repressed, disruptive side is complicated by the necessity of the former's removal by death before Kay can commit herself fully to Louis. Rather than a liberation, an exorcism of buried guilt allows Kay to move on, without the elimination of her dread of the hidden, inexorable vitality symbolised by trees.

A more prosaic but no less painful narrative of familial pressures and connections between siblings is found in *The Last Days of Chez Nous* (Gillian Armstrong, 1991). Armstrong's elucidation of individual feminine experience from *My Brilliant Career* onwards reaches a peak in this Rohmer-like tale of misjudgement and infidelity. Previously the director had considered the entrapment for the single woman contained in liberation from and commitment to children (*High Tide* (1987)), and completed a series of documentaries following the lives of three women from their teens into their twenties which explore 'female sex roles, ambitions and attitudes in an Australian working class environment'.[15] In treating the affection, tension and competition between sisters Beth and Vicky, and the latter's attraction to the former's husband Jean Paul, Armstrong delivers a concise chamber drama whose stylistic restraint matches the selective deafness, dumbness and blindness of the family members. The group's cohesion succumbs to a series of crises (Vicky's unplanned pregnancy and abortion, stifling mealtimes and parties, and the breakdown of Beth's and Jean Paul's marriage), and the affair between Vicky and Jean Paul begins when Beth is absent, attempting to patch up her relationship with her father (Bill Hunter) during a driving holiday. Ironically her sister and husband capitalise on the removal of Beth's control over the house while she strives to wear down her father's obstinacy. Resolution of one long-standing family conflict provokes another, which paradoxically also comes to represent a conclusion to unspoken strife:

> Just as in *Sweetie*, we are left with the feeling that the bond between sisters, forged as it is within the family, can be so destructive that only death (or, as in the case of Beth and Vicki, estrangement) can

allow at least one sister to flourish. There is a sense in which Beth can now become a good and real mother to [her daughter] Annie whose needs were hitherto overshadowed by the demands of Vicki, the pretend daughter.[16]

The ironic inclusion of a (trans)formative journey in *The Last Days of Chez Nous* reflects another strain of generic Australian film-making, in which the natural and human landscape and the rite of passage narrative are combined in the indigenisation of an American genre: the road movie.

Australian road movies

Given the initial polarisation of Australian film production towards the extremes of art and commerce, the appearance of Australian road movies might have been predicted in the latter category from an early stage of the revival. However, though road- and car-oriented films did appear from the mid-seventies, with the exception of the *Mad Max* trilogy they did not necessarily exhibit a purely commercial motivation in their scripting or iconography.

In the road movie, the travel undertaken by the protagonists serves as 'a metaphor for life itself', with 'freedom and social mobility' being analogous to 'physical mobility'.[17] Several Australian films reflect both the internationalisation of the national cinema in the adoption of imported generic bases, and the indigenisation of such conventional forms to suit local conditions. *Oz* (Ned Lander, 1981) transplants and modernises the narrative of *The Wizard of Oz* (Victor Fleming, 1939) while *Road Games* (Richard Franklin, 1981) employs American stars in its commercially-oriented horror narrative. However, some notable examples of early Australian road films stress entrapment and stasis rather than liberation through movement, and also address contemporary social and racial issues in the process of emphasising the futility of travel. In *Queensland* (John Ruane, 1976) and *The FJ Holden* (Michael Thornhill, 1977), the symbolic car offers no escape from the suffocation and disillusionment of modern life, in distinct contrast to the anticipated freedom of the rural highways:

The FJ Holden is a suburban road-movie in which the protagonists ... get nowhere, trapped in the maze of Sydney's western suburbs: Bankstown, Panania, Chullora. This is another essential of the Australian landscape, not one that asks through the camera to be claimed by the senses, but one which claims – or at least accommodates – the Australian heart.[18]

Against the mythologised but unknown natural landscape, the known but unfulfilling urban environment appears safe but unchallenging. Travel beyond the fringe of cities into the under-populated land constitutes a freeing, and testing of the (national) character. In *Backroads* (Phillip Noyce, 1977), a critical commentary on social structures and racial prejudices is contained within the generic format. The friendship between an archetypal white Australian (played by Bill Hunter) and his Aboriginal companion is strained by their travel through the inhospitable, sparsely-populated rural environment. The promise of liberation is sabotaged by their usage of a stolen car, with the sense of entrapment exacerbated by the film's compositions, based on images of the vacant landscape viewed through the car windows. The anticipated flight from authority is undermined by the replication of contemporary social tensions within the microcosm of the car.

In later examples, the social and cultural aspects of the road movie's significance have been advanced alongside generic innovation. *Over the Hill* (George Miller, 1992) depicts the lifestyle of an older, itinerant generation. The 'grey nomads' are travellers of retirement age who trek along the rural back roads as 'middle-class gypsies'. Alma, an American widow (Olympia Dukakis) comes to Sydney uninvited to visit her daughter. Unresolved problems in their relationship cause her to leave on an unplanned trip in a classic American car, renovated by her granddaughter's boyfriend. In the country she meets Dutchly, a divorced, retired dentist, and her experiences (participating in rituals with Aboriginal women, and exploring her own and the car's full potential) reveal the remedy for strained family relationships. However, she discovers she can no longer accept internment in the homes of her children, and returns to the road with Dutchly as her new partner. The film's conclusion, with images of their two vehicles heading towards the sunrise emphasises the transcendence and optimism offered by the motif of movement, but in this example the age and experience of the travellers alter the significance and impact of the generic format.

A more conventional and predictable example of the Australian road movie, again centred on the differences between generations, is seen in *Spider and Rose* (Bill Bennett, 1994). Brad ('Spider'), a young ambulance driver, is detailed to take Rose home to her son's farm by road on his last day before leaving the service. Her obstinacy and his resentment of this unwelcome assignment combine to make the journey intolerable for both parties, but in the course of their travel the circumstances inspiring their attitudes emerge. A year previously, Rose's husband died in a car crash, and it is the pain of being unable to help fatally injured accident victims that has disillusioned Spider. They discover other, unexpected similarities in their experiences of lean-tos in the Depression and squats by the unemployed in the present, and gradually a grudging respect grows on each side. When their ambulance crashes and Spider suffers a broken leg, Rose takes the wheel and gives him her walking stick. However, as in the case of *Over the Hill*, reaching the first destination does not complete the journey. Rose's family do not want her to live with them and plan to put her into a home. Leaving them but also turning down the offer of an alternative partnership with a widower she met *en route*, Rose sets out on the road on her own, leaving Spider to return to the city as best he can. Although the age differences between characters in these films are unusual, their narratives utilise the road movie motif of formative, symbolic travel quite conventionally. The travellers and those they meet undergo changes. Rose and Alma gain insight into their own weaknesses and mistakes, and their determination affects those with whom they travel (Spider and Dutchly). Their family crises are admitted and addressed, if not always resolved, and the freedom of the road (even for those of pensionable age) is asserted unequivocally. The opinions and experiences of one generation throw the assumptions and life style of the other into perspective, without sentimentalisation of the young or old.

An unabashed popular youth appeal is discernible in other Australian road movies, in emulation of the violence and momentum of comparable American films. *Kiss or Kill* (Bill Bennett, 1997) and *Heaven's Burning* (Craig Lahiff, 1997) depict criminal odysseys across the Australian landscape by young couples on the run from the law, but ally contemporary issues and aspects of Australian Gothic to their conventional, commercial impetus. In *Kiss or Kill*, Alan and Nicole flee from Adelaide after committing a series of robberies and acquiring an incriminating video tape. They are followed across country by detectives and an ageing football star, who is featured on the tape and fearful of blackmail. The couple's route is exposed by a trail of murder victims. The crimes may have been committed by either Alan (who cannot explain where he gets the money to finance their escape) or by Nicole (who sleepwalks and cannot account for her actions). Their suspicion of each other heightens as the chase continues. The couple's paranoia finds a graphic expression in the film's use of jump-cuts, which exaggerate the lacunae in the narrative and engender their (and the viewer's) uncertainty over events. Rather than to escape from justice, their journey becomes an attempt to overcome their distrust, arising from present circumstances and childhood traumas. In depicting headlong flight across a treacherous geographical and human environment, the film provides a Gothic endnote to the landscape cinema. The land, like the characters, preserves its anonymity and unfathomability, with the couple's limited knowledge of each other not being rectified by their journey. The city detectives eventually solve the riddle of the serial murders, but Alan and Nicole remain ignorant of the truth and of each other's defining but unrevealed secrets.

Heaven's Burning follows the doomed romance between a Japanese woman who leaves her husband and a getaway driver from a botched bank raid. Having faked her own kidnapping to leave her honeymoon hotel, Midori is subsequently taken hostage by the survivors of the gang, but Colin (Russell Crowe) kills his associates when they decide to shoot her. They go on the run from the police, Midori's husband and the survivors of the Afghan crime family that planned the robbery. While neither the Australian driver nor the errant Japanese wife intend harm, their circumstances victimise them and as they become lovers they leave a trail of shootings, robberies, fights and car chases for their pursuers to follow. The punctuation of their trip by violent episodes meets generic expectations and emphasises the couple's ultimate fate. The line of the road they follow to the coast mimics the lifeline on Midori's palm, which a fortune teller says predicts the death of a loved one. The bandages she ties around her hand to avert this fate preview the bandages she applies to Colin's hands after he is nailed to a table by the vengeful gang. He manages to free himself when Midori is threatened again, and this episode appears almost as a modern inversion of the climactic event in *A Town Like Alice*. Instead of opposing the Japanese in war and suffering crucifixion for a British woman, Colin the Australian male endures the torture on behalf of a modern Japanese woman who craves the perceived freedom of Australian citizenship. This reappraisal of national divisions in line with contemporary Australian links with Asia is seen in contrast to remarks made by Colin's father to Midori's husband, cursing him with the 'bad Karma' spawned by the Second World War. The film's caricatured portrayal of the Afghan family, whose sadism is linked explicitly to the war with the Soviet Union, is reinforced by racist remarks (referring to the 'yodelling' of the muezzin in the local mosque) made by the cops investigating the bank robbery. As such, the positive pairing of the central couple is undermined by the surrounding characters' prejudices. The unattainability of an earthly paradise of multicultural tolerance is demonstrated by the couple's fatal crash, just as their shared immolation in the flames which engulf their car confirms the film's title.

Australian road movies from the 1970s to the 1990s have foregrounded contemporary social and racial issues within an (imported) generic format. The road movie is particularised by the depiction of the local landscape, and the problematisation of individual and communal identity which recurs throughout the revival. In the most recent example, *Paperback Hero* (Anthony Bowman, 1999), constructions of masculine identity dependent on working life and sexual relationships are examined in a comedic, road movie format. It is in the cross-breeding of indigenous genres (the rite of passage and the Gothic) and imported ones (the road movie and the musical) that the keystone successes of '90s Australian cinema achieve a definitive expression of new Australian cultural and filmic identity.

Glamour, kitsch and camp

The trio of popular successes of the 1990s (*Strictly Ballroom*, *Muriel's Wedding* and *Priscilla*) were seen by local and overseas critics to inaugurate a 'new, distinctively Australian genre ... "kitsch comedy"'.[19] The three films share self-conscious narrative strategies and a playful approach to convention and expectation, but their distinctiveness lies more in innovation upon established formulae rather than the initiation of new forms. The basis for all three resides in the musical genre, with its progression through gruelling rehearsals prior to the perfection of performance. Dance routines in *Strictly Ballroom* and the lip-synch drag act in *Priscilla* advance through stages of development and exhibition for varied spectators, before the ultimate spectacle takes place in front of the intended audience. In *Muriel*, the music is present not in performance but consumption reflecting the heroine's definition of her life and identity in terms of the lyrics of pop songs.

The musical format had first been 'Australianised'[20] in *Starstruck* (Gillian Armstrong, 1982). The Hollywood narrative of MGM's star vehicles for Judy Garland and Mickey Rooney is transplanted to Sydney, where two teenagers dream of performing in the Opera House. An allusion to Marlene Dietrich's 'Hot Voodoo' number in *Blonde Venus* (Josef von Sternberg, 1932), in Jackie's (Jo Kennedy) emergence from a kangaroo costume, illustrates the film's combination of parody of and homage to the brashness of the musical. Stuart Cunningham contends that in imitating the optimism of the Hollywood musical, *Starstruck* offers a utopian vision for the success of Australian film (and culture), which conciliates the embarrassment of the Ocker films and the self-reproach of the Gothic.[21] In appropriating a superficially unsuitable 'foreign' genre, *Starstruck* recruits the positivism of utopian entertainment to the cause of individual and national wish-fulfilment.

Strictly Ballroom deploys the same motifs in a similarly knowing way, and is as susceptible to reading in terms of Richard Dyer's definition of the musical's entertainment value.[22] The film's wry manipulation of the backstage musical (velvet curtains opening at the beginning and closing at the end), the untruthful flashback (in the reminscences of yesteryear) and mimicry of documentary interviews (with each of the key characters) exemplify the affirmation and parodying of conventions and related expectations seen in *Starstruck*. It is through the juxtaposition of disparate and incongruous filmic features (slow-motion images, freeze-frames, mock-documentary and parodied Gothic), included alongside the romantic plot and its integrated musical numbers, that *Strictly Ballroom* undertakes its teasing and self-conscious rejuvenation of well-known conventions, with the audience's collusion:

Ballroom works not despite its absurdities, but because of them – and exactly the same goes for Baz Luhrmann's film ... its plot is a compendium of cliches, signalled well in advance, so that we all wait in happy complicity for the moment when Fran takes off her glasses and metamorphoses into beauty.[23]

In generic terms Scott Hastings' dancing embodies energy and spontaneity, indicative of the *bricoleur*'s improvisation rather than the professional's stale efficiency. His rebellion against the prescriptions of the Australian Dance Federation becomes an individual quest for identity beyond conformity to the group. In challenging the Gothic, patriarchal authority of Federation president Barry Fife (Bill Hunter), Scott undergoes a rite of passage which precipitates a reappraisal of his future and his family's past.

Scott's personal development encompasses appreciation of the skills (and attractiveness) of someone other than himself (Fran), and recognition that personal integrity is connected with cultural authenticity. His initial arrogance in dismissing her comments on his innovative steps prompts an angry response from Fran: her outburst sees her slip from the vernacular of Australian English into impassioned, proverbial Spanish. Similarly, Fran's grandmother insists on Scott sensing the rhythm of the dance in his heart, not his feet. The ballroom version of Paso Doble is a pale, mechanical imitation of the original dance. The authentic dance expresses personal passion and intuitive intimacy, illustrating the inseparability of cultural veracity and emotional integrity.

The limitation of the Federation's authorised steps reflects the artificiality of the emotions displayed in standardised ballroom performances. Where the genre musical celebrates community, in the unifying work of show business, in *Strictly Ballroom* the conformist community is the romantic couple's adversary. Scott's and Fran's individually-crafted dance distinguishes them from the crowd, but links them with Fran's family's Spanish roots, 'the ethnic gift of culture and style which rejuvenates Australian institutions'.[24] The transparency of the genuine feeling which inspires their performance at the Pan Pacific Championships (where they dance in love, not in competition) validates their Paso Doble emotionally as well as culturally, as a quintessential, multicultural, New Australian spectacle. Paradoxically but fittingly, this reconnects them with the dance community, as the competitors and spectators recognise 'the future of dance' in Australia and overthrow the tyranny of the Federation. The couple's triumph also reverses the humiliation of Scott's father Doug (Barry Otto) thirty years before, when Barry Fife frustrated Doug's attempts to introduce innovative dance steps, and also suggests the integration of Fran's family into wider society. The victory of the young multicultural couple over a timeworn, conservative establishment again suggests the emergence of a new, authenticated but diverse Australian-ness distinct from the patterns of the past.

Muriel Heslop's transformative experiences are also devoted to the discovery of an authentic and secure identity. Her unhappiness is attributable to the absence of cohesion and contentment in her family environment: instead of compensating for her inability to fit in with her competitive and shallow peers, members of her family corroborate society's devaluation of Muriel's intelligence, looks and prospects. Her father Bill (Bill Hunter) despises his wife and children as 'no-hopers'. He uses his authority as a local councillor for his own and his friends' benefit. His long-standing affair with beauty consultant Deidre Chambers leads to Muriel gaining a poorly-paid job as a cosmetics representative. In the parochial town of Porpoise Spit, Muriel's difference from her make-up- and marriage-obsessed peers bolsters their self-esteem even as it demolishes Muriel's. She consoles herself with wedding fantasies and the music of Abba, whose lyrics allow her to experience beauty, romance and freedom vicariously. The vacuity of the lives of Tania, Cheryl and Janine, and the unreliability of the men they chase are mollified by the certainty that no one will ask Muriel out, let alone marry her. Her desire to fit in drives her to cash her father's blank cheque in order to follow her 'friends' on holiday to Hibiscus Island, but this journey transforms her life in unexpected ways.

When she meets Rhonda, a forgotten school friend on the island, a previously unimagined alternative lifestyle opens up. Rhonda scorns Tania and her friends and attaches herself to Muriel, who she takes to be a kindred free spirit and Abba fan. However, to conform to Rhonda's expectations, Muriel fabricates a fantasy life. She tells Rhonda her holiday is a last fling before she marries, so that the trip taken in emulation of her arrogant peers becomes a hedonistic indulgence of which her new friend can approve. In effect, Muriel is still attempting to harmonise her fantasies with the standards and expectations of others: dissipation on one side and marriage on the other. Despite the apparent rebellion of going to live with Rhonda in Sydney after the holiday, instead of returning home to her father's wrath, Muriel maintains her illusion (and delusion) by letting her friend think she has jilted her husband-to-be. She embellishes her fantasy further in 'the city of brides' in the wake of Rhonda's illness. Using the story of a critically-ill mother to garner sympathy, Muriel tries on and is photographed in a series of wedding dresses. She hoards these images in an album like 'a *Madame Bovary* for the *Photo Love* generation'[25] until Rhonda discovers them.

The disillusionment felt by both characters on the revelation of Muriel's secret betrays the degree to which even Rhonda adheres to the standards of female success measured in marriage and desirability. Without a genuine admirer or Rhonda's support, Muriel determines to marry immediately as this will fend off the threat of a forced return to Porpoise Spit. It will also provide proof that she is not 'nothing'. She responds to an advertisement posted by a South African swimmer, who seeks an Australian passport through a 'greencard marriage' in order to compete in the Olympics. Since the wedding will outshine those of her friends in cost and media coverage Muriel agrees, but changes her name to 'Mariel' to distance herself from her family and her former life. David Van Arkle's obsessive desire to succeed is therefore equated to Muriel's, at the cost of Rhonda's respect.

Although she seeks to avoid entrapment as 'Muriel' in her home town, Mariel's choices have suggested the likelihood of her following her mother into ridiculed anonymity. Muriel is suspected of shoplifting when she acquires a new dress to attend Tania's wedding, and her mother Betty (Jeanie Drynan) actually commits an absent-minded theft due to the stress of her daughter's disappearance and her husband's infidelity. Identical compositions (humiliated woman in the foreground, Bill dealing with their misdemeanour in the background) link these incidents to the danger Muriel courts by defining herself via marriage. Betty's eventual suicide, covered up as a heart attack in order to get Bill off charges of corruption through a sympathy vote, alerts Mariel to the hazards of her conduct. Despite a growing affection in her marriage to David, she abandons him to return home for a showdown with her father and to rescue the wheelchair bound Rhonda from Tania. The mutually supportive female friendship supersedes marriage for its own sake and even heterosexual love. The couple's return to Sydney marks the beginning rather than the end of Muriel's brilliant career.

The title of *Muriel's Wedding* is significant since, on examination, we discern that the titular event never takes place. Muriel weds as Mariel, in a public denial of her actual identity. Mariel's wedding is styled to impress her shallow friends and to replace dowdy Muriel Heslop with exotic Mariel Van Arkle. Contentment with, rather than resignation to being Muriel at the end of her travels and experiences does not discount the possibility, but does defuse the desire, for marriage. The Abba songs which featured prominently in Muriel's consolatory fantasies (listening to 'Dancing Queen' in her room at home, insisting on 'I Do, I Do, I Do' for her entrance to the church on her wedding day) are also reduced to the stature of kitsch, popular cultural references shared in a tongue-in-cheek way by Rhonda, Muriel and the audience. Only Tania and her cronies consider retro '70s music out of place in the 1990s.

As in the case of *Strictly Ballroom*, P.J. Hogan's debut feature plays upon the expectations of a variety of popular cultural forms. The portrayal of Muriel's indolent and idiotic family 'updated a tradition of Australian storytelling centring on the antics of a 'daggy' family ... the archetypal Rudd family story retold this time in a coastal city and contemporary context.'[26] The film's ironic humour does not detract from Muriel's rite of passage towards independence and adulthood, which is couched in the terms of the soap opera and television confessional show:

Hogan plays this melodramatic stuff for laughs, using humour as a bulwark against mawkishness. But slipped into this comedy is a morality tale, suggesting the downside of psychobabble through its depiction of Muriel's self-obsession. Although we are invited to approve of Muriel's growth, and cheer along at the film's close ... her behaviour along the way suggests an underdog's potential for a blind cruelty equal to that she receives from Tania.[27]

While it exhibits some of the same kitsch comedic potential as *Strictly Ballroom*, *Muriel's Wedding* is centred in the rite of passage format. Its stress on the experience of an unpromising heroine who learns to accept herself while improving her circumstances reflects the film's qualification and 'customisation' of 'Hollywood's "feel-good" formula'.[28]

The Adventures of Priscilla, Queen of the Desert extends the motifs of personal growth allied to travel seen in *Muriel's Wedding* by adhering closely to the road movie genre. Three drag performers (two transvestites and a transsexual) journey from Sydney to Alice Springs to put on a show. Their motives for signing up for the trip vary: Bernardette (formerly Ralph, played by Terence Stamp) escapes the loneliness of bereavement; Adam (Felicia, played by soap opera star Guy Pearce) relishes the opportunity to scandalise the locals *en route*; and Tick (Mitzi, played by Hugo Weaving) responds to a hidden, personal obligation. In addition to the road movie, *Priscilla* incorporates elements of the Western (in the group's desert trek), the musical (in the rehearsals which build towards the climactic performance) and the Gothic (in the isolated and unfriendly towns through which they pass). The film's scatological and sexual humour also updates aspects of the Ocker films.[29] The film employs reflexive techniques and exploits the audience's complicity in their effects in a similar fashion to *Strictly Ballroom*, and revels in the gaudiness of camp costuming to an even greater extent than either Luhrmann's or Hogan's films. The vivid clothes, make-up and language of the trio contrast dramatically with those of the insular communities they visit. In exaggerating the difference between urban and rural characters, the trio represent a drastic departure from the stereotype of Australian masculinity perpetuated elsewhere in the national cinema:

The film relies on the spectacular and sometimes hilarious contrast between the gorgeous artifice of drag and the stark and alien landscape. Echoed by Adam's dream of climbing King's Canyon in full drag ('a cock in a frock on a rock'), Elliott dreams a movie based on the incongruous spectacle of drag culture and, by implication, gay culture, in the outback.[30]

While they encounter prejudice and hostility on their journey (which escalates from insults in Broken Hill to violence in Coober Pedy), the acquisition of the landscape through the realisation of Adam's dream represents a qualification or redefinition of the image of Australian masculinity, and national identity. The group's positive encounters in the desert with Aborigines and Bob the mechanic (Bill Hunter) are balanced by the homophobia and aggression of the predominantly male population. This criticism of the aggressively masculine stereotype is countered by Bob's characterisation as a 'gentleman'. Despite his appearance as the epitome of stoicism and self-sufficiency, Bob's likeness to the iconic bushman is undermined by his attraction to the drag queens. Cynthia, his 'mail-order' Filipino bride, suggests his susceptibility to sex tourism, and when she leaves him her accusations of sexual inadequacy are accompanied by the mocking laughter of kookaburras. The implied admonition of judging by appearances contained in the film's plot and characterisation peaks with the revelation that Tick is not only married but has a son, Benji, at Alice Springs. In attempting to assume the role of father, Tick adopts the beer-drinking masculine stereotype which has dogged the group *en route*. This uncharacteristic performance is deflated by Benji's enquiries about Tick's boyfriends and his renowned Abba impersonation.

Travelling to the geographical and metaphorical centre of the country, the trio stake a claim upon a (human and physical) landscape which seeks to repel them. The affirmation of their expedition is undermined by the acknowledgement that, once the climb and their shows are completed, they will return to the city where they belong. The declining reception of their performances (participation and enthusiasm from the Aborigines, dismissal in the face of competition from Cynthia's pornographic party piece, muted applause from the crowd at Alice Springs) runs contrary to the increasing perfection and tempo of numbers in the conventional musical, and shows that the troupe's presence in and effect on the physical and human landscape is impermanent. The differences between city and country, between communities and sexualities are registered, with the hope rather than the certainty of conversion or tolerance. However, each side has affected the other, as is suggested by the vestiges of feathered costumes left in the desert, and the incorporation of indigenous details (such as the costumes resembling frilled lizards) in the final performance. The subdued response to their act reflects the road movie truism that experiences on the road are more important than the motivation or destination of the journey.

The Western's sense of nationhood and the musical's utopian tone form the basis of *Priscilla*'s criticism of social formations and prejudices. The unique landscape, and the troupe's odyssey across it, are crucial to the film's optimistic but problematic unification of gay and straight, male and female, bisexual and transsexual characteristics in multicultural Australia. The characterisation of the protagonists is central to such analysis:

Bold drag queens have always been the revolutionaries of the gay movement: disfranchised, near the bottom of any community's pecking order (including their own), but empowered by lessons of nonattachment [sic] and the realisation that they stand with those who have the least to lose in their fight against social injustice.[31]

Although the advocation of tolerance is qualified by the retreat to the safety of Sydney (home of the Gay and Lesbian Mardi Gras), Pamela Robertson sees the championing of the drag queens as obscuring other existing prejudices. Prevalent social inequalities are oversimplified or reiterated. The token inclusion of Aborigines, the humiliation of Shirl in Broken Hill and demonisation of Cynthia reveal the endurance of other forms of chauvinism:

The joke [against Shirley] fulfils the stereotype of gay male misogyny by asserting that drag queens and transsexuals are more appealing than biological women ... If Shirley represents failed femininity as sexual lack, Cynthia represents an excess that also marks her as failure. Whereas the drag act parodies female stereotypes, Cynthia seemingly inhabits them. Her act appears to represent her true self as genuinely perverse ... by privileging the Aboriginal people, and portraying them as happy singing and dancing natives, naturally and automatically tolerant, the film ultimately represents a stereotype as egregious as the grotesque Filipino. The Aboriginal characters are not so much united with the white drag queens but existing *for* them.[32]

The racial and sexual characterisation of Cynthia 'reveals current white male alarm over shifting ethnicities of Australia'.[33] The film's advancement of one peripheralised group (the drag queens, even though they themselves represent particular definitions of gender and sexuality which the film conflates) is at the expense of the reaffirmation of other forms of racial and sexual prejudice. Arguably its portrayal of gayness and ostracism is defused and centred, with the drag queens and their *risqué*, Ockerish comedy restating conservative principles (the couple formed by Bernardette and Bob, Tick's assumption of fatherhood, and the containment of gayness through the withdrawal to the enclave of Sydney). The perception of sanitised gayness and lesbian subtexts to *Muriel's Wedding* (in which the heroine's intimate conversation with Rhonda on holiday is the 'one really erotic scene'[34]), and *Strictly Ballroom* (in which, despite the elevation of Paul Mercurio as a gay pin-up, Scott is 'saved' from the effeminate artificiality of ballroom by the heterosexuality of authentic dance'[35]), strengthen such criticisms. The mainstreaming of non-heterosexuality in concert with retrospective, kitsch culture and the spectacle of 'vestigial or assimilated camp'[36] excess unites these three films, suggesting a conservative contrivance to their optimistic, liberal, multicultural narratives of personal transformation:

Because gay men have been obliged by the homophobic elision of sexuality and gender identity to pay critical attention to gender, camp has emerged as a radical paradigm within which gender becomes artificial and open to deconstruction ... [However] camp is less a product of access to the machinery of representation and more a product of *compromised* access to that machinery.[37]

Conclusion

One of the great achievements of the past thirty years has been the remaking of Australian society into one where liberal values (and even many of those once dismissed as impossibly radical) hold sway. We live in a society where tens of thousands of people will take to the streets to protest against racism, to oppose war, to defend trade unions, to celebrate lifestyles.[38]

The Australian cinema's signal successes of the 1990s have attained consistent international acclaim, through the combination of local and imported materials. At home (with *Strictly Ballroom* becoming the highest grossing Australian film of 1992, and *Muriel's Wedding* receiving the 1994 AFI award for Best Feature Film) and abroad (with *Muriel*, *Strictly Ballroom* and *Priscilla* being screened at Cannes, *Bad Boy Bubby* winning four awards at the Venice Film Festival and *Shine* garnering seven Academy Award nominations[39]), a second renaissance of Australian film has been welcomed with critical and commercial rewards. The 'internationalisation' of Australian filmmaking has been achieved through a synthesis of American popular genres (the musical, the road movie) and Australian ones (the Gothic, the rite of passage) and the articulation of nationally-specific content (debates on multiculturalism, masculinity, authority and identity). Inevitably in such popular forms, the rationalisation of serious questions is simplified if not simplistic, optimistic if not utopian, but the treatment of pertinent contemporary issues by the national film industry in entertainment films with wide appeal represents an advance over the unadventurous recapitulation of colonial history. Addressing such issues in feature films follows on from the commitment to wider cultural and ethnic representation on national television, with the inauguration of the SBS (Special Broadcasting Service) channel in 1980.[40] The commercial imperatives of AFFC funding (behind films like *Priscilla*, *Chez Nous*, *Death in Brunswick*, *Bad Boy Bubby*, *Strictly Ballroom*, *Heaven's Burning* and *Sirens*) have facilitated the emergence of a successful and creditable popular cinematic product, which nonetheless contains pertinent criticisms of relevant, contemporary social issues.

Significantly, the individual or communal rite of passage remains central to Australian narrative. Even the imported mainstream genres concentrate on peripheralised identities, distinguished by age, gender, race and sexuality. The rite of passage appears to be *the* Australian genre, recurring through and cross-fertilising the Gothic, the male ensemble, the 'female ensemble' such as *The Last Days of Chez Nous* or *Island* (Paul Cox, 1989), the period film and the recent quirky comedies. As surrogates of the nation overcoming colonial inferiority and attaining nationhood, the tribulations of troubled, innocent, fallible and impressionable youth searching for meaning and identity appear consistently, tackling social and historical forces with varying conviction and success. Within the family, even grown-up and middle-aged children (Carl in *Death in Brunswick*, Scott in *Strictly Ballroom*, Stan in *Stan and George's New Life* (Brian McKenzie, 1992)) struggle to escape from a stifling but ageing authority.

In comparison with the treatment of diversity and tolerance seen in AFFC-funded successes like *Strictly Ballroom*, *Muriel's Wedding* and *Priscilla*, *Dead Letter Office* (John Ruane, 1998) provides a low-key, slow-paced rite of passage narrative which, like *Deadly*'s handling of race issues, foregrounds multiculturalism in the family context. Alice (Miranda Otto) joins the Dead Letter Office, the receptacle for all undeliverable mail, in the hope of tracing her father. The prologue follows the progress of her letters written in childhood, which were collected in the Office when the intended recipient proved untraceable. Alice hopes her employment there will help her to track down her father. Her life has reached an impasse because of her unacknowledged and unreciprocated love, and she believes that discovering his whereabouts will give her life a purpose.

At work she meets a range of characters similarly adrift, waiting for the threatened cuts in the postal service which will mean the closure of the Office. The only source of motivation within the Office's futile activity is its manager Frank (George Delhoyo), a Chilean immigrant whose family was destroyed during the military dictatorship. His emigration to Australia was unplanned, and his avoidance of other refugees leaves him bereft of human contact outside work. The similarity of Alice's and Frank's positions prefigures their mutual attraction. Alice's reliance on Frank's dedication to track down her father is balanced by his example inspiring her to intervene in other cases of personal anguish which the Office's letters contain. However, her naivety leads her to misjudge the case of an Argentinian woman, and her ignorance of Frank's background frustrates their embryonic relationship. By the time Frank finds her father, Alice has begun to learn, studying Chile's contemporary history in order to understand him. Her eventual meeting with her father (Barry Otto) reveals that she has outgrown him, having found an emotional partner and a life purpose in Frank.

While it contains examples of eccentricity and quirky humour, Ruane's film evinces both an emotional authenticity and a structured and satisfying narrative. The Office is at once a concrete and metaphorical environment, embodying a successfully concluded quest amidst innumerable disappointments. The fulfilment of Frank's and Alice's relationship is affecting, with its predictability in plot terms modified by their differences in age, experience and ethnicity. At the end the couple depart from the city to view the mountains (and compare them with those in Frank's home country), and again a real journey succeeds a psychological one. Without the exaggeration of horror, camp or kitsch sensibilities, *Dead Letter Office* articulates a personal and national development. Alice seeks a vanished parent, driven by the childish faith that he holds an answer for her. A bereaved father from another country takes the place of her biological parent, in writing her the letter she has dreamed of receiving and by loving her as an adult. A mixed couple emerges from the grief of two individuals. The real father, and the defunct office are irrelevant to their new multicultural (republican?) future. While not approaching other AFFC-funded productions in box office success, *Dead Letter Office* epitomises the hybridity of Australian generic patterns developed since 1970, and the consistent subject matter of the revival: personal, communal and national identity.

Notes

1 Tom O'Regan, *Australian National Cinema* (London, Routledge, 1994), p. 195.

2 Ibid., p. 54.

3 Elizabeth Jacka, The Media Industries: Film, in Stuart Cunningham and Graeme Turner (eds), *The Media in Australia: Industries, Texts, Audiences* (St Leonards, Allen & Unwin, 1993), p. 84.

4 Australian Film Finance Corporation Pty Ltd, Funding Guidelines October 1992, p. 2.

5 Ibid., pp. 3–4.

6 Elizabeth Jacka, The Production Process: Film, in Cunningham and Turner (eds) (1993), p. 191.

7 Kim Newman, *Death in Brunswick*, *Sight and Sound* vol. 1 no. 10 (1992), pp. 42–3 (p. 43).

8 Jonathan Romney, *Proof*, *Sight and Sound* vol. 1 no. 8 (1991) pp. 48–9 (p. 49).

9 Ibid.

10 Philip Kemp, *Bad Boy Bubby*, *Sight and Sound* vol. 4 no. 11 (1994), pp. 39–40 (p. 40).

11 Jocelyn Robinson and Beverley Zalcock, *Girls' Own Stories: Australian and New Zealand Women's Films* (London, Scarlet Press, 1997), pp. 64–5.

12 Jill Forbes, *Celia*, *Monthly Film Bulletin* vol. 57 no. 673 (1990), pp. 63–4 (p. 64).

13 Steve Jenkins, *Sweetie*, *Monthly Film Bulletin* vol. 57 no. 676 (1990), pp. 142–3 (p. 143).

14 Robinson and Zalcock (1997), p. 78.

15 Mark Mordue, Homeward Bound: Interview with Gillian Armstrong, *Sight and Sound* vol. 58 no. 4 (1989), pp. 270–2 (p. 270).

16 Robinson and Zalcock (1997), p. 85.

17 Ron Eyerman and Orvar Lofgren, Romancing the Road: Road Movies and Images of Mobility, *Theory, Culture and Society* vol. 12 no. 1 (1995), pp. 53–79 (pp. 54–5).

18 Susan Dermody and Elizabeth Jacka, *The Screening of Australia Vol. II: Anatomy of a National Cinema* (Sydney, Currency, 1988a), p. 119.

19 Adrian Martin, More Than Muriel, *Sight and Sound* vol. 5 no. 6 (1995), pp. 30–2 (p. 30).

20 Stuart Cunningham, Hollywood Genres, Australian Movies, in Albert Moran and Tom O'Regan (eds), *An Australian Film Reader* (Sydney, Currency, 1985), p. 237.

21 Ibid., p. 239.

22 Richard Dyer, Entertainment and Utopia, *Movie* no. 24 (1977), pp. 2– 13 (pp. 4–5).

23 Philip Kemp, *Strictly Ballroom*, *Sight and Sound* vol. 2 no. 6 (1992), p. 56.

24 O'Regan (1994), p. 310.

25 Robert Yates, *Muriel's Wedding*, *Sight and Sound* vol. 5 no. 4 (1995), p. 49.

26 O'Regan (1994), p. 39.

27 Yates (1995), p. 49.

28 Martin (1995), p. 32.

29 Susan Barber, *The Adventures of Priscilla, Queen of the Desert*, *Film Quarterly* vol. 50 no. 2 (1996–97), pp. 41–5 (pp. 41–2).

30 Pamela Robertson, Home and Away: Friends of Dorothy on the Road in Oz, in Steven Cohan and Ina Rae Hark (eds), *The Road Movie Book* (London, Routledge, 1997), p. 276.

31 Mark Thompson, Children of Paradise: A Brief History of Queens, in Corey K. Creekmuir and Alexander Doty (eds), *Out in Culture: Gay, Lesbian and Queer Essays on Popular Culture* (London, Cassell, 1995), p. 451.

32 Robertson (1997), pp. 278–80.

33 Barber (1996–97), p. 44.

34 O'Regan (1994), p. 272.

35 Tamsin Wilton, On Not Being Lady Macbeth: Some (Troubled) Thoughts on Lesbian Spectatorship, in Tamsin Wilton (ed.), *Immortal, Invisible: Lesbians and the Moving Image* (London, Routledge, 1995), pp. 153–5.

36 Ibid., p. 152.

37 Ibid., p. 145.

38 Graham Willett, Minorities Can Win: The Gay Movement, the Left and the Transformation of Australian Society, *Overland* no. 149 (1997), pp. 64–8 (p. 68).

39 Information from *Australian Directors: A Quick Reference Guide*, published by the Australian Film Commission, April 1999.

40 See Stuart Cunningham, Television, in Cunningham and Turner (eds) (1993), pp. 20–6. See also Craig Brown, Ethnic Stereotypes in Television, *Cinema Papers* 87 (1992), pp. 54–6, for discussion of representation of cultural diversity within Australian broadcasting.

Conclusion

In the beginning (the late 1960s) when the desire for an Australian cinema began to be voiced actively, the project was basically anti-cultural imperialist. To be sure, some of the groups voicing anti-imperialist sentiments were doing so opportunistically, with secret dreams of a 'Hollywood-south'; but this at least was the argument which was supposed to justify government subsidisation. The whole project then surely included the notion of a cinema capable of challenging existing film conventions, existing audience viewing patterns and to offer films which illuminated, criticised and analysed Australian culture and history, and those of other societies as well – particularly the ones which had traditionally provided the greater parts of Australia's cultural material.[1]

The recreation of the Australian film industry in the 1970s, and its subsequent survival on economic as well as aesthetic terms, have been inseparable from debate over sources of finance. Governmental support and public funding of the first years of indigenous production ensured completion and exhibition of the early films in a less than hospitable environment. Such high profile assistance was itself an integral part of the cultural project the cinematic renaissance represented, and it has been paralleled by contemporary and subsequent initiatives in Britain and other filmmaking countries. The value of a national cinematic enterprise appears as a given, of equal stature and importance as the perceived cultural and commercial strength of the opposition:

Even a cursory examination of media history reveals that no country in the Western world, other than the US, has sustained a film and television industry without some sort of regulation or other measures designed to support it.[2]

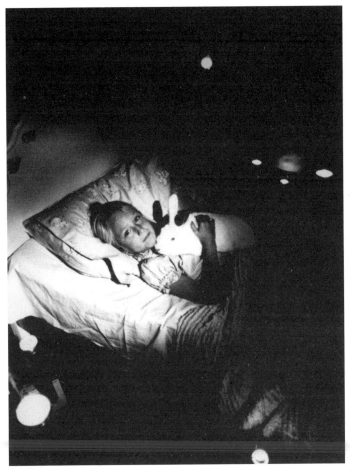

6 *Celia*

However, assistance was seen to rely increasingly on approval of cultural value, irrespective of artistic worth or true representativeness. The reception and encouragement of the period film cycle has been taken as evidence of a regimentation of treatment in the service of a primary political objective: to define and broadcast an expedient, respectable and marketable form of Australian identity at a crucial moment in the development of national consciousness. It is to the credit of the emergent filmmakers and the diversity of their individual work that alternatives, opposites and challenges to the stated or unstated rubric for Australian cinema have continued to appear. The evolution of home-grown genres, which adapt or hybridise existing narrative or iconographic patterns or emulate conventional forms without modification, has been central to commercial and art film aspirations in Australian filmmaking, and to conservative and radical readings of the resultant film texts.

Having been proposed by lobbyists in journals and written into being via governmental legislation, the Australian film industry has been subjected to concerted critical attention ever since. It is arguable that the Australian cinema has had as vital existence on paper as it has on film: 'The Australian film industry is not only the least productive in the world; it is also, in a sense, the most written about.'[3] In addition to being the most 'written about', it has also been the most frequently written *off*, with exaggerated reports of its demise in the 1920s, 1950s and 1980s. Again, available sources of funding had an impact on the orientation and critical reception of films made in the 1980s:

> Tax concessions made possible high budget Australian themed films like *Mad Max III: Beyond Thunderdome* (Dr Miller and Ogilvie 1985) and *Crocodile Dundee*; in their absence in the 1990s, high budget films became internationally themed, as in Chris Noonan's *Babe* (1995).[4]

Indirect governmental support came in the form of tax concessions to film investors (the '10BA' scheme of tax relief which operated between 1981 and 1988). In the wake of the commercial and artistic successes garnered by Australian films in the first decade and a half of the revival, dissatisfaction with the industry's goals and disappointment in its products became apparent:

> Received opinion in the industry and the film community itself is now that the feature film industry is a disaster ... by most people's standards the period 1984-88 is not one we can be 'proud' of in the feature film. The Australian cinema has lost its way.[5]

Yet the criteria for 'disasters' in the feature category are as questionable as those for success. The preceding decade witnessed the 'failure' of certain Gothic films on the same narrative and melodramatic terms which were the basis for the 'successes' of *The Man from Snowy River* and *Crocodile Dundee*. Susan Dermody and Elizabeth Jacka also note the commercial failure of *Melvin, Son of Alvin* (John Eastway, 1984) and *Razorback* (Russell Mulcahy, 1984). These films sought to recapture the success of the first Ocker comedies and Gothic films, but both failed to find an audience despite, in the case of *Razorback*, being pre-sold to and re-edited by Warner Brothers.[6] Such unrewarding deference to American finance, conventions and demands has been an abiding feature of commercial production, and this connects with the inevitable exodus of Australian (and New Zealand) filmmakers to Hollywood during the 1980s. The first generations of notable directors and creative personnel from both countries were tempted to pursue their careers across the Pacific, and the majority have never returned to filmmaking at home. The Hollywood films of Bruce Beresford, Fred Schepisi and Phillip Noyce have enjoyed a variable critical reception. After the revival landmark of *Breaker Morant*,[7] Beresford's films have ranged from the disastrous (*King David*, (1985)) to the profitable (*Driving Miss Daisy*, (1989)) to the merely competent (*Rich in Love* (1992)). Schepisi's output has included work in the UK and Japan, and maintained a consistent craftsmanship and commitment. In being recruited to direct high-profile star vehicles and big budget entertainment films, Phillip Noyce has moved the furthest from the political as well as aesthetic standpoint of his previous work. The simplicity of *Dead Calm* (1989), the sensationalism of *Sliver* (1993) and the reactionary perspective of *Patriot Games* (1992) and *Clear and Present Danger* (1994) seem far removed from the social criticism of *Newsfront* (1979) and *Heatwave* (1982).[8] The New Zealand directors Roger Donaldson and Geoff Murphy have also become subsumed within the American film industry, and the originality and personality of their work has declined as a result. Their countrymen Peter Jackson and Vincent Ward seem, so far at least, to have been able to follow up their successes within their national cinema with unconventional and individual films funded from or made overseas. Peter Weir's productions in America have, by comparison, consolidated his reputation as a gifted and intuitive filmmaker, whose successes (*Witness* (1985), *Dead Poets Society* (1989) and *The Truman Show* (1998)) have proved popular with audiences and critics and garnered numerous Oscar nominations. Weir's films continue to revise Hollywood genres and to provide a critique of Western (American) society. His best film in this regard, and the closest in tone and detail to his Australian work, is the undervalued *Fearless* (1994). Many other filmmakers, including John Duigan, Baz Luhrmann (who, through the success of *Strictly Ballroom*, has enjoyed a preferential contract with 20th Century-Fox to write, direct and produce his own films), Dr George Miller, Simon Wincer and Philippe Mora, have also worked partly or entirely in the US after early successes in Australia.

The female directors Gillian Armstrong, Jane Campion and Jocelyn Moorhouse have also pursued projects in America, which often appear to be sanitised versions of their earlier Australian work. Armstrong may have been attracted to the film adaptation of *Little Women* (1994) because of its similarity to *My Brilliant Career*, but the American film's treatment of family life and marriage are distinctly different from the Australian film's trenchant criticism. Moorhouse followed *Proof* with *How to Make an American Quilt* (1995), which avoided cliché and subverted its own soap-operatic narrative. Rather than concentrating on the doubts of a young woman on the verge of marriage, the film provides insights to the disappointments and losses of the women of an older generation who come together to sew her traditional matrimonial quilt. The integration of each individual's recollections is reminiscent of but superior to the format adopted in *The Company of Strangers* (Cynthia Scott, 1990). The certainty of the marriage being a success (and the likelihood of the wedding even taking place) are sufficiently undercut during the film's progression to suggest that perceptions of some key American institutions (marriage and melodramatic narrative) have been reworked to telling effect. The tone of Jane Campion's articulation of female experience has altered from black comedic (*Sweetie* (1989)) to biographical (*An Angel at My Table* (1990)) to novelistic (*The Piano* (1993), *The Portrait of a Lady* (1996)). The demands of mainstream Hollywood production have reduced the tendency towards episodic and deliberately unstructured narrative technique which had previously characterised her work, but in so doing have also removed some depth and discernment from the observation of character. The capacity for criticism of or divergence from mainstream filmmaking within the American films made by Australasian directors has, therefore, varied greatly, in relation to their personalities and opportunities.

Commercialism at home is as controversial an issue as the 'talent drain' abroad. John Hinde has argued that the Ocker comedy represented the original and authentic Australian cinema, and that failure to repeat and capitalise on its success in the 1970s has produced an unprofitable, cultural cinema aimed more at the international rather than local audience.[9] The vehement critical reaction against the Ocker and sex comedies was a crucial moment in deciding what the new Australian cinema was to be, if only by determining what it should *not* be. The danger of these films enshrining rather than satirising perceptions of Australian-ness (with recognition rather than repulsion being the basis of their success with local audiences[10]) precluded their perpetuation. If the particular subject matter proved unacceptable, the principle of generic filmmaking did not, and the inception of indigenous conventionalised forms has been central to subsequent developments. However, in some ways the popular demand has followed rather than preceded repetitious or formulaic production. The Gothic emerged at the same time as the Ocker films, and yet it has outlasted them as a characteristic Australian tone in many later films. The financial encouragement of the period film cycle may have been instrumental in the heritage cinema ethos adopted subsequently by the popular, uncontentious television mini-series. Films from the early 1990s onwards (such as *Muriel's Wedding*) have institutionalised the entertaining eccentricity and trademark 'quirkiness' of Australian filmmaking which now appears equally restrictive.

The development of indigenous genres or conventions, recognisable for home audiences and not inaccessible to those abroad, is certainly preferable to the unimaginative mimicry of American models. However, the nature of Hollywood filmmaking has also moved away from the patterns of plot and causality enshrined in the classical era. The difficulty of classifying contemporary trends filmically as well as nationally is acute, especially in those countries subject to American influences. While accepting that 'even a British viewer is a cultural tourist in a Merchant-Ivory film', Nick Roddick has criticised the assimilation of fashions and styles from other media into recent feature films. In seeking to appeal to a youth audience, young British filmmakers have adopted:

a style that will be recognizable to that audience: the spot-welded style of modern American movies rather than the seamless one of classic Hollywood ... the influence of music videos goes without saying ... *Shopping, Beyond Bedlam* and [*Welcome to the*] *Terrordome* set action and atmosphere above motivation, camera movements before characterisation. As in *Lethal Weapon* and *Basic Instinct*, impact is all.[11]

Such stylistic features are representative of a cross-over between media forms, and are not indicative of experimentation in the medium of film itself. That the British films listed by Roddick were equally unpopular with critics and audiences underlines the short-sightedness of following rather than establishing cinematic trends. If the Australian cinema has not been as instrumental in the further development of film form as some critics may have hoped,[12] it has been able to discuss national identity and cultural influences through the revision and subversion of existing generic forms. In this respect, a close resemblance between the 'colonised' Canadian cinema and the Australian film industry becomes discernible, as both use the generic vocabulary of Hollywood to articulate difference and criticise cultural imperialism. The subversion of genre is central to the definition of national character:

The reliance on established genres provides a general security blanket: the producer knows what he or she is investing in, the distributor has an 'angle' to exploit, the director knows that the film will find an audience, and the audience knows what to expect and how to respond. This sense of security is precisely what is lacking, almost by definition, in the more traditional (progressive?) Canadian cinema that explores (often painfully) the uncertainties of Canadian experience.[13]

The groups of films addressed in this book have been categorised by critics or have aligned themselves with generic patterns, in response to their maker's intentions and their audience's expectations. Stereotypical representations of Australian masculinity such as those found in *The Overlanders*, *They're A Weird Mob* and *Crocodile Dundee* strive to designate the white, classless, individualistic male as the archetypal Australian, defined strictly by or in relation to outsiders. The natural landscape is the male's habitat and is also the crucible for the stoical and self-reliant aspects of national character which he incarnates. The AFC genre institutionalises Australian-ness in relation to romantic pastoral ideals (as in *The Man from Snowy River*), or an uncomplicated distillation of colonial, cultural heritage. The Australian Gothic also defines Australian characteristics in relation to the features of the natural, rural landscape, but perceives the same environmental influences as unremittingly negative (as in *Wake in Fright*, *Shame*, and *The Cars That Ate Paris*). The only qualification of this might be that the human environment (the social construct in either the rural or urban setting) is conceived as vitiated or perverse in itself (as in *Summerfield* and *Heatwave*), and that geographical isolation (of the rural communities, the coastal cities and the island continent itself) merely reveals inherent characteristics. This caveat allows the incorporation of period films which embody a Gothic criticism of establishment authority and its relationship with the colonial past (such as *Picnic at Hanging Rock* or *The Getting of Wisdom*). The male ensemble films represent an extension to the images of masculinity established in the first group and a codicil to the period film's depiction of female experience. National character is explored through communal activities undertaken by composite heroes, with the stereotypical characteristics validated by their portrayal across and incarnation by groups rather than emblematic individuals. The groups' frequent involvement in historical events of national and international importance again serves to define Australian-ness almost by default, in relation to other countries. The representativeness of groups and individuals, and their growing awareness of colonial and historical realities, links the male ensemble and the period cycle with the rite of passage films. The gradual understanding or dramatic revelation of injustice and the compromises of adulthood which the rite of passage films (such as *The Year My Voice Broke*) contain are analogous to the growth of national consciousness and identity encapsulated in historically-based male ensemble pieces (like *Breaker Morant* and *The Odd Angry Shot*). From such an analysis it becomes clear that it is not only the development of indigenous genres which indicates a burgeoning national and filmic culture, but also the motifs, continuities and conventions within those genres which provide insight into contemporary concepts of national identity. The 'aesthetic processes' of the national cinema have both served and exposed film's 'ideological function', and engaged with the prevalent social and political realities. From inside and outside Australia, the advent of indigenous genres has punctuated specific periods of production and assisted in the recognition of the national cinema as a broad 'Australian' genre identified by its consistencies of cast, theme, narration and *mise-en-scène*. However, for a narrow production base spawning limited numbers of high-profile successes, the generic perception of Australian film production becomes more forcefully instilled:

Generic understandings of Australian cinema are probably inevitable because of the circumstances of their viewing. For the general audience Australian titles might optimistically make up one in ten cinema titles viewed, one in twenty or so video titles viewed ... The audience notes the Australian setting, *mise-en-scène*, actors (known and marked as Australian) and publicity (if a success) this noting of Australianness provides sufficient materials to create a generic sense of Australian cinema, no matter what the differences are among films.[14]

This does not devalue the analysis of generic characteristics and individual texts sub-dividing the Australian national cinema. Exceptions are too numerous and significant to any definition of the national 'genre' (such as tendencies towards meandering narrative, the disappointment of expectation, a masculine emphasis, and an anti-authoritarian stance) to sustain the generalisation. Rather, understanding the use made of specific genres and their tropes informs the examination of Australian filmmaking. The science fiction, horror and fantasy bases of the Gothic have been dismissed in the past as exploitative genres aimed at adolescent audiences. However, the Australian Gothic embodies a serious critique of establishment authority and raises objections to accepted and pervasive social forms. Period films which ratify the colonial cultural heritage on a superficial level, on closer inspection can be seen to ridicule the imposition of outmoded, imported cultural forms. Their abandonment in the contemporary sphere is sought through their portrayal as idiosyncrasies or irrelevances in representations of the past. The male ensemble and the rite of passage treat personal and national definitions of self-hood as equally problematic, and equally necessary. Representations of Australians in war become the rites of passage for mature males, re-configuring national maturity through the loss of innocence. The recurrent motif of birth or rebirth out of death (in films as diverse as *Ground Zero, Georgia, Gallipoli, Mad Max* and *Muriel's Wedding*) recognises the struggle towards realisation, personally and nationally, as a traumatic inevitability. It is noticeable that later films attempt the re-definition of Australian-ness (or rather the definition of New Australians and a new kind of Australian-ness) through recourse to the revision of imported and indigenous genres: the Gothic in *Proof, Death in Brunswick* and *Welcome to Woop Woop* (Stephan Elliott, 1997); the rite of passage in *Muriel's Wedding* and *Dead Letter Office*; the musical and the Gothic in *Strictly Ballroom* and *The Adventures of Priscilla, Queen of the Desert*. Far from advocating conformity, demanding consistency or championing communality, the evolution of film genres represents a reinforcement of and parallel to the formulation of national identity:

Nations, like genres, are born through a process that does not disappear with that birth. The imagining of community, like the genrification process, always operates dialectically, through the transformation of an already existing community/genre.[15]

Generic revision and hybridisation are crucial to the Australian cinema and to national identity, in furnishing the idiomatic forms which facilitate popular reception, elucidate Australian culture and character, and criticise the colonial and neo-colonial influences on Australian societal development.

The cohort of Australian actors who have performed in local productions since the revival and incarnated the variations on nationality they have proposed are an equally significant factor in the development and success of the new national cinema. Certain (male) stars, in conjunction with and inseparable from specific dramatic personae and filmic texts, have been recognised as emblematic national types. The laconic bushman of pioneer legend and formative literature was personified on the screen by Chips Rafferty, and subsequent Australian film heroes have evolved from this archetype. Individuality, resourcefulness, reticence and wry humour remain crucial characteristics of Australian masculinity as represented in the cinema by Jack Thompson, Bryan Brown, Mel Gibson and Paul Hogan. However, tinges of melancholy and defeatism also afflict the larrikin, whose belligerence towards authority is the clearest admission of inferiority. An older generation of male actors, such as Bill Kerr, Bill Hunter and John Meillon have offered both positive and negative images of conservative masculinity and patriarchal control. Bill Hunter's roles in some of the most successful films of the 1990s (*The Last Days of Chez Nous*, *Strictly Ballroom*, *Muriel's Wedding*, and *The Adventures of Priscilla, Queen of the Desert*) reflect this range, with the self-centred and destructive fathers and father-figures of the first films being succeeded by the unexpected re-orientation of Outback masculinity effected by his performance in *Priscilla*. The invalid, parodied authority his characters represent in *Strictly Ballroom* and *Muriel's Wedding* is duly overthrown, in contrast to the benevolent but doomed figures, representative of the nation, which Hunter played in 1980s films such as *Newsfront* and *Gallipoli*:

The avuncular Major Barton ... actually renounces his authority in the suicidal last attack; and declaring that he will not ask his men to do anything he would not do himself, he dies with them. So that the only recommended authority is, paradoxically, an egalitarian one.[16]

Notions of noble sacrifice and national victimhood lying behind the characterisation of the 'Aussie Battler' have been extended by portraits of youthful weakness and male uncertainty in recent films. The physical and emotional vulnerability suggested by Hugo Weaving's performances (in *Proof* and *Priscilla*) is distinct from images of capable and undemonstrative males in the same and other films. The taciturn, potentially violent, alienated and ill-fated characters played by Russell Crowe (in *Romper Stomper* and *Heaven's Burning*) appear as descendants of Max transposed to contemporary settings. The ubiquity of Noah Taylor, portraying insecure, loquacious teenagers in *The Year My Voice Broke*, *Flirting*, *Secrets* and *Shine*, provides more examples of voluble but vulnerable males hampered as much by their nationality as their age and circumstances. Barry Otto's incarnation of the pantaloon figure (in *Bliss*, *Strictly Ballroom*, *Kiss or Kill* and *Dead Letter Office*) suggests another variant on the humiliated and powerless Australian male, but adds personal and enigmatic depth to the melancholic humour of defeat and disappointment. Within the abidingly masculine cinema, female roles continue to be circumscribed, but Judy Davis' pigeon-holing in roles as a feminist and non-conformist produces female characters whose strength represents an equality with and a threat to masculinity. After her appearances in films of the revival, she has gone on to perform in films by David Cronenberg and Woody Allen. The downtrodden female, disadvantaged in work and marriage, has been played by Jeanie Drynan from *Don's Party* to *Cappuccino* to *Muriel's Wedding*.

Another prominent consistency within the films made in Australia since the revival is the number of narratives which turn on or are resolved by the timely or untimely revelation of a secret. While the discovery of hidden and unpalatable truth is a central feature of Gothic films, examples of the 'dark secret' can be found in all the generic categories. Within the Australian Gothic the rural town is characterised as the repository of dreadful, unacknowledged truth: Paris' economy of horror in *Cars*; adultery and racism leading to murder in *Deadly*; personal and communal sexual secrets in *Summerfield*, *Secrets* and *The Year My Voice Broke*; and the desolation of rural existence itself in *Wake in Fright*. The secrets of certain central characters have varying sources and repercussions. Sexual repression and release lie behind the economy with the truth seen in *Sirens* and *Golden Braid*. Adultery, incest and abortion incite judgement from the natural landscape or supernatural agencies in *Long Weekend*, *Bliss* and *Incident at Raven's Gate*. Relationships threatened by racial prejudice are kept secret in *Death in Brunswick* and *Nirvana Street Murder*.

Secrets dividing or shared by parents and offspring characterise *Celia* (the mother's complicity in the daughter's crime) and *Death in Brunswick* (the mother's withholding of the son's inheritance). Ignorance of a partner's past characterises the relationships in *Kiss or Kill*, *Spider and Rose* and *Heaven's Burning*. The denial or concealment of marriage and parenthood, and the resultant, unacknowledged loss connects *Georgia*, *Dead Letter Office* and *The Adventures of Priscilla, Queen of the Desert*. The secret of the sand in the tanker allows Max to redefine himself as a hero, but the secret album of fake wedding photos epitomises Muriel's inability to accept herself as she is. Within portrayals of institutions, the secrecy of establishment control (*Homesdale*), unstated political agendas (*Ground Zero*) and the pervasive authority of covert and conservative forces (*Between Wars* and *The Everlasting Secret Family*) have been explored in films of the revival. Deliberate obfuscation and secrecy are revealed as the iniquities of capitalism in *Heatwave* and *Bliss*. Class-based authority is reasserted by the planting of evidence in *Heatwave* and *The Plumber*. Destructive competitiveness and spiteful vendettas precipitate self-perpetuating lies in *The Club* and *Strictly Ballroom*. However, the entirety of Western (and Australian) civilisation is undermined by the re-discovery of atavistic beliefs and behaviour in *Walkabout* and *The Last Wave*, in which the secret of tribal existence is buried beneath the modern city. The hiding of the world from the protagonist, or of the protagonist from the world features in *Proof*, *Shine*, and *Bad Boy Bubby*, and also appears in *The Truman Show*.

The difficulty remains of how to interpret this remarkable consistency across many years and examples of Australian filmmaking. Secrecy, guilt, deceit and disavowal provide the basis for many narratives and the motivation for numerous individual characters, and must therefore connect with an innate Australian quality of perspective or identity. In the cases of films addressing the treatment of the landscape and Aboriginal population, the significance of the revelation of a hidden, bitter truth becomes obvious:

Many Australians share with a moral vengeance the guilt *Walkabout* deals with, and perceive the white history of Australia as invasive, destructive and life-threatening, like a cancer. The guilt is felt as deepening sexual repression, economic rapacity and phobia-ridden relations with the land.[17]

Unlike the 'problem' identity for other Australians, Aboriginal and Islanders are seen as having a secure identity and sense of belongingness ... Their dispossession is becoming – like slavery and the US state – the settler culture's 'original sin', its genocide, its holocaust, its guilty history ... Aboriginal survival and activism ensures that the settler culture has to re-imagine itself not as victim of imperial predation and colonial or neo-colonial servitude, but as a perpetrator and oppressor of indigenous peoples.[18]

While not all narrative secrets are related directly to the initial seizure of the continent and subsequent treatment of its original inhabitants, the connection is explicit in enough films to justify the extension of this specific moral burden to other instances and forms of secrecy, guilt and repression. Implicit in all the examples of the 'dark secret' in Australian narrative is the recognition of incompleteness, ignorance or immaturity. There is the realisation and acceptance of the need for questing and questioning in order to clarify the circumstances in which groups and individuals find themselves, and to determine a problematic personal and national identity. The film industry may have been conceived as part of a response to Australia's supposed 'cultural cringe', the admission of cultural immaturity in comparison with the settlers' mother countries. At a more fundamental level, the projects of self-realisation which Australian protagonists undertake and the concealed truths they search for are symptoms of and reactions against an 'identity cringe' inherent in a colonial culture. The definition of national identity may have been foregrounded as the revival's unequivocal goal, but in any case has represented the clandestine agenda of many of its products since 1970.

At the end of the 1990s, after three decades of rejuvenated Australian filmmaking, the diversity, popularity and representativeness of the national cinematic output continue to be causes for celebration and criticism. When interviewed by David Stratton in 1979, Peter Weir concluded that the Australian film industry would never survive without the financial support of the government. His contemporaries within the industry at that time bemoaned the scarcity of overseas sales, criticised the relatively inconsequential sums invested by the government in the first ten years, or advised that smaller, not greater numbers of films should be made per year in the future.[19] The national industry has maintained a respectable if modest level of production, giving opportunities to second and third 'waves' of directors, actors and technicians, and continuing to contemplate the nature of the country and society which has shaped its practitioners and products:

Australianness is a powerful *construct*. As a call to some kind of national consciousness, to a generalised consensus about national 'type', behaviour and identity, it is a political construct or at least a construct in the service of a political idea, however undeclared the idea may be ... the strongest body of work on national self-images has been inflected by a white, male Anglo-celtic, 'common man' point of view, larrikin and spirited at its most endearing moments, but populist and conservative at its heart.[20]

This is not to suggest that the conservative portrayals of the Australian male stereotype, standing for the entirety of the European-derived society and by extension the entirety of Australia, have been conceived in nationalistic terms or, for that matter, that succeeding contradictory representations have had a political origination either. The commercial exercise (purveying and profiting from popular films) fuses with the 'social practice' of consumption, adoption or interrogation of their denotative and connotative elements, and animates the *cultural* practice of reflection, interpretation and absorption in which filmmakers and audiences engage. After thirty years the Australian cinema has largely accomplished its commercial and artistic filmmaking objectives, and created a recognisable local and global identity as well as markets and consumers for its productions. At the time of writing, Australia's national identity and international standing are under scrutiny because of the commanding role taken by Australian defence forces in the East Timor crisis and the imminent national poll on republican status. Australian leadership of Interfet (the International Force for East Timor) represents an assumption of responsibility within the Pacific sphere of influence, and presupposes a national and political maturity in directing rather than deputising in an emergency overseas. It will be instructive to observe how and when these experiences are delineated within the Australian cinema, in positive generic formats, unproblematic ensemble narratives, or downbeat documentary dramas. The nature of their representation will denote the formal refinement of the Australian film industry, just as the outcome of the republican poll and Interfet's mission will redefine Australia's regional and global prestige.

The incarnations of the Australian cinema as a commercial enterprise, an aesthetic experiment, a political manifesto and a national representation have typified the contradictions inherent in the industry's (re)creation. The industry, its funding, its productions and their reception have been subjected to prolonged and critical perusal, just as the composition, realisation and representation of the nation have been examined and disputed during the same period. James Ricketson's praise for the small-scale, eloquent, demanding and unexpectedly popular films of the 1970s maintains its relevance twenty years later, as a curriculum and a series of objectives for the future of Australian film: 'It is contemporary, socially relevant, intelligent without being elitist, entertaining without compromising its content, challenging but not didactic, aware of its audience but not pandering to its expectations.'[21] Undertaking or maintaining this agenda for the national film industry, producing a hybridised generic cinema which corresponds with a multicultural national audience at home and an international audience overseas, would represent the highest achievement of the Australian New Wave.

Notes

1 Susan Dermody and Elizabeth Jacka, *The Screening of Australia Vol. I: Anatomy of a Film Industry* (Sydney, Currency, 1987), p. 158.

2 Elizabeth Jacka, The Media Industries: Film, in Stuart Cunningham and Graeme Turner (eds), *The Media in Australia: Industries, Texts, Audiences* (St Leonards, Allen & Unwin, 1993), p. 85.

3 Sylvia Lawson, Australian Film, 1969, in Albert Moran and Tom O'Regan (eds), *An Australian Film Reader* (Sydney, Currency, 1985), p. 175.

4 Tom O'Regan, *Australian National Cinema* (London, Routledge, 1996), p. 14.

5 Elizabeth Jacka, Critical Positions, in Susan Dermody and Elizabeth Jacka (eds), *The Imaginary Industry: Australian Film in the Late '80s* (North Ryde, AFTRS Publications, 1988b), p. 69.

6 Elizabeth Jacka, The Changing Production Environment, in Dermody and Jacka (eds) (1988b), p. 35.

7 Voted the best film of the revival in a poll of critics and filmmakers in 1984. See Anon., The top ten films, in *Cinema Papers* nos 44–5 (1984), pp. 62–5.

8 O'Regan (1996), p. 24.

9 John Hinde, *Barry McKenzie* and *Alvin* Ten Years Later, in Moran and O'Regan (eds) (1985), pp. 184–7.

10 Scott Murray, Australian Cinema in the 1970s and 1980s, in Scott Murray (ed.), *Australian Cinema* (St Leonards, Allen & Unwin, 1994), p. 79.

11 Nick Roddick, Welcome to the Multiplex, *Sight and Sound* vol. 4 no. 6 (1994), pp. 26–8 (pp. 27–8).

12 James Ricketson, Poor Movies, Rich Movies, in Moran and O'Regan (eds) (1985), p. 225.

13 Jim Leach, The Body Snatchers: Genre and Canadian Cinema, in Barry Keith Grant (ed.), *Film Genre Reader* (Austin, University of Texas Press, 1986), p. 358.

14 O'Regan (1996), p. 194.

15 Rick Altman, *Film/Genre* (London, BFI, 1999), p. 203.

16 Graeme Turner, Representing the nation, in Tony Bennett (ed.), *Popular Fictions: Technology, Ideology, Production, Reading* (London, Routledge, 1990), p. 121.

17 Susan Dermody and Elizabeth Jacka, *The Screening of Australia Vol. II: Anatomy of a National Cinema* (Sydney, Currency, 1988a), p. 82.

18 O'Regan (1996), p. 276.

19 David Stratton, *The Last New Wave: The Australian Film Revival* (London, Angus and Robertson, 1980), pp. 293–5.

20 Dermody and Jacka (1987), p. 35.

21 Ricketson (1985), p. 226.

Filmography

The following is not an exhaustive list of Australian film production since 1970, but covers the features discussed in the text.

Adventures of Barry McKenzie, The (1972, Longford Productions)

director	Bruce Beresford
producer	Phillip Adams
photography	Don McAlpine
screenplay	Barry Humphries, Bruce Beresford
starring	Barry Crocker, Barry Humphries

Adventures of Priscilla, Queen of the Desert, The (1994, Latent Image/Specific Films Production)

director	Stephan Elliott
producer	Al Clark, Michael Hamlyn
photography	Brian J. Breheny
screenplay	Stephan Elliott
starring	Terence Stamp, Hugo Weaving, Guy Pearce, Bill Hunter

Alvin Purple (1973, Hexagon)

director	Tim Burstall
producer	Tim Burstall
photography	Robin Copping
screenplay	Alan Hopgood
starring	Graeme Blundell, Abigail, Lynette Curran

Attack Force Z (1982, John McCallum/Central Motion Picture Corporation)

director	Tim Burstall
producer	Lee Robinson
photography	Lin Hung-Chung
screenplay	Roger Marshall
starring	Mel Gibson, Chris Haywood, Sam Neill, John Philip Law

Bad Boy Bubby (1993, Fandango/Bubby Pty Productions)

director	Rolf de Heer
producer	Domenico Procacci, Giorgio Draskovic, Rolf de Heer
photography	Ian Jones
screenplay	Rolf de Heer
starring	Nicholas Hope, Carmel Johnson

Between Wars (1974, A Michael Thornhill Production)

director	Michael Thornhill
producer	Michael Thornhill
photography	Russell Boyd
screenplay	Frank Moorhouse
starring	Corin Redgrave, Arthur Dignam, Judy Morris

Bliss (1985, Window III Productions)

director	Ray Lawrence
producer	Anthony Buckley
photography	Paul Murphy
screenplay	Peter Carey, Ray Lawrence, from the novel by Peter Carey
starring	Barry Otto, Lynette Curran, Helen Jones

Breaker Morant (1979, South Australian Film Corporation)

director	Bruce Beresford
producer	Matthew Carroll
photography	Donald McAlpine
screenplay	Jonathon Hardy, David Stevens, Bruce Beresford, from the play by Kenneth Ross
starring	Edward Woodward, Bryan Brown, Jack Thompson

Break of Day (1976, Clare Beach Films)

director	Ken Hannam
producer	Patricia Lovell
photography	Russell Boyd
screenplay	Cliff Green
starring	Sara Kestelman, Andrew McFarlane

Caddie (1975, Anthony Buckley Productions)

director	Donald Crombie
producer	Anthony Buckley
photography	Peter James
screenplay	Joan Long
starring	Helen Morse, Jack Thompson

Cappuccino (1989, Archer Films)

director	Anthony Bowman
producer	Anthony Bowman, Sue Wild
photography	Danny Batterman
screenplay	Anthony Bowman
starring	John Clayton, Rowena Wallace, Jeanie Drynan

Cars That Ate Paris, The (1974, Salt Pan Productions/Royce Smeal Film Productions)

director	Peter Weir
producer	Hal McElroy, Jim McElroy
photography	John McLean
screenplay	Peter Weir, Keith Gow, Piers Davies
starring	Terry Camilleri, John Meillon

Celia (1988, Seon Films)

  director Ann Turner
  producer Timothy White, Gordon Glenn
  photography Geoffrey Simpson
  screenplay Ann Turner
  starring Rebecca Smart, Nicholas Ede, Mary-Anne Fahey

Chant of Jimmie Blacksmith, The (1978, The Film House)

  director Fred Schepisi
  producer Fred Schepisi
  photography Ian Baker
  screenplay Fred Schepisi, from the novel by Thomas Keneally
  starring Tommy Lewis, Freddy Reynolds, Jack Thompson

Club, The (1980, South Australian
Film Corporation/New South Wales Film Corporation)

  director Bruce Beresford
  producer Matt Carroll
  photography Don McAlpine
  screenplay David Williamson, adapted from his play
  starring Jack Thompson, Graham Kennedy, Harold Hopkins,
                John Howard

Crocodile Dundee (1986, Paramount/Hoyts/Rimfire)

  director Peter Faiman
  producer John Cornell
  photography Russell Boyd
  screenplay Paul Hogan, Ken Shadie
  starring Paul Hogan, Linda Koslowski, John Meillon, David Gulpilil

Crocodile Dundee II (1988, Rimfire Films/Paramount)

  director John Cornell
  producer John Cornell, Jane Scott
  photography Russell Boyd
  screenplay Paul Hogan, Brett Hogan
  starring Paul Hogan, Linda Koslowski, John Meillon, Ernie Dingo

Dead Calm (1988, Warner Bros./Kennedy-Miller Productions)

  director Phillip Noyce
  producer Terry Hayes, Doug Mitchell, George Miller
  photography Dean Semler
  screenplay Terry Hayes, from the novel by Charles Williams
  starring Sam Neill, Nicole Kidman, Billy Zane

Dead Letter Office (1998, BBC Films/Artist Services Production)

  director John Ruane
  producer Denise Patience
  photography Ellery Ryan
  screenplay Deb Cox
  starring Miranda Otto, George DelHoyo, Barry Otto

Deadly (1990, Moirstorm Productions)

  director Esben Storm
  producer Richard Moir
  photography Geoffrey Simpson
  screenplay Esben Storm, Richard Moir, Ranald Allan
  starring Jerome Ehlers, Frank Gallagher

Death in Brunswick (1990, Meridian Films)

director	John Ruane
producer	Timothy White
photography	Ellery Ryan
screenplay	John Ruane, Boyd Oxlade, based on the novel by Boyd Oxlade
starring	Sam Neill, Zoe Carides, John Clarke

Devil's Playground, The (1976, The Film House)

director	Fred Schepisi
producer	Fred Schepisi
photography	Ian Baker
screenplay	Fred Schepisi
starring	Arthur Dignam, Nick Tate

Don's Party (1976, Double Head Productions)

director	Bruce Beresford
producer	Phillip Adams
photography	Don McAlpine
screenplay	David Williamson, based on his play
starring	John Hargreaves, Ray Barrett, Graeme Blundell, Jeanie Drynan

Emma's War (1985, Belinon Productions)

director	Clytie Jessop
producer	Adrena Finlay, Clytie Jessop
photography	Tom Cowan
screenplay	Peter Smalley, Clytie Jessop
starring	Lee Remick, Miranda Otto, Mark Lee

Everlasting Secret Family, The (1987, Indian Pacific Films)

director	Michael Thornhill
producer	Michael Thornhill
photography	Julian Penney
screenplay	Frank Moorhouse, based on his own collection of short stories
starring	Arthur Dignam, Mark Lee

FJ Holden, The (1977, FJ Films)

director	Michael Thornhill
producer	Michael Thornhill
photography	David Gribble
screenplay	Terry Larsen
starring	Paul Couzens, Eva Dickinson

Flirting (1989, Kennedy-Miller Productions)

director	John Duigan
producer	Dr George Miller, Terry Hayes, Doug Mitchell
photography	Geoff Burton
screenplay	John Duigan
starring	Noah Taylor, Thandie Newton, Nicole Kidman

Fringe Dwellers, The (1986,
Virgin Films/Damien Nolan Productions/Ozfilms Ltd)

director Bruce Beresford
producer Sue Milliken
photography Don McAlpine
screenplay Bruce Beresford, Rhoisin Beresford
starring Kristina Nehm, Justine Saunders, Bob Maza

Gallipoli (1981, Paramount)

director Peter Weir
producer Robert Stigwood, Patricia Lovell
photography Russell Boyd
screenplay David Williamson, Peter Weir
starring Mark Lee, Mel Gibson, Bill Kerr, Bill Hunter

Georgia (1988, Jethro Films Production)

director Ben Lewin
producer Bob Weis
photography Yuri Sokol
screenplay Ben Lewin, Joanna Murray Smith, Bob Weis,
based on an original story by Mac Gudgeon
starring Judy Davis

Getting of Wisdom, The (1977,
Southern Cross Film Productions)

director Bruce Beresford
producer Phillip Adams
photography Don McAlpine
screenplay Eleanor Witcombe,
based on the novel by Henry Handel Richardson
starring Susannah Fowle, Barry Humphries, John Waters

Golden Braid (1990, Film Victoria/Illumination Films)

director Paul Cox
producer Paul Cox
photography Nino G. Martinetti
screenplay Paul Cox, Barry Dickins
starring Chris Haywood, Gosia Dobrowolska, Paul Chubb

Ground Zero (1987, Avenue Pictures)

director Michael Pattinson, Bruce Myles
producer Michael Pattinson
photography Steven Dobson
screenplay Mac Gudgeon, Jan Sardi
starring Colin Friels, Donald Pleasance, Jack Thompson

Harlequin (1980, F.G. Film Productions)

director Simon Wincer
producer Antony I. Ginnane
photography Gary Hansen
screenplay Everett De Roche
starring Robert Powell, David Hemmings

Filmography

Heatwave (1981, Heatwave Films/M&L Enterprises/Preston Crothers)

director	Phillip Noyce
producer	Hilary Linstead
photography	Vincent Monton
screenplay	Marc Rosenberg, Phillip Noyce, based on an original screeplay by Mark Stiles
starring	Judy Davis, Richard Moir, Bill Hunter, John Meillon

Heaven's Burning (1997, Craig Lahiff, Duo Art Production)

director	Craig Lahiff
producer	Al Clark, Helen Leake
photography	Brian Breheny
screenplay	Louis Nowra
starring	Russell Crowe, Youki Kudoh

High Tide (1987, FGH/SJL Productions)

director	Gillian Armstrong
producer	Sandra Levy
photography	Russell Boyd
screenplay	Laura Jones
starring	Judy Davis, Colin Friels

Holidays on the River Yarra (1990, Jungle Pictures)

director	Leo Berkeley
producer	Fiona Cochrane
photography	Brendan Lavelle
screenplay	Leo Berkeley
starring	Craig Adams, Luke Elliot

Homesdale (1971)

director	Peter Weir
producer	Richard Brennan, Grahame Bond
photography	Anthony Wallis
screenplay	Peter Weir, Piers Davies
starring	Grahame Bond, Geoff Malone, James Dellit

Incident at Raven's Gate aka Encounter at Raven's Gate (1988, Hemdale Film Corporation/An Acquabay Production)

director	Rolf de Heer
producer	Rolf de Heer, Marc Rosenberg
photography	Richard Michalak
screenplay	Marc Rosenberg, Rolf de Heer, from an original screenplay by James Michael Vernon
starring	Steven Vidler, Celin Griffin, Ritchie Singer

Island (1989, Illuminations Films/Film Victoria)

director	Paul Cox
producer	Paul Cox, Santhana K. Naidu
photography	Michael Edols
screenplay	Paul Cox
starring	Irene Papas, Eva Sitta, Anoja Weerasinghe, Chris Haywood

Journey Among Women (1977, KoAn Film Productions)

- *director* Tom Cowan
- *producer* John Weiley
- *photography* Tom Cowan
- *screenplay* Dorothy Hewett, Tom Cowan, John Weiley
- *starring* Lillian Crombie, June Pritchard, Martin Phelan

Kiss or Kill (1997, Bill Bennett Productions)

- *director* Bill Bennett
- *producer* Bill Bennett, Jennifer Bennett
- *photography* Malcolm McCulloch
- *screenplay* Bill Bennett
- *starring* Frances O'Connor, Matt Day, Chris Haywood, Barry Otto

Last Days of Chez Nous, The (1991, Jan Chapman Productions Pty Ltd)

- *director* Gillian Armstrong
- *producer* Jan Chapman
- *photography* Geoffrey Simpson
- *screenplay* Helen Garner
- *starring* Lisa Harrow, Bruno Ganz, Kerry Fox, Miranda Otto, Bill Hunter

Last Wave, The (1977, Ayer Productions)

- director Peter Weir
- *producer* Hal McElroy, Jim McElroy
- *photography* Russell Boyd
- *screenplay* Tony Morphett, Petru Popescu, Peter Weir
- *starring* Richard Chamberlain, David Gulpilil, Nandjiwarra Amagula

Lighthorsemen, The (1987, Picture Show/RKO)

- *director* Simon Wincer
- *producer* Ian Jones, Simon Wincer
- *photography* Dean Semler
- *screenplay* Ian Jones
- *starring* Peter Phelps, Gary Sweet, John Walton

Long Weekend (1977, Dugong Films)

- *director* Colin Eggleston
- *producer* Colin Eggleston
- *photography* Vincent Monton
- *screenplay* Everett De Roche
- *starring* John Hargreaves, Briony Behets

Mad Max (1979, Warner Bros/Mad Max Pty Ltd)

- *director* Dr George Miller
- *producer* Byron Kennedy
- *photography* David Eggby
- *screenplay* James McCausland, George Miller
- *starring* Mel Gibson, Steve Bisley, Joanne Samuel

Filmography

Mad Max 2 (1981, Warner Bros/Kennedy-Miller)

director Dr George Miller
producer Byron Kennedy
photography Dean Semler
screenplay Terry Hayes, George Miller, Brian Hannant
starring Mel Gibson, Vernon Wells, Emil Minty

Mad Max Beyond Thunderdome (1985, Warner Bros/Kennedy-Miller)

director Dr George Miller, George Ogilvie
producer George Miller
photography Dean Semler
screenplay Terry Hayes, George Miller
starring Mel Gibson, Tina Turner, Angry Anderson

Man From Snowy River, The (1982, Cambridge Films/Michael Edgley International)

director George Miller
producer Geoff Burrows
photography Keith Wagstaff
screenplay John Dixon, Fred Cullen
starring Kirk Douglas, Jack Thompson, Tom Burlinson

Mango Tree, The (1977, Pisces Production)

director Kevin Dobson
producer Michael Pate
photography Brian Probyn
screenplay Michael Pate, based on the novel by Ronald McKie
starring Geraldine Fitzgerald, Robert Helpmann

Melvin, Son of Alvin (1985, Memorelle)

director John Eastway
producer Jim McElroy
photography John Eastway
screenplay Morris Gleitzman
starring Graeme Blundell, David Argue, Abigail

Muriel's Wedding (1994, CIBY 2000/House and Moorhouse Film Production

director P.J. Hogan
producer Lynda House, Jocelyn Moorhouse
photography Martin McGrath
screenplay P.J. Hogan
starring Toni Collette, Rachel Griffiths, Bill Hunter, Jeanie Drynan

My Brilliant Career (1979, Margaret Fink Films)

director Gillian Armstrong
producer Margaret Fink
photography Don McAlpine
screenplay Eleanor Witcombe, based on the novel by Miles Franklin
starring Judy Davis, Sam Neill

Newsfront (1978, Palm Beach Pictures)

director Phillip Noyce
producer David Elfick
photography Vincent Monton
screenplay Phillip Noyce, based on an original screenplay by Bob Ellis
starring Bill Hunter, Chris Haywood

Night The Prowler, The (1978, Chariot Films)

 director Jim Sharman
 producer Anthony Buckley
 photography David Sanderson
 screenplay Patrick White, based on his own short story
 starring Kerry Walker, Ruth Cracknell, Terry Camilleri

Nirvana Street Murder (1990, Australian Film Commission)

 director Aleksi Vellis
 producer Fiona Cochrane
 photography Mark Lane
 screenplay Aleksi Vellis
 starring Mark Little, Ben Mendelsohn

Odd Angry Shot, The (1979, Samson Productions Pty Ltd)

 director Tom Jeffrey
 producer Sue Milliken, Tom Jeffrey
 photography Don McAlpine
 screenplay Tom Jeffrey, based on the novel by William Nagle
 starring Graham Kennedy, John Jarrett, John Hargreaves, Bryan Brown

Overlanders, The (1946, Ealing Studios)

 director Harry Watt
 producer Michael Balcon
 photography Osmond Borrodale
 screenplay Harry Watt
 starring Chips Rafferty, John Heyward, Daphne Campbell

Over the Hill (1992,
Village Roadshow Pictures/Glasshouse Pictures Production)

 director George Miller
 producer Robert Caswell, Bernard Terry
 photography David Connell
 screenplay Robert Caswell
 starring Olympia Dukakis, Derek Fowlds, Bill Kerr

Piano, The (1993, CIBY 2000/Jan Chapman Productions Pty Ltd)

 director Jane Campion
 producer Jan Chapman
 photography Stuart Dryburgh
 screenplay Jane Campion
 starring Holly Hunter, Sam Neill, Harvey Keitel, Anna Paquin

Picnic at Hanging Rock (1975, South Australian Film Corporation)

 director Peter Weir
 producer Hal McElroy, Jim McElroy, Patricia Lovell
 photography Russell Boyd
 screenplay Cliff Green, from the novel by Joan Lindsay
 starring Rachel Roberts, Anne Lambert, Helen Morse, Dominic Guard

Filmography

Plumber, The (1979, South Australian Film Corporation)

director	Peter Weir
producer	Matt Carroll
photography	David Sanderson
screenplay	Peter Weir
starring	Judy Morris, Ivar Kants

Proof (1991, House and Moorhouse Film Pty Ltd)

director	Jocelyn Moorhouse
producer	Lynda House
photography	Martin McGrath
screenplay	Jocelyn Moorhouse
starring	Hugo Weaving, Russell Crowe, Genevieve Picot

Razorback (1984, UAA/Western)

director	Russell Mulcahy
producer	Hal McElroy
photography	Dean Semler
screenplay	Everett De Roche
starring	Gregory Harrison, Arkie Whiteley, Bill Kerr, Chris Haywood

Romper Stomper (1992, Seon Films)

director	Geoffrey Wright
producer	Daniel Scharf, Ian Pringle
photography	Ron Hagen
screenplay	Geoffrey Wright
starring	Russell Crowe, Daniel Pollock, Jacqueline McKenzie

Secrets (1992, Beyond Films/Victorian International Pictures/Avalon NFU Studios)

director	Michael Pattinson
producer	Michael Pattinson
photography	David Cornell
screenplay	Jan Sardi
starring	Beth Champion, Malcolm Kennard, Noah Taylor, Willa O'Neill

Shame (1987, Barron Films)

director	Steve Jodrell
producer	Damien Parer, Paul D. Barron
photography	Joseph Pickering
screenplay	Beverly Blankenship, Michael Brindley
starring	Deborra-Lee Furness, Tony Barry, Simone Buchanan

Shine (1996, Momentum Films Pty Ltd)

director	Scott Hicks
producer	Jane Scott
photography	Geoffrey Simpson
screenplay	Jan Sardi
starring	Geoffrey Rush, Noah Taylor, Lynn Redgrave, Sir John Gielgud

Sirens (1994, Samson Productions Two Pty
Ltd/Sarah Radclyffe Productions – Sirens Ltd)

director	John Duigan
producer	Sue Milliken
photography	Geoff Burton
screenplay	John Duigan
starring	Hugh Grant, Tara Fitzgerald, Sam Neill, Elle MacPherson

Spider and Rose (1994, Dendy Films)

director	Bill Bennett
producer	Lyn McCarthy, Graeme Tubbenhauer
photography	Andrew Lesnie
screenplay	Bill Bennett
starring	Ruth Cracknell, Simon Bossell

Stan and George's New Life (1992, Lea Films Pty Ltd)

director	Brian McKenzie
producer	Margot McDonald
photography	Ray Argall
screenplay	Brian McKenzie, Deborah Cox
starring	Paul Chubb, Julie Forsyth

Starstruck (1982, Palm Beach Pictures)

director	Gillian Armstrong
producer	Richard Brennan
photography	Russell Boyd
screenplay	Stephen Maclean
starring	Jo Kennedy, Ross O'Donovan, Max Cullen

Stork (1971, Tim Burstall
& Associates/Bilcock & Copping Film Productions)

director	Tim Burstall
producer	Tim Burstall
photography	Robin Copping
screenplay	David Williamson, adapted from his own play
starring	Bruce Spence, Graeme Blundell

Strictly Ballroom (1992, M&A Film Corporation)

director	Baz Luhrmann
producer	Tristam Miall
photography	Steve Mason
screenplay	Baz Luhrmann, Craig Pierce
starring	Paul Mercurio, Tara Morice, Bill Hunter

Summerfield (1977, Clare Beach Films)

director	Ken Hannam
producer	Patricia Lovell
photography	Mike Molloy
screenplay	Cliff Green
starring	Nick Tate, Elizabeth Alexander, John Waters

Sunday Too Far Away (1974, South Australian Film Corporation)

director	Ken Hannam
producer	Gil Brealey, Matt Carroll
photography	Geoff Burton
screenplay	John Dingwall
starring	Jack Thompson, Max Cullen, Reg Lye, Peter Cummins

Survivor, The (1980, Tuesday Films)

director	David Hemmings
producer	Antony I. Ginnane
photography	John Seale
screenplay	David Ambrose, based on the novel by James Herbert
starring	Robert Powell, Jenny Agutter

Sweetie (1989, Electric/Arena Film)

director	Jane Campion
producer	John Maynard
photography	Sally Bongers
screenplay	Gerard Lee, Jane Campion
starring	Genevieve Lemon, Karen Colston

Tender Hooks (1988, Tru Vu Pictures)

director	Mary Callaghan
producer	Chris Oliver
photography	Ray Argall
screenplay	Mary Callaghan
starring	Jo Kennedy, Nique Needles

They're a Weird Mob (1966, Williamson-Powell Production)

director	Michael Powell
producer	Michael Powell
photography	Arthur Grant
screenplay	Richard Imrie from the book by Nino Culotta
starring	Walter Chiari, Claire Dunne, Chips Rafferty, John Meillon

Three To Go (1971, Commonwealth Film Unit)

director	Peter Weir (*Michael*), Oliver Howes (*Toula*), Brian Hannant (*Judy*)
producer	Gil Brearley
photography	Kerry Brown
screenplays	Peter Weir, Oliver Howes, Brian Hannant
starring	(*Michael*) Grahame Bond, Matthew Burton; (*Toula*) Gabrial Battikha, Erica Crown; (*Judy*) Judy Morris, Brian Anderson

The Umbrella Woman, aka **The Good Wife** (1987, A Laughing Kookaburra Production)

director	Ken Cameron
producer	Jan Sharp, Helen Watts
photography	James Bartle
screenplay	Peter Kenna
starring	Rachel Ward, Bryan Brown, Sam Neill

Wake in Fright, aka **Outback** (1971, NLT/Group W Production)

director	Ted Kotcheff
producer	George Willoughby
photography	Brian West
screenplay	Evan Jones, based on the novel by Kenneth Cook
starring	Gary Bond, Donald Pleasance

Walkabout (1970, Max L. Rabb/Si Litvinoff Films Pty. Ltd)

director	Nicolas Roeg
producer	Si Litvinoff
photography	Nicolas Roeg
screenplay	Edward Bond, based on the novel by James Vance Marshall
starring	David Gulpilil, Jenny Agutter, John Meillon

Welcome to Woop Woop (1998, The Big Red Pty Ltd)

director	Stephan Elliott
producer	Finola Dwyer
photography	Mike Molloy
screenplay	Michael Thomas, based on the novel *The Dead Heart* by Douglas Kennedy
starring	Johnathon Schaech, Rod Taylor

Wide Sargasso Sea (1992, Sargasso Productions/A Laughing Kookaburra Production)

director	John Duigan
producer	Jan Sharp
photography	Geoff Burton
screenplay	Jan Sharp, Carole Angier, John Duigan, based on the novel by Jean Rhys
starring	Karina Lombard, Nathaniel Parker, Rachel Ward, Michael York

Year My Voice Broke, The (1987, Kennedy-Miller Productions)

director	John Duigan
producer	Terry Hayes, Doug Mitchell, George Miller
photography	Geoff Burton
screenplay	John Duigan
starring	Noah Taylor, Loene Carmen

Year of Living Dangerously, The (1982, Wayang Productions/MGM)

director	Peter Weir
producer	Hal McElroy, Jim McElroy
photography	Russell Boyd
screenplay	David Williamson, C.J. Koch, Peter Weir, from the novel by C.J. Koch
starring	Mel Gibson, Sigourney Weaver, Linda Hunt, Bill Kerr

Young Einstein (1988, Serious Productions)

director	Yahoo Serious
producer	Yahoo Serious, Warwick Ross, David Roach
photography	Jeff Darling
screenplay	Yahoo Serious, David Roach
starring	Yahoo Serious, Odile Le Clezio

Bibliography

Australian film

Baxter, John, The Australian Cinema (Sydney, Angus and Robertson, 1970)

Bertrand, Ina and Diane Collins, Government and Film in Australia (Sydney, Currency/AFI, 1981)

Cunningham, Stuart, Featuring Australia: The Cinema of Charles Chauvel (Sydney, Allen and Unwin, 1991)

Cunningham, Stuart and Graeme Turner (eds), The Media in Australia: Industries, Texts, Audiences (St Leonards, Allen & Unwin, 1993)

Dermody, Susan and Elizabeth Jacka, The Screening of Australia Vol. I: Anatomy of a Film Industry (Sydney, Currency, 1987)

Dermody, Susan and Elizabeth Jacka, The Screening of Australia Vol. II: Anatomy of a National Cinema (Sydney, Currency, 1988a)

Dermody, Susan and Elizabeth Jacka (eds), The Imaginary Industry: Australian Film in the Late '80s (North Ryde, AFTRS, 1988b)

Hall, Sandra, Critical Business: The New Australian Cinema in Review (London, Rigby, 1985)

Hamilton, Peter and Sue Mathews, American Dreams, Australian Movies (Sydney, Currency, 1986)

Mathews, Sue 35mm Dreams: Conversations with Five Directors About the Australian Film Revival (Melbourne, Penguin, 1984)

McFarlane, Brian, Words and Images: Australian Novels into Film (Richmond, Heinemann, 1983)

McFarlane, Brian, Australian Cinema 1970–1985 (London, Secker & Warburg, 1987)

McFarlane, Brian and Geoff Mayer, New Australian Cinema: Sources and Parallels in American and British Film (Cambridge, Cambridge University Press, 1992)

Moran, Albert and Tom O'Regan (eds), An Australian Film Reader (Sydney, Currency, 1985)

Moran, Albert and Tom O'Regan (eds), *The Australian Screen* (Harmondsworth, Penguin, 1989)

Murray, Scott (ed.), *The New Australian Cinema* (Melbourne, Thomas Nelson, 1980)

Murray, Scott (ed.), *Australian Cinema* (St Leonards, Allen & Unwin, 1994)

O'Regan, Tom, *Australian National Cinema* (London, Routledge, 1996)

Pike, Andrew and Ross Cooper, *Australian Film 1900–1977: A Guide to Feature Film Production* (Melbourne, Oxford University Press, 1980)

Robinson, Jocelyn and Beverley Zalcock, *Girls' Own Stories: Australian and New Zealand Women's Films* (London, Scarlet Press, 1997)

Shirley, Graham and Brian Adams, *Australian Cinema: The First Eighty Years* (revised edn) (Sydney, Currency, 1989)

Stewart, John, *An Encyclopaedia of Australian Film* (Frenchs Forest, Reed Books, 1984)

Stratton, David, *The Last New Wave: The Australian Film Revival* (London, Angus and Robertson, 1980)

Treole, Victoria (ed.), *Australian Independent Film* (Sydney, AFC, 1982)

Tulloch, John, *Legends on the Screen: The Narrative Film in Australia 1919–1929* (Sydney, Currency, 1981)

Tulloch, John, *Australian Cinema: Industry, Narrative and Meaning* (Sydney, Allen and Unwin, 1982)

Turner, Graeme, *National Fictions: Literature, Film and the Construction of Australian Narrative* (London, Allen & Unwin, 1986)

Film and media: general

Allen, Robert C. and Douglas Gomery, *Film History: Theory and Practice* (London, McGraw-Hill, 1985)

Altman, Rick, *Film/Genre* (London, BFI, 1999)

Andrew, Dudley, *Concepts in Film Theory* (Oxford, Oxford University Press, 1984)

Bennett, Tony (ed.), *Popular Fiction: Technology, Ideology, Production, Reading* (London, Routledge, 1990)

Bennett, Tony, Susan Boyd-Bowman, Colin Mercer and Janet Woollacott (eds), *Popular Television and Film: A Reader* (London, BFI, 1981)

Caughie, John (ed.), *Theories of Authorship* (London, Routledge & Kegan Paul, 1981)

Cohan, Steven and Ina Rae Hark (eds), *The Road Movie Book* (London, Routledge, 1997)

Creekmuir, Corey K. and Alexander Doty (eds), *Out in Culture: Gay, Lesbian and Queer Essays on Popular Culture* (London, Cassell, 1995)

Fell, John L. (ed.), *Film Before Griffith* (London, University of California Press, 1983)

Grant, Barry Keith (ed.), *Film Genre Reader* (Austin, University of Texas Press, 1990)

Hall, Stuart, Dorothy Hobson, Andrew Lowe and Paul Willis (eds), *Culture, Media, Language* (London, Hutchinson, 1980)

Hedges, Inez, *Breaking the Frame: Film Language and the Experience of Limits* (Indianapolis, Indiana University Press, 1991)

Higson, Andrew, *Waving the Flag: Constructing a National Cinema in Britain* (Oxford, Clarendon, 1995)

Hill, John and Pamela Church Gibson (eds), *The Oxford Guide to Film Studies* (Oxford, Oxford University Press, 1998)

Kaminsky, Stuart M., *American Film Genres* (2nd edn) (Chicago, Nelson Hall, 1985)

Martin, Helen and Sam Edwards, *New Zealand Film 1912–1996* (Auckland, Oxford University Press, 1997)

Mast, Gerald, *Film Cinema Movie* (London, University of Chicago Press, 1983)

Mast, Gerald and Marshall Cohen (eds), *Film Theory and Criticism* (3rd edn) (Oxford, Oxford University Press, 1985)

Monaco, James, *How to Read a Film* (revised edn) (Oxford, Oxford University Press, 1981)

Nowell-Smith, Geoffrey (ed.), *The Oxford History of World Cinema* (Oxford, Oxford University Press, 1996)

Orr, John and Colin Nicholson (eds), *Cinema and Fiction: New Modes of Adapting 1950–1990* (Edinburgh, Edinburgh University Press, 1992)

Rayner, Jonathan, *The Films of Peter Weir* (London, Cassell, 1998)

Richards, Jeffrey, *Films and British National Identity: From Dickens to Dad's Army* (Manchester, Manchester University Press, 1997)

Smith, Joseph H. and William Kerrigan (eds), *Images in Our Souls: Cavell, Psychoanalysis and Cinema* (London, Johns Hopkins University Press, 1987)

Thompson, Kristin and David Bordwell, *Film History: An Introduction* (London, McGraw-Hill, 1994)

Tudor, Andrew, *Theories of Film* (London, Secker & Warburg, 1973)

Turner, Graeme, *Film as Social Practice* (London, Routledge, 1988)

Wilton, Tamsin, *Immortal, Invisible: Lesbians and the Moving Image* (London, Routledge, 1995)

Articles

Anon., The Top Ten Films, *Cinema Papers* nos 44–5 (1984): 62–5

Bachmann, Gideon, Films in Australia, *Sight and Sound* vol. 46 no. 1 (1976–77): 32–6

Barber, Susan, *The Adventures of Priscilla, Queen of the Desert*, *Film Quarterly* vol. 50 no. 2 (1996–97): 41–5

Brennan, Richard, Peter Weir – profile, *Cinema Papers* no. 1 (1974): 16–7

Brennan, Richard, A Pain in the Industry?, *Cinema Papers* no. 11 (1977): 218–19

Bromby, Robin, In the Picture: Australia, *Sight and Sound* vol. 48 no. 4 (1979): 230–1

Brown, Craig, Ethnic Stereotypes in Television, *Cinema Papers* no. 87 (1992): 54–6

Buckley, Anthony, We Know Where We've Been But ..., *Cinema Papers* no. 4 (1975): 31–4

Chute, David, The Ayatollah of the Moviola: Interview with Dr George Miller, *Film Comment* vol. 18 no. 4 (1982): 26–31

Clancy, Jack, The Triumph of Mateship – The Failure of the Australian War Film Since 1970, *Overland* no. 105 (1986): 4–10

Crowdus, Gary and Udayan Gupta, An Aussie in Hollywood: An Interview with Bruce Beresford, *Cineaste* vol. 12 no. 4 (1983): 20–5

Cunningham, Stuart, Australian Film, *The Australian Journal of Screen Theory* nos 5–6 (1980): 36–47

Dawson, Jan, Australian Film Culture, *Cinema Papers* no. 12 (1977): 307, 373

Freebury, Jane, Screening Australia: *Gallipoli* – A Study of Nationalism in Film, *Media Information Australia* no. 43 (1987): 5–8

Fonda-Bonardi, P. and C. Fonda-Bonardi, The Birth of a Nation – An Interview with Peter Weir, *Cineaste* vol. 11 no. 4 (1982): 41–2

Gibson, Ross, Camera Natura: Landscape in Australian Feature Films, *Framework* nos 22–3 (1983): 47–51

Glaessner, Verina, In the Picture: Australia, *Sight and Sound* vol. 46 no. 3 (1977): 150

Glenn, Gordon and Scott Murray, Production Report – *The Cars That Ate Paris* Cinema Papers no. 1 (1974): 18–26

Hentzi, Gary, Peter Weir and the Cinema of New Age Humanism, *Film Quarterly* vol. 44 no. 2 (1990): 2–12

Hutton, Anne B., Nationalism in Australian Cinema, *Cinema Papers* no. 26 (1980): 96–100

Jacka, Liz, The Film Industry in Australia: Trends in the Eighties, *Media Information Australia* no. 42 (1986): 17–21

Jacobs, Diane, Australian Originals, *American Film* vol. 4 no. 7 (1979): 52–6

Kennedy, Harlan, The New Wizards of Oz, *Film Comment* vol. 25 no. 5 (1989): 73–7

Martin, Adrian, More Than Muriel, *Sight and Sound* vol. 5 no. 6 (1995): 30–2

McFarlane, Brian, The films of Peter Weir, *Cinema Papers* no. 26 (1980) Special Supplement: 1–24

McFarlane, Brian and Tom Ryan, Peter Weir – towards the centre, *Cinema Papers* no. 34 (1981): 322–9

Mordue, Mark, Homeward Bound: Interview with Gillian Armstrong, *Sight and Sound* vol. 58 no. 4 (1989): 270–2

Moore, Catriona and Stephen Muecke, Racism and the Representation of Aborigines in Film, *Australian Journal of Cultural Studies* vol. 2 no. 1 (1984): 36–53

Murray, Scott, Hal and James McElroy – Producers, *Cinema Papers* no. 14 (1977): 148–53

Murray, Scott and Antony I. Ginnane, Producing *Picnic*: Pat Lovell, *Cinema Papers* no. 8 (1976): 298–301, 377

Pinkus, Margot, The Government and the Film Industry, *Cinema Papers* no. 33 (1981): 230–1, 305

Roddick, Nick, Welcome to the Multiplex, *Sight and Sound* vol. 4 no. 6 (1994): 26–8

Shirley, Graham, Entertainment is Big Business: The PDGA Seminar 1976, *Cinema Papers* no. 11 (1977): 212–14, 284

Travers, T.H.E., *Gallipoli* – Film and the Tradition of Australian History, *Film and History* vol. 14 no. 1 (1984): 14–20

Weis, Bob, The Last Word [AFFC Funding], *Cinema Papers* no. 73 (1989): 80

Willett, Graham, Minorities Can Win: The Gay Movement, the Left and the Transformation of Australian Society, *Overland* no. 149 (1997): 64–8

Reviews

Adair, Gilbert, *My Brilliant Career*, *Monthly Film Bulletin* vol. 47 no. 553 (1980): 25

Brown, Geoff, *The Cars That Ate Paris*, *Sight and Sound* vol. 44 no. 3 (1975): 192

Clancy, Jack, *The Last Wave*, *Cinema Papers* no. 15 (1978): 259

Clancy, Jack, *The Plumber*, *Cinema Papers* no. 23 (1979): 569, 571

Combs, Richard, *Picnic at Hanging Rock*, *Monthly Film Bulletin* vol. 43 no. 512 (1976): 196–7

Combs, Richard, *The Last Wave*, *Sight and Sound* vol. 47 no. 2 (1978): 121–2

Cook, Diane, *Dead Letter Office*, *Cinema Papers* no. 127 (1998): 40–1

Dawson, Jan, *Walkabout*, *Monthly Film Bulletin* vol. 38 no. 454 (1971): 227–8

Epstein, Jan, *Welcome to Woop Woop*, *Cinema Papers* no. 127 (1998): 37–8

Flaus, John, *The Cars That Ate Paris*, *Cinema Papers* no. 3 (1974): 274–5

Forbes, Jill, *Celia*, *Monthly Film Bulletin* vol. 57 no. 673 (1990): 63–4

Francke, Lizzie, *The Adventures of Priscilla, Queen of the Desert*, *Sight and Sound* vol. 4 no. 11 (1994): 38

Glaessner, Verina, *High Tide*, *Monthly Film Bulletin* vol. 55 no. 659 (1988): 364

Glaessner, Verina, *Shame*, *Monthly Film Bulletin* vol. 56 no. 665 (1989): 188–9

Greenfield, Pierre, *Picnic at Hanging Rock*, *Movietone News* nos 62–3 (1979): 8–10

Jaehne, Karen, *Gallipoli*, *Cineaste* vol. 11 no. 4 (1982): 40–3

Jenkins, Steve, *Sweetie*, *Monthly Film Bulletin* vol. 57 no. 676 (1990): 142–3

Johnston, Trevor, *Romper Stomper*, *Sight and Sound* vol. 3 no. 4 (1993): 55–6

Kemp, Philip, *Flirting*, *Sight and Sound* vol. 1 no. 7 (1991): 44

Kemp, Philip, *Strictly Ballroom*, *Sight and Sound* vol. 2 no. 6 (1992): 56

Kemp, Philip, *Bad Boy Bubby*, *Sight and Sound* vol. 4 no. 11 (1994): 39–40

Lipman, Amanda, *Sirens*, *Sight and Sound* vol. 4 no. 8 (1994): 53–4

Murray, Scott, *Picnic at Hanging Rock*, *Cinema Papers* no. 7 (1975): 264–5

Newman, Kim, *Young Einstein*, *Monthly Film Bulletin* vol. 56 no. 669 (1989): 313–4

Newman, Kim, *Death in Brunswick*, *Sight and Sound* vol. 1 no. 10 (1992): 42–3

Pulleine, Tim, *The Last Wave*, *Monthly Film Bulletin* vol. 45 no. 531 (1978): 66–7

Pulleine, Tim, *Harlequin*, *Monthly Film Bulletin* vol. 47 no. 560 (1980): 176

Pulleine, Tim, *Breaker Morant*, *Monthly Film Bulletin* vol. 47 no. 559 (1980): 153

Pulleine, Tim, *Heatwave*, *Monthly Film Bulletin* vol. 49 no. 584 (1982): 200

Pulleine, Tim, *The Lighthorsemen*, *Monthly Film Bulletin* vol. 55 no. 658 (1988): 335–6

Pulleine, Tim, *The Year My Voice Broke*, *Monthly Film Bulletin* vol. 56 no. 664 (1989): 158–9

Romney, Jonathan, *Proof*, *Sight and Sound* vol. 1 no. 8 (1991): 49

Sharrett, Christopher, *Mad Max Beyond Thunderdome*, *Film Quarterly* vol. 40 no. 3 (1987): 59

Strick, Philip, *The Cars That Ate Paris*, *Monthly Film Bulletin* vol. 42 no. 496 (1975): 101–2

Strick, Philip, *The Everlasting Secret Family*, *Monthly Film Bulletin* vol. 55 no. 659 (1988): 362

Strick, Philip, *Encounter at Raven's Gate*, *Monthly Film Bulletin* vol. 57 no. 675 (1990): 103

Turner, Adrian, *Gallipoli*, *Films and Filming* no. 327 (1981): 33

Yates, Robert, *Muriel's Wedding*, *Sight and Sound* vol. 5 no. 4 (1995): 49

Index